Susan J. White

Art, Architecture, and Liturgical Reform

Pueblo Publishing Company

New York

Design: Frank Kacmarcik

ISBN: 0-925127-01-9

Printed in the United States of America

Contents

List of Abbreviations

LA   *Liturgical* Arts Quarterly

The abbreviations below refer to collections housed in the University of Notre Dame Archives, Hesburgh Library, University of Notre Dame, Notre Dame, Indiana:

LAS   Liturgical Arts Society Collection

ML   Maurice Lavanoux Papers

SRCA   Society for the Renewal of Christian Art, Inc. Collection

The number following abbreviations LAS, ML, and SRCA indicates the number of the archival box within a given collection in which the material referred to can be found.

Preface

"This is manifestly the moment when such a project as you have in mind should be initiated," wrote neo-Gothicist architect Ralph Adams Cram in 1927 upon hearing plans for an organization devoted to the liturgical arts. The 40-year history of the Liturgical Arts Society is eloquent testimony to the truth of Cram's observation. During the decade between 1920 and 1930, Roman Catholics increasingly sought a more sophisticated approach to the Christian life, and this search resulted in an array of social, political, and literary movements. A truly American liturgical movement was born during those years, and the language of liturgical renewal would soon become common currency among the Roman Catholic avant-garde, including the men and women who founded the Liturgical Arts Society.

But even the Roman Catholic intelligentsia had refused to affirm the revolution in art and architecture that had been sending shock waves through Europe and America since the late-19th century. The radical subjectivity of Impressionism and Cubism, the socio-political agenda of Dadaism and Futurism, the sterility of Bauhaus design, and the anarchy of Surrealism were simply too dangerous to be approached by Roman Catholics in an era of persistent anti-modernism in the Church. And so the Roman Catholic avant-garde was forced to look elsewhere for a suitable artistic vocabulary. In the academic medieval Romanticism of the day, many found a form of artistic expression which would allow them to affirm their religious identity while maintaining a degree of intellectual respectability. But most Roman Catholics, both in Europe and in the United States, found a safe haven from the "shock of the new" in saccharine and sentimental religious arts. While these provided comfort, they offered little in the way of artistic merit or theological depth. At the same time, the early pioneers of the Roman Catholic liturgical movement recognized that liturgical renewal must necessarily involve all of the fundamental aspects of Christian life. Politics, social welfare, ecclesiology, and piety would all be touched by the transformative power of liturgical reform in the years to come. It is not surprising, then, that the arts of the Church also came under scrutiny.

The Liturgical Arts Society was established in 1928 as a national effort to "devise ways and means for improving the standards of taste, craftsmanship, and liturgical correctness in the practice of Catholic art in the United States" (Masthead, *Liturgical Arts*, volumes 1:1 to 40:3). Founded and led by lay people, the Liturgical Arts Society's membership included men and women from all levels in the Church who felt that objects of art used in public worship should be in keeping with the spirit of the liturgy and would, in this way, aid in the revitalization of Christianity and society as a whole. In 1931, the Society began publication of a quarterly magazine. For four decades, *Liturgical Arts* exerted one of the single strongest influences on American artists and architects concerned with the design and furnishing of Roman Catholic churches; it also provided a forum for the views of the leaders of the liturgical movement, American and European, on the place of the arts in liturgical renewal.

This study focuses on the work of the Liturgical Arts Society, its quarterly journal *Liturgical Arts*, and the specific theological, ecclesiastical, and social context within which it operated. Divided into two major parts, the book first traces the history of the Society from its founding meetings in 1927-1928 to its dissolution in 1972. Relying upon previously unresearched archival materials, this section chronicles the Society's links with the American Roman Catholic liturgical movement, Church leaders, and artists and architects concerned with ecclesiastical building and furnishing.

Part II examines the liturgical, aesthetic, and theological underpinnings of the Liturgical Arts Society's agenda. Beginning with a discussion of the Society's views on the liturgy and liturgical reform, the investigation proceeds to document its theology of art. The question of legitimate authority in the matter of religious art and architecture is paid particular attention and serves to expose the ecclesiological presuppositions beneath the Society's work. The discussion then turns to the role of the Liturgical Arts Society within the debate over modern religious art, and concludes by considering its work as part of the social, historical, and theological world of which it was a part.

Four appendices are added to the text. The first is the original Constitution and Bylaws under which the Liturgical Arts Society was incorporated in 1928. This is followed by a biographical gazetteer of persons influential in the organization and a list of elected officers. Finally, Maurice Lavanoux's "Notes Submitted to the Subcommission on Sacred Art Preparatory to Vatican Council II" are included because they reflect the Society's mature thinking on the subject of religious art and architecture.

SOURCES
When the Liturgical Arts Society disbanded and *Liturgical Arts* ceased publication in 1972, the papers of the Society were given to the University of Notre Dame where they remain, largely uncataloged, in the Archives. These materials include important correspondence between the Society's leadership and most, if not all, of the central figures in the American and European liturgical movement and religious art. The minutes of meetings, financial statements, lecture notes, photographs, and, material for *Liturgical Arts* complete the Liturgical Arts Society Collection, which was donated to the University of Notre Dame by Maurice Lavanoux, the editor of *Liturgical Arts* for more than 35 years.

There are 114,500 items in the Liturgical Arts Society Collection, contained in 229 boxes. They have been arranged in five groups:

1) correspondence, 1922-1949 (arranged alphabetically by surname of correspondent)
2) correspondence, 1938-1972 (arranged chronologically)
3) photographs (arranged alphabetically by subject)
4) photographs (arranged alphabetically by location of subject)
5) related materials (financial and business papers related to the formation of the Society, lectures by Maurice Lavanoux, articles for *Liturgical Arts*)

Two other collections in the University of Notre Dame Archives are of additional interest. The personal papers of Lavanoux include letters, diaries, and the manuscript of a 559-page autobiography, and were donated to the University upon Lavanoux's death in 1974. The archives of the Society for the Renewal of Christian Art, Inc., the legitimate heir to the Liturgical Arts Society, contain information about the events immediately following the Society's demise. Taken together, these not only chronicle the history of the Society and its work, but also trace the important connections with persons of significance to the American and European liturgical movement, Church leaders, and artists, architects, and craftspeople concerned with church building and furnishing.

In addition, the 159 issues of *Liturgical Arts* are a significant primary source for information on the place of the arts in the work of the Society, in the program of liturgical renewal and in the Roman Catholic Church as a whole. Forty years of editorial commentary, feature articles, reviews, correspondence, and advertising (which was carefully chosen to reflect the Society's values) are important witnesses to a particular stance toward the liturgy and the arts that serve it.

Secondary sources directly related to the Liturgical Arts Society and *Liturgical Arts* magazine are few. Occasional reference is made to the group and its activities in the religious or secular press, or in biographical studies of persons with whom it had contact. On the whole, however, the Society did its work quietly and with little fanfare, changing the face of ecclesiastical art and architecture with small, decisive strokes.

Throughout its 40-year history, the Liturgical Arts Society monitored the progress of liturgical renewal and translated it into design principles for the architect, artist, pastor, and liturgist. In so doing, the Society assisted in the transformation of Roman Catholic ecclesiastical art and architecture. Although the Liturgical Arts Society no longer exists, the work of the architects and artists it encouraged and the liturgical movement of which it was a part survive and continue to shape the worship of the Roman Catholic Church. A careful analysis of the criteria by which the Liturgical Arts Society judged and promoted ecclesiastical building and furnishing cannot help but make us more sensitive to the influence it continues to exert.

ACKNOWLEDGMENTS

Many people have made invaluable contributions to the successful completion of this study. I especially wish to acknowledge the assistance of the Cushwa Center for the Study of American Catholicism and the Department of Theology of the University of Notre Dame; their generous financial support allowed me to work on this project with few distractions. The knowledgeable staff of the University of Notre Dame Archives spent innumerable hours unravelling the intricacies of the Liturgical Arts Society Collection. I am particularly indebted to Sharon Sumpter of the Archives staff whose good cheer and efficiency made the work much simpler.

Many friends and colleagues have given liberally of their time, their insights, their comfort, and their encouragement. Special thanks are due to Robert Rambusch for his infectious enthusiasm for this topic, Professor Robert D. Hawkins for hours spent acquainting me with the mysteries of the computer, and Philip Schatz, Michael Moriarty, and the Reverends Gail M. Snodgrass and Stanley Robertson Hall whose comradeship and pastoral care were invaluable at every stage.

I am profoundly grateful to Professor Thomas F. O'Meara, O.P. , of the University of Notre Dame for his perceptive and meticulous attention to the text and to those who read and commented on the manuscript: Professors Mark Searle, William G. Storey, and the late Niels K. Rasmussen, O.P. This work, like its author, has benefited immeasurably from their care. And finally, I wish to thank my husband James. His gentle encouragement, his generous comfort, and his endless patience in the face of considerable neglect have made this study a reality.

Susan J. White
24 November 1988
South Bend, Indiana

CHAPTER ONE

The Founding of the Liturgical Arts Society

EVERITT HARMAN AND THE PORTSMOUTH PRIORY
RETREATS

"Sir: A letter published in the February *Journal* said that artists and
architects were '. . . characterized by one trait, a desire for fame . . .
and were filled with but one ideal — to flood the world with
beauty.'

"I wonder if there are not a few — especially those interested in ecclesiastical art and architecture — who (as so many medieval artists were) are interested only in the latter ideal? . . . I know of two
or three in America — are there any more? who are interested in
such an idealistic work as architecture, to the ultimate benefit of the
profession and the public alike. I should like to establish contact
with them if there are any — whether their interest be great or
slight, and whether it be a personal one or only a cooperative one."[1]

A Benedictine, AIA

In the early spring of 1925, a young American architect appeared at
the Benedictine Abbey of Fort Augustus, Scotland, to undertake
theological studies. Everitt Radcliffe Harman, a 32-year-old graduate of the Massachusetts Institute of Technology School of Architecture (1921) and son of a wealthy Beverly Hills, California, family,
was a novice[2] at Fort Augustus' struggling American foundation,
Portsmouth (Rhode Island) Priory of St. Gregory the Great.[3] His initial attraction to the Portsmouth Foundation, in all likelihood, had
been fired by Fort Augustus' reputation as a patron of ecclesiastical
arts, and now he had the opportunity to see for himself.

During the next two years, Harman became convinced that what he
observed happening at Fort Augustus (and at Beuron, Caldey, and

1

Maredsous, which he also visited during that time) could be transplanted to the United States with even more fruitful results. "A great deal has been done by the Benedictines in this country and on the continent towards a beginning [of a renewal of ecclesiastical art]," Harman wrote to one of the men who responded to his plaintive letter to the *American Institute of Architects Journal*, "but the opportunities are far greater in America than anywhere else, should God so will to draw us together as he appears to be doing." [4]

Upon his return from Scotland in the spring of 1927, Harman re-established himself at Portsmouth Priory, which was itself also beginning to manifest an interest in the renewal of Christian art. Encouraged by the positive response he had received to his letter in the *Journal*, he organized at Portsmouth the first retreat for individuals who shared his own despair about the level to which American Roman Catholic Church art had fallen and his desire to do something about it.[5] The Portsmouth retreatants had more in common than their interest in the renewal of Church art, however. With few exceptions, they were Roman Catholic laymen from wealthy families, fledgling architects, draftsmen, and artists, and graduates of prestigious East Coast universities: Harvard, Yale, Princeton, Columbia. They were destined to become part of that great American Roman Catholic cultural and intellectual revival that marked the period between the two World Wars.[6]

A BENEDICTINE OBLATES GUILD OF ARCHITECTS, ARTISTS, AND CRAFTSMEN

It was to this group gathered at Portsmouth Priory in the summer of 1927 that Everitt Harman presented his vision, a vision shaped by his own Benedictine formation that combined artistic excellence with monastic organization, discipline, and spirituality. The organizational scheme was entitled "A Benedictine Oblates Guild of Architects, Artists, and Craftsmen." The plan as outlined[7] was tripartite and consisted of: 1) a small, select group of artists and educators, who wished to enter deeply into the spiritual and artistic life of the Church by following the Rule of St. Benedict and living in seclusion, "in order that they may inspire both their life and their art"; 2) a wider oblate movement among those Roman Catholics "generally interested in the better things of the Church, especially

2

in getting a better artistic expression," whose principal function would be to provide financial support to the select group.[8] Both groups would work toward the eventual establishment of 3) a regular monastery, under the guidance of Fort Augustus. This monastery was conceived of as "the crowning feature, the final result and flower of the lay movement." [9]

In other words, in its full incarnation, Harman's movement, and especially his Benedictine foundation, was intended to stand as a shining example to which the whole Church would eventually turn for guidance in reforming the artistic expression of its faith. It was designed, said one supporter of the group, to do battle against:

"prison stone churches looking like jails on the outside and either wedding cakes or vaudeville theatres in the inside ... cardboard chasubles and lace curtain albs and surplices, against gold fringe frontlets and female angels in pink and blue dance frocks, against fret-saw shrines and confessionals, against factory statues in 'natural' colors tattooed with gold-leaf 'decorations' on religious habits, against wood painted to imitate grained marble, against any and every sort of imitation."[10]

The members of the Portsmouth Priory group, most of whom were based in New York, met there with Harman in September[11] and again for a retreat at Portsmouth in January of the new year.[12] By the January meeting, it was evident that the balance of power within the group was beginning to shift. Among a number of the original retreatant's group there had grown the feeling that Everitt Harman (referred to occasionally as "Brother Wilfrid") could not manage the rather delicate political matters necessary to making the plan a reality. Wrote one of the members:

"Brother Wilfrid, . . . who was more or less the leader of this affair when I came into it, has not been very wise in his handling of matters. He has deluged the Abbot [McDonald of Fort Augustus] with rambling and pointless letters, which, I fear, are beginning to make him sick of the whole affair."[13]

The letter goes on to say that even the Prior of Portsmouth had strongly advised the group to have the plan presented by those who can "talk about the thing a little more coherently and soundly," so that it will not be thought to be "merely a sort of aimless brainstorm on the part of willing but not very significant men."[14] In spite of these reservations, several members of the group continued to support Harman's original scheme, namely, a guild comprised mainly of oblates (or whose control at least would be in oblate hands) and an eventual Benedictine monastic community under Fort Augustus.[15] But by January, 1928, when the next retreat was held, a second group had formed and prepared another organizational scheme.[16]

The chief spokesman of this second body of opinion was a young New York draftsman who had attended the first Portsmouth Priory retreat. Idesbald Walter Paulus Joseph Maria von Water- schoot van der Gracht was a Hollander, the son of a famous Dutch geologist and an Austrian countess.[17] During his twelve years in the United States, van der Gracht had become increasingly distressed by the low esteem with which the Roman Catholic Church was held within society at large. Although he strongly supported the need for action, he had come to believe that Harman's scheme would not be sufficient to turn the tide of popular opinion in the Church's favor:

"Brother W. obviously thinks primarily of the spiritual welfare of the members, [but] we, as laymen, must keep in mind its missionary function toward the public, else there is no real need for a primarily devotional foundation."[18]

In a 10,000-word essay, which was presented to the group at the third Portsmouth Priory retreat, June 16-18, 1928, van der Gracht outlined his assessment of the problem of Roman Catholic intellectual life in America and the solution that he proposed.[19] His argument can be summarized as follows:

1) The Roman Catholic Church in the United States is regarded with fear, suspicion, and scorn by the largely Protestant and Anglo-Saxon intellectual establishment.[20]

2) The main reason for this situation is the fact that there was no recognized Roman Catholic element in America until "the great

waves of Irish, German, Latin, and Slavic immigration began to pour into the country."[21]

3) Because of the low socioeconomic status of these immigrants, the Church as a whole was perceived and labeled as lacking higher cultural values.

4) At the same time, the Church had many, many internal problems to solve, with a vast mission field and millions of Roman Catholics in need of pastoral care.

5) These demands on the Church and its clergy made it unable to retain its historic commitment to the intellectual and artistic expression of its faith.

6) But in recent years there had come into being a "body of cultured Catholics within the Church to whom many of her higher inspirational treasures are unavailable."[22]

7) Although their needs were not being met, the members of "this enlightened element within the Church . . . must lead in restoring her full inspirational and guiding qualities."[23]

8) Only in restoring these qualities can the Church "be more effective within, and also manifest to all her full beauty and wisdom and take her rightful place in the cultural life of the nation."[24]

Although it was criticized by some for taking too critical and "European" a view of the American situation,[25] the paper quickly became a sort of manifesto for the group as a whole. In addition to its appraisal of the current status of American Roman Catholicism, it contained the blueprint of an organizational scheme that, it was suggested, would be most effective in solving the problems of the Church's limited cultural influence in the United States.

Unlike Harman's plan, the van der Gracht plan for the renewal of Christian art did not end with, but rather began with a monastic community. Van der Gracht believed that the key to the entire project was to immediately establish a Benedictine monastery which would be a:

"center of liturgical observance and of higher Catholic culture as practiced in the arts and general intellectual pursuits. A place where young men — and older — could come and have certain contact with people of their own cultural status, where they could find those things in their faith that are at present almost entirely inaccessible to them: its real relationship to their artistic and intellectual life."[26]

Van der Gracht's supporters believed that one of the major difficulties with Harman's "Oblates Guild" was that the demand for the oblate vocation (so integral a part of the Harman plan) was a matter of such personal import that it could not be made a qualifying factor in an organization of this kind. Van der Gracht himself criticized Harman's plan for an oblate movement because it:

"presumes that all artists of our ideals would wish to become oblates; what about those who do not? Oblateship is not something that can be quasi-required; if a man had not felt the urge to do it himself, it is doubtful whether he should be pushed into it as a condition to active participation."[27]

It was felt that some qualified individuals might be kept from joining the group by the demand of oblateship, while persons of little artistic talent might be included simply because they were oblates.

"It is quite conceivable that there would be a great deal more understanding of the real problems involved among many non-oblates, which would not only react on the efficiency of the organization and its professional prestige, but tend to eliminate the interest of the — conceivably more capable — non-oblate members, and put an undesirable premium on a matter which is purely one of conscience, whose value is certainly great, but no guarantee of excellence in artistic, or even intellectual and spiritual matters."[28]

Van der Gracht believed that if an already-established monastery would undertake to establish a foundation devoted to the arts, it would not only increase the prestige of the Roman Catholic Church as a whole, but also encourage oblate vocations among lay Roman Catholic artists and architects.

Just as Everitt Harman had investigated the willingness of Fort Augustus to support his own monastic plan,[29] so too had the van der Gracht group thoroughly explored the question of leadership. The members were convinced that they had found the man that they were seeking in Dom Suibert Kramer, monk of Beuron Abbey. Dom Kramer, the former *Glockensachverständiger* (bell-master) of the Beuronese Congregation (and a distant cousin of van der Gracht), had spent the previous year in the United States working for his abbey.[30] Overtures had been made to him by van der Gracht, with the intention that he become superior of the proposed foundation,[31] but it was recognized that the problems of the approval of ecclesiastical authorities, the willingness of Beuron itself to undertake such a foundation, and the funding of the project were enormous. (And indeed, it was largely the matter of money that finally kept the monastic component of either the Harman or van der Gracht plan from ever becoming a reality.[32])

But the monastic community, although at the heart of the van der Gracht scheme, was not the whole of it:

"A second and more specialized element of the movement would be an organization of artists, architects, craftsmen, and such others as are actively interested in these particular phases of the Church's material aspects. Working toward a betterment of the aesthetic expression of the Catholic ideal, it is founded on the belief that the full beauty of this expression requires most intimate union between the Church and the artist."[33]

It is from this "more specialized" element of the movement proposed by Ides van der Gracht that the Liturgical Arts Society was eventually forged. The van der Gracht group[34] envisioned a lay guild:

"of all those embued by our spirit, whose control is vested in Catholic hands, but in which oblateship is — though urged as very valuable and helpful and desirable — not written into the Constitution . . . we organize primarily as spiritually minded artists, not primarily as oblates with artistic inclinations."[35]

At the June 16-18, 1928 retreat at Portsmouth Priory, led by Abbot McDonald of Fort Augustus,[36] both Everitt Harman and Ides van der Gracht presented their individual proposals to the group. Each man had drawn up a set of programmatic guidelines; in addition, Harman had produced a full Constitution and Bylaws of the Benedictine Oblates Guild of Architects, Artists, and Craftsmen.

But van der Gracht clearly had the upper hand, and he openly challenged Harman on the feasibility of demanding that all potential
members become oblates and the ability of the group to sustain itself without the guiding hand of a monastic community (which in
the Harman scheme, van der Gracht alleged, would not be possible
for at least nine years).[37] Harman's response is not recorded, but
after the retreat no further mention of the oblate plan is made, and
even Harman's staunchest supporters eventually saw merit to the
van der Gracht plan. One wrote:

"Van der Gracht has certain ideals in connection with this thing,
and while I don't mean to say I'm not in sympathy with them,
they're so foreign to what our original group had in mind that I am
not always sure that they meet with the approval of you other original members. The thing, however, seems to be shaping into something definite and practical, and most of the schemes we've had
haven't been either."[38]

THE LITURGICAL ARTS SOCIETY: A REALISTIC PLAN

Despite general support for the entire van der Gracht scheme, the
core idea of founding a Benedictine monastic community seems to
have been seen as unworkable and was practically abandoned
within three months of the June, 1928 retreat. It had been thought
that wealthy patrons could be found who would donate to the effort a landholding in Connecticut or New York and sufficient funds
to support the foundation through its early years.[39] In spite of a
certain amount of solicitation by Ides van der Gracht, no one came
forward with more than good will and kind words for a monastery;
the idea of a Benedictine house devoted to the arts had to be surren-
dered.[41]

Ides van der Gracht spent the months following the June retreat preparing, revising, and soliciting advice on a complete set of bylaws
and a constitution for the group. The result was essentially a flesh-
ing out of the second element in his original plan, namely: a Society
whose purpose was to "increase the interest of its members in the
spiritual value of the liturgical arts, and to co-ordinate the efforts of
those concerned with its development."[42] A draft Constitution and
Bylaws of the Liturgical Arts Society were finalized and approved
at a meeting at van der Gracht's New York apartment on Septem-

8

ber 24, 1928. One month later, on October 22, 1928, the Liturgical Arts Society was incorporated in the State of New York with nine of the original Portsmouth Priory group as subscribers to the Certificate of Incorporation. The names Everitt Harman and Ides van der Gracht both appear on the list.[43]

ORGANIZATIONAL DECISIONS

Once the Society believed itself to be on fairly firm ground, with By-Laws, Constitution, and statement-of-purpose, the young founders felt confident enough to reach out for support to the older and more well-established members of the Roman Catholic intellectual community. On August 27, 1928, Everitt Harman traveled to Boston to visit Charles Maginnis, who was quickly becoming the foremost Roman Catholic ecclesiastical architect in the country, and acquainted him with the Society's vision.[44] Michael Williams, editor of *The Commonweal*, had been one of the Portsmouth Priory retreatants, although not among the first, but now John LaFarge, S.J., an editor of *America*, was also approached.[45] Both Maginnis and LaFarge gave their wholehearted support, and both would soon assume leadership roles in the Society.[46]

The full Society met for the first time late in December of 1930[47] at the offices of *America*. At this meeting, permanent committees were formed, officers elected, and the directorate of the Society approved. Individuals from both the original Portsmouth Priory group and from the group of more recent, professionally well-established individuals served in leadership positions. Charles Maginnis, head of the successful Boston architectural firm of Maginnis & Walsh, was elected the Society's first president. His extensive contacts, both with the leadership of the Roman Catholic Church and with the most influential architects in the United States and Europe, were a valuable resource for the fledgling organization. In all, Charles Maginnis would serve four terms as president, giving the Liturgical Arts Society prestige at a critical time in its history. Ides van der Gracht continued his service to the group as vice president. But since Charles Maginnis had a rather autocratic presidential style, van der Gracht was given little opportunity to exercise his leadership skills. Another member of the Portsmouth Priory group, Joseph Shanley, a young New York architect, was elected treasurer.

The Society's first secretary, Maurice Lavanoux, had also been present at the Portsmouth Priory meetings, having been one of the first to respond to Everitt Harman's letter to the *AIA Journal*.[48] When he was elected, he was a draftsman with the Boston offices of Maginnis & Walsh. In the end, Maurice Lavanoux would prove to be the most influential of the Society's founding members, serving as secretary for 42 years. The directorate, for obvious reasons, was entirely made up of the more successful members of the Society, many of whom also served on the boards of directors of other Roman Catholic organizations. (For example, the Reverend T. Lawrason Riggs was a director of *The Commonweal*, the St. Hilda Guild, and the Calvert Associates as well as the Liturgical Arts Society.) Throughout the Society's existence, the members of the directorate continued to be chosen from among the most influential men and women the Roman Catholic Church had to offer.[49]

THE QUESTION OF MEMBERSHIP

Once the plan for a "Benedictine Guild" comprised mainly of oblates had been abandoned, a number of practical problems surfaced for the new Society. In order to work some of them out, a set of temporary directors, standing committees, and officers was elected on November 2, 1929.[50] One of the first orders of business for this leadership was to delineate the qualifications necessary for inclusion in the Liturgical Arts Society. The makeshift "Membership Committee" met in January of 1928, and its earliest deliberations are reported by the "President *pro tem:*"[51]

"The Membership Committee finally got together about the first of this year (LaFarge is chairman, and I put van der Gracht and George N. Schuster of *The Commonweal* on it) and recommended as a policy—at least for the present if not permanently—that the membership should be quite limited—and of an extremely high quality. Schuster voiced the opinion—which is based upon his very broad contacts with things via *The Commonweal*—that a very limited membership of really high-calibre men could accomplish something eminently worthwhile whereas a wide membership of a more average quality could do very little lasting good."[52]

Ides van der Gracht, still wielding significant influence in the New York group, was even more precise about the quality of prospective members: "As far as membership is concerned," he wrote Lavanoux on the occasion of the public announcement of the group's existence, "it seems to me that we should make it our policy to do this by INVITATION ONLY . . . rather than a carryall for every Tom, Dick, and Harry."[53]

But the general announcements of the formation of the group which appeared in such publications as *America*[54] and *The Commonweal*[55] caused some unsettling difficulties in carrying out this plan. In response to the publicity, letters expressing interest and support came in from all parts of the country. Many were from individuals whom the Society would consider "acceptable" candidates for membership, but "on the other hand," lamented van der Gracht, "there come some rather embarrassing ones, which we should have a policy for, while hurting as few feelings as possible."[56]

Many of these difficulties were handled by an organizational scheme which admitted various classes of members. When the Bylaws Committee met in January, 1931, the qualifications for each class of membership were more exactly defined. Van der Gracht reported that:

"The Committee was guided in its deliberations by the general principle that there should be two classes of membership: first, a Corporate membership, a comparatively small body in the nature of an Academy composed of Catholics of the highest standing both as practicing artists and as vitally interested in the aims of the Society in whose hands the government of its affairs would be vested; and, secondly, a larger Sustaining Membership to which would be admitted all those who evince an active interest in the propagation of its ideals."[57]

The final draft of the Bylaws and Constitution of the Society reflected this relatively strong sense of exclusiveness in its section on membership.[58]

By June of 1931, a list of 200 to 300 persons to be invited to Sustaining Membership had been drawn up, and they were contacted by letter. The Executive Secretary reported that in May and June of 1931 he had sent out more than 100 invitations and had had, as of the 18th of June, "over 25 responses enclosing cheques."[59] In spite of the rigorous requirements for joining the Society, within six months, membership figures bespoke some degree of success: 58 corporate members and 94 sustaining members had been added to the ranks of the Liturgical Arts Society.[60]

But it appears that the selection of individuals to be nominated to membership was not guided solely by the Society's perception of a candidate's professional stature or contribution to the furthering of the Society's aims. The Executive Secretary was pleased to report that the membership campaign was "at last reaching a number of the very wealthy people."[61] Maurice Lavanoux, however, had long been suspicious of the New York group's reliance on wealthy patrons. "I am afraid," he wrote to Harman on one occasion, "that they pin their faith on the help of 'social' connections. I dread such social connections because they become so many 'strings' that hinder the work afterwards."[62] The Society's years of precarious financial status would lend support to Lavanoux's contention that wealthy patrons could not be relied upon to any great degree.

The gauging of a potential member's true "aesthetic sensibilities" was also part of the selection process, as is evidenced by the case of Charles Connick, who was noted for his craftsmanship in stained glass. Although not a Roman Catholic, Connick was on the list of those to be invited to Sustaining Membership, presumably by virtue of the quality and quantity of the "Connick Glass" that adorned the finest Roman Catholic Church buildings of the period.[63] Maurice Lavanoux questions Connick's inclusion, partly because he was "under the impression that only Catholics were to be invited as such."[64] But his deeper reasons have little to do with Connick's denominational identity:

"I know Mr. Connick very well, but personally I would exclude him... because, while his knowledge of ecclesiastical art is extensive, his sympathies are of the sentimental variety. By this I mean the kind of understanding that raves over St. Francis' love of birds, etc., but forgets the saint's place in the Church militant."[65]

ADVISORS

In October of 1930, a list of persons to serve as members of an "Advisory Board" to the Society was drawn up. It was intended that they could be called upon to act as knowledgeable resources for the Society's proposed "Information Bureau;" liturgists,[66] journalists,[67] diocesan clergy,[68] architects,[69] and educators[70] were included on the list. Even though the Liturgical Arts Society was founded by lay people, 17 of the 21 prospective advisory board members were clergymen. Benedictines were well-represented on the advisory board, since, as Maurice Lavanoux explained, "it has always seemed right to me that a name of a Benedictine abbot should appear in connection with our work, because of the close cooperation and guidance of the Order with the liturgical revival at the present time."[71] In the end, four Benedictines agreed to serve in an advisory capacity, three of whom (Dom Hugh Diman of Portsmouth Priory, Dom P. Raphael of St. Anselm's, Manchester, New Hampshire, and Dom Alcuin Deutsch of St. John's, Collegeville, Minnesota) were priors or abbots of their respective communities.

"The purpose of these names on the letterhead," according to Lavanoux, who, as secretary of the Society, issued the invitations to board membership, "is mainly to furnish a guarantee that the plans have been approved by competent persons and [are] not merely the result of misguided enthusiasm."[72] In the end, 19 of the 21 invited men accepted the Society's request to serve.[73] Father Joseph Walsh and Father Robert Lord, both faculty members of St. John's Seminary, Boston, Massachusetts, excused themselves, and it was assumed that their refusal was "because of the Cardinal's [O'Connell's] limited approval."[74] (Neither man declared this to be his explicit reason for declining, but rather cited other pressing obligations.) Within a few years, the advisory board had served its purpose as guarantor that the Society was not simply a momentary whim of Roman Catholic eccentrics, and the list was dropped from the letterhead in 1934.

NON-ROMAN CATHOLIC PARTICIPATION

Although the group's self-identity was clearly Roman Catholic, the question of the role of non-Roman Catholic Christians in the life of the Liturgical Arts Society arose almost immediately after it had been decided to abandon the idea of a Benedictine-related organization. There was concern as early as 1929 that the presence of non-Roman Catholics in visible positions in the Society might make it appear that "we were admitting from the very start that we cannot stand on our own feet."[75] But it was Ralph Adams Cram (1863-1942), the dean of the neo-Gothic school of American architecture and a devout Anglican, who served as catalyst for the whole ecumenical debate during the Society's formative period.

Throughout his career, Ralph Adams Cram was dedicated to returning the Church to the purity and harmony it had enjoyed prior to the upheaval caused by the Reformation, Renaissance, and the Industrial Revolution. In order to recover what he called "the Gothic Spirit" of the Church, Cram worked for the restoration of organic unity between religion, art, modes of production, and social organization. Ralph Adams Cram was the most vocal and visible of the American Gothicists, and his architectural designs embodied his romantic medievalism. Cram's quest for the true Gothic Spirit of the Church, resulted in a substantial number of notable religious buildings in Gothic style, not only for Episcopalians, but for Presbyterians, Methodists, Congregationalists, and Unitarians as well. By reproducing a medieval environment, re-establishing craft guilds, restoring monarchical systems of government, and returning to hierarchical Church polity, Cram sought to reform and reunite all of Christianity.[76]

As one committed to the "true Catholic spirit," Cram influenced many of the leading Roman Catholic intellectual movements of the time. He was an early and important supporter of *The Commonweal*[77] and of the Calvert Associates, both of which were dedicated to restoring the Catholic Church to its proper place in American intellectual life. His volume in the "Calvert Series" (Hillaire Belloc, general editor) bore the Nihil Obstat and Imprimatur.[78]

Cram's close connections with Roman Catholic artists and architects made him aware almost immediately of any stirrings of organized involvement in the advancement of ecclesiastical art. Indeed, in making plans for the very first formal meeting of those who had become interested in his plan, Everitt Harman broaches the subject of Cram:

"I have heard from Wright Goodhue (Bertram's nephew in Boston) who will also come down [for the September 10 organizational meeting] and he says that Cram would like to come if he could make it. But I am inclined to make the gathering a more personal affair until we get a definite plan outlined."[79]

Cram did not attend the meeting.

On August 27, 1928, Harman traveled to Boston from Portsmouth Priory and paid a call on Cram (and on Charles Maginnis as well)[80] in order to acquaint him with recent developments in the journey toward an organization for the advancement of liturgical art. Without hesitation, Cram responded with his full endorsement of Harman's proposal for a "Catholic Arts League" and wrote a letter to that effect on the spot:

"Your whole project is one which I have thought about a great deal during the past twenty years on my own account, but I have hardly seen just how this end was to be accomplished. Many years' experience in dealing with Catholic architecture and the allied arts has convinced me that this is manifestly the moment when such a project as you have in mind should be initiated. There is an extraordinary recrudescence of interest in Catholic art of every kind. This interest must be canalized and made operative. Furthermore, the demand for good art must be met. It seems to me that your plans cover both these considerations, and just in so far as I can be of any assistance along these lines, you may count on my enthusiastic cooperation and support."[81]

In addition to his promise of personal support, Cram presented Harman with $50 "to help defray incorporation expenses." He was the only individual outside the original group to make a monetary contribution.[82]

Unfortunately, personal and professional antagonism toward Ralph Adams Cram became entangled with and colored the entire question of non-Roman Catholic participation in the Liturgical Arts Society. At the center of the active opposition to Cram's involvement was Maurice Lavanoux, a member of the original Portsmouth Priory group, whose judgment may have been guided somewhat by his position as draftsman in the firm of Maginnis & Walsh, at that time the Cram firm's major competitor.[83] Lavanoux's animosity toward Cram was perhaps more open and strident than that of other members of the early group, but it is indicative of the sentiments of at least one faction and also of the extent to which personal, professional, and programmatic inclinations intertwined in setting policy for the Society.[84]

In 1929, Maurice Lavanoux had approached the managing editor of *The Commonweal*, George N. Schuster (himself later a member of the Membership Committee of the Society), about the possibility of writing a review of Cram's *The Catholic Church and Art*[85] for publication. Schuster agreed that such a review would be of interest to his readers, and in a short time Lavanoux received a review copy of the book from the publisher, Macmillan & Company. Upon receipt of a copy of Lavanoux's review (which he admits was "not a very flattering one"),[86] Macmillan informed him that *The Commonweal* had "made other arrangements" for review of the book. Lavanoux immediately wrote Schuster for an explanation. He was told that the review could not be published because "Mr. Cram has helped *The Commonweal* from the beginning" and "he is a very lovable man."[87] Wrote Lavanoux, relating the incident to Harman[88]; "I do not see what a 'very lovable man' has to do with the publication of a review which calls attention to misrepresentations. . . ." Lavanoux contended that Cram's insistence on one architectural style to the "practical exclusion of any other" amounted to "moral dishonesty," and that this was especially offensive from "one who is continually on the fence and playing two camps." (He added that the whole business reminded him of "the Anglican 'Malines' group."[89])

The incident had clearly pushed Lavanoux past the point of toleration, for he concluded his letter to Harman by saying: "For my part, I will object to Mr. Cram's *active* participation in our plans to the extent of withdrawing should anyone insist that he be given any control."

Harman was greatly disturbed by Lavanoux's uncompromising stance:

"There can be no doubt that your attitude towards Cram . . . will certainly cause you great difficulty, and it is perhaps the cause of New York's slowness to act. The Cardinal's office will take the same attitude (if they know about it), I am sure . . . . I have felt all along that you are unjustly prejudiced against Cram (perhaps on religious grounds), as in *this* case *we* are the 'heterodox' — at least insofar as

16

we try to reconcile opposing camps under one banner. His principles are Catholic, and he may teach his doctrine as exclusively true until condemned by the Church or proven wrong to his own satisfaction."[90]

In the matter of Lavanoux's refusal to participate in the Society if Cram were given any influence, Harman spoke even more emphatically:

"I could not condemn strongly enough such an attitude on your part. It is like saying I shall have nothing to do with anyone who has any real convictions! I would say that it is the *only way you can find the truth* (until the Church pronounces) — get both the pro and con of it — work up discussions and arguments *from both sides* — *open forum* — let them have it out! To me that is the whole purpose of the idea, and *Cram is indispensable.*"[91]

In the end, both "sides" can claim a victory of sorts in the matter of Ralph Adams Cram. Cram's name was not among those on the list of Advisory Board members. This was especially disturbing to Everitt Harman, who reminded the group that Cram was the only one who had offered them cash at the outset of their venture.[92] Lavanoux explained in response that it was his own belief that "all officers and members of the Advisory Board should be Catholics."[93] But on May 28, 1931, nearly three years after he first gave his personal and financial support to Everitt Harman's plan for a "Catholic Arts League," Ralph Adams Cram was invited to Sustaining (not the higher-ranking Corporate) Membership in the Liturgical Arts Society. His name was also prominent in the press releases announcing the publication of Vol. 1 No. 1 of *Liturgical Arts*, November 20, 1931:

"The presence of Mr. Cram among the members, although he is not a member of the Roman Catholic communion, is indicative of the interest felt by many outside the Church, who have nevertheless joined the Society to further its purposes."[94]

But that was not to be the end of the debate over Cram's brand of "Catholicism" and that of the Society. Two years later, on July 10, 1933, Ralph Adams Cram wrote to the Society,[95] asking if it might be interested in setting up a display at the exhibition of ecclesiastical arts and crafts to be held in Boston (October 15-22, 1933) to mark the 100th anniversary of the Oxford Movement. The Society's secretary, Maurice Lavanoux, wrote to a number of the directors for their opinion of the proposal and, at the same time, expressed his own reservations:

"The fact that this Boston exhibition is to be held in connection with the 100th anniversary of the Oxford Movement seems to put the matter in a curious light. In view of the recent pronouncement by the Rt. Rev. William Moreland Hall, Bishop of Sacramento in the Cathedral of St. John the Divine (*Brooklyn Tablet*, July 8, 1933), I wondered whether any cooperation by the society might be understood as a sympathetic attitude toward the Anglican celebration of the Oxford Movement. Mr. Binsse and myself feel very strongly that an acceptance on our part to send the New York exhibits to Boston would be construed as an endorsement of the idea . . . that, after all, the Anglican is really a Catholic and can be termed as such even tho' he disclaims any allegiance to Rome and can disbelieve any dogma which he deems to be contrary to his reason."[96]

Lavanoux was certainly not alone in his strong reaction against any Roman Catholic recognition of the Oxford Movement centenary. Throughout 1933, Roman Catholics in England and the United States saw the event as an occasion for extended commentary on Anglican-Roman Catholic relations. Unfortunately, the discussion was hardly an irenic one, with divisiveness fueled by several articles in the Catholic press quoting inflammatory statements made by Anglican clergy.

In the *Brooklyn Tablet*,[97] the Rt. Reverend William Moreland Hall, Episcopal Bishop of Sacramento, California, is reported to have said in a sermon at the Cathedral of St. John the Divine, New York, that "it was due to God's guidance that Columbus' course veered to the south, leaving North America to be civilized by Anglo-Saxons rather than by slaves of any king or vassals to a Pope." He went on to credit the American system of public education with transforming the masses of those immigrant people who are still inclined to such slavery into "real Americans."

The reaction of the English-speaking Roman Catholic press to the centennial of the Oxford Movement was uniformly negative. In the same issue of the *Brooklyn Tablet* (page 8), an article titled "Are Protestants Catholics?" suggests that the best way for Anglicans to celebrate the centennial would be "by following in the footsteps of its greatest figure — John Henry Newman. Let them come out of the 'encircling gloom' and into the 'kindly light.' "

The London *Tablet* was perhaps stronger in its deprecation of the centennial and the churchmanship which underlay it. In its July 8, 1933, edition, an editorial stated:

"We contend that the Oxford Movement originated in Catholicism — in that only true Catholicism which is in full communion with the Holy See of Rome — and that no man was or is a legitimate son who failed or is failing to let it carry him to its Catholic — not 'Anglo-Catholic' — goal . . . . We, on our side, maintain that the only men who were true to the [Oxford] Movement were those who moved along its divinely-traced course all the way to Rome, instead of side-tracking themselves in that falsely-named 'Anglo-Catholicism' which has added one more to England's hundreds of sects."

All of this made Cram's suggestion that the Society participate in a celebration of the Oxford Movement exceedingly problematic. One of the Society's directors, Bishop James Cassidy of Fall River, Massachusetts, replied that it would indeed be unwise to participate in the exhibition for the very reasons that Lavanoux had set forth in his circular letter.[98] Several other directors responded, expressing similar sentiments.[99] "Obviously as Catholics," Charles Maginnis wrote, "we cannot be expected to share this particular current of enthusiasm over the Oxford Movement."[100] On July 28, 1933, Lavanoux declined Cram's invitation to participate in the Boston exhibition. "Of course I think this is a mistake," Cram wrote in response to Lavanoux's letter, "and I should have supposed that the Directors would have been only too glad to bring the influence of Catholic art to bear on any of those at present outside the fold."[101]

Cram kept up his membership in the Liturgical Arts Society for the next 11 years. On Page 1 of the November, 1942 issue of *Liturgical Arts*,[102] there appears a substantial, if restrained, obituary by Charles Maginnis, marking the death of Ralph Adams Cram. It fails to mention Cram's interest in and support of the Society and steers very wide of any issue that might be tagged "religious." In fact, most of the obituary is not devoted to Cram at all, but rather to the work of Bertram Grosvenor Goodhue, a Roman Catholic who had been Cram's partner for many years.

It is difficult to judge to what degree the Society's policy regarding the involvement of non-Roman Catholics in its work was the direct result of the founding members' reaction to this one provocative personality. Clearly, the fear of "contamination" of a Roman Catholic endeavor did not deter such enterprises as *The Commonweal*, its organizational arm The New Review, the St. Hilda Guild (devoted to the restoration of Gothic Church vesture), and the Calvert Associates from welcoming Cram's full participation. Indeed, advertisements for the St. Hilda Guild and for the Calvert Associates appeared in 1:1 and 1:2 of *Liturgical Arts*. Each advertisement contained a list of individuals who served in leadership positions for the organization, and at the top of both lists was the name "Ralph Adams Cram." Given this evidence, one might suspect that the explanations offered for excluding Cram from a position of influence in the Liturgical Arts Society were more a mask for professional jealousy than an expression of ecclesiastical purism.

Whatever the truth of the matter, it seems that the decisions made about the inclusion of Cram set theprecedent for a substantial portion of the Society's history. The Society had clearly set its course on the path of Roman Catholic interests and concerns almost exclusively; with the passing of Ralph Adams Cram, the urgency of the question of non-Roman Catholic involvement passed too.

THE SOCIETY AND THE ROMAN CATHOLIC HIERARCHY

In addition to these membership issues, it became necessary to rethink the relationship between the Society and the hierarchy of the Roman Catholic Church once the plan to form a Benedictine Guild was abandoned. It was clear to all concerned that if the Society was to be more than simply a group that gathered privately to exchange ideas on the state of ecclesiastical art, then a close link with Church leaders was imperative.

But in the absence of any definite plan of action, it seemed premature to approach the Archbishop of New York (within whose jurisdiction the Society had been incorporated in October of 1928) for an endorsement. As the months went by, however, there was growing concern that Cardinal Hayes might hear of the group's plans before a formal statement of the aims and workings of the organization could be drafted, and that he might be given a "false impression through adverse channels." (It is suggested that among these "adverse channels" is "Barclay Street or their outlying protégées," the commercial vendors of ecclesiastical furnishings whom the Society viewed as its primary opposition.[103]) By the spring of 1930, the group was at last ready to present its program to Cardinal Hayes for approval, and Charles Maginnis, who had done a considerable amount of architectural work for the archdiocese, was enlisted to serve as go-between. Maginnis sent the Cardinal a statement of purpose outlining the Society's proposed objectives and requested an audience. This was scheduled for January 12, 1931. But at the last minute, Hayes's office canceled the meeting, and the fears that the plan had been sabotaged by those unfriendly to the Society's aims were rekindled. Nearly a year passed with no word from the Cardinal, and the group in New York began to despair of ever seeing its goals realized. "You can't get anywhere," exclaimed one member of the group, "unless you have the approval of the members of the hierarchy!"[104]

Finally, in November of 1931, the meeting was rescheduled. On December 7, 1931, Henry Lorin Binsse, the Society's paid Executive Secretary,[105] and Ides van der Gracht had "a long and very positive discussion" of the Liturgical Arts Society with Cardinal Hayes, whose formal approval for the Society's activities was secured. "His Eminence was most encouraging," van der Gracht reported to Maginnis the following day, "and asked us particularly to convey his appreciative thanks to you for thinking of him in this connection."[106] As a result, the words "Under the Patronage of His Eminence Patrick Cardinal Hayes, Archbishop of New York," were added to the upper left-hand corner of the Society's letterhead.

Things did not go as smoothly, however, with the leadership of the Church in Boston. Maurice Lavanoux seemed aware from the beginning that he would have to tread carefully where Archbishop O'Connell was concerned and wrote to the New York group seeking advice on the politics of the situation:

"Would it not be well to plan a visit to Cardinal O'Connell immediately after the visit to Cardinal Hayes so that it may seem a simultaneous affair? We hope to be fairly active in Boston, and naturally we will rely upon the Cardinal's good will. From what I have heard he will be touchy about it."[107]

On July 19, 1930, Lavanoux wrote to O'Connell describing the Society and outlining its anticipated programs for the "improvement of ecclesiastical art." (The same letter, drafted by George Schuster of *The Commonweal*, had already been sent to Cardinal Hayes.[108])

"These considerations are submitted to Your Eminence [the letter concludes] with the hope that you will be pleased to give us your cooperation and endorse our efforts with your approval. The undersigned, [Lavanoux], delegated by the aforesaid group of architects, begs the privilege of an audience to further explain our plans and hopes for the future."[109]

But it appears that the Cardinal was not as pleased as Lavanoux had hoped, as evidenced by the rather terse reply that came back from O'Connell's secretary, the Rev. F. A. Burke: "His Eminence the Cardinal directs me to say that the purpose which you outline is admirable and that he wishes you every success in this regard."[110] But Lavanoux was not to be put off, and once again he wrote to Burke, explaining that what the Society really needed was an explicit statement of approval from the Cardinal himself. The Cardinal, it appears, was unmoved by this plea (or unaware of it), and in a conversation with Burke early in September, 1931, Lavanoux was told that "he should be satisfied with the knowledge that the Cardinal had cordially received the plans of the Society."[111]

Without the Boston Archibishop's expressed approval and the possibility of using his name as a sponsor of its activities, the Society had added difficulties in Boston. When the time came to publicize the formation of the Society in the Catholic press, the Boston diocesan newspaper was reluctant to say very much. "The *Pilot* refuses to list the names of patrons," lamented Lavanoux in a letter to van der Gracht, "because the Cardinal's name cannot be used."[112]

THE LITURGICAL ARTS SOCIETY CHAPLAIN
The naming of a chaplain to the Society was another matter in

which the difficulties with the Boston hierarchy surfaced. The by-laws and constitution of the Society specified the office of chaplain, to the Society, whose duties were described as follows:

"a) A Chaplain shall be invited by the Board of Directors of the Society to serve for a term of three years. He shall be *ex officio* member of the Executive Committee.

"b) He shall celebrate annually a Mass for the welfare of the Society at a time and place to be specified by the Executive Committee."[113]

Maurice Lavanoux had suggested that it might be politically advantageous to include the appointment of a chaplain as one of the items on the agenda for the meeting with the archbishop of New York. The person appointed:

"would be our spiritual director, and through him we could arrange for semi-monthly meetings when we could be given instructions on questions of theology, etc. To these meetings could come all craftsmen and others who are actively interested in art. The same could be done in Boston and, eventually, in any other dioceses that would join the movement."[114]

Indeed, the appointment of a Society chaplain ("who would give us monthly talks on points of doctrine, the liturgy, and canon law") was one of the goals outlined in the letter sent to both Cardinal Hayes and Cardinal O'Connell, but there was no request that the Cardinals themselves make such an appointment. But once it became apparent that O'Connell was going to withhold his personal endorsement of the Society, Lavanoux decided that the Society's need of a chaplain might be used as something of a bargaining chip, and once again he wrote to Monsignor Burke on August 23, 1930, presenting a broad vision of the role of chaplain:

"Any development of our sources of information will always depend on a thorough understanding of the laws of the Church. The spiritual aspect of the whole question will color and dictate logical policy . . . . Questions on symbolism in general can be answered by laymen, but it is conceivable that other equally important questions may touch on matters within the exclusive province of a priest. Meetings could be held monthly, at which the chaplain could, for example, explain the nature of the sacraments. On such lectures we could base our logical interpretation and understanding of symbolism."[115]

Two weeks later, on September 4, 1930, having had no response from the Cardinal's office, Lavanoux paid Monsignor Burke a call. "He explained that His Eminence 'would not appoint a chaplain at the present time.' There was no explanation," Lavanoux wrote to the New York group.[116] This is the last record of contact between the Society and the Archbishop of the Boston diocese. (A month later, Charles Maginnis offered to write to various members of the Roman Catholic hierarchy on the Society's behalf. The name of Cardinal O'Connell is conspicuously absent from the list.[117])

Undoubtedly, Maurice Lavanoux found this entire episode discouraging, having hoped that Boston would be a major center of the Society's activity, and in September of 1932, he himself left Boston and moved to New York to spearhead the work of the organization there.

Since 1928, Fr. John LaFarge, S.J., son of the famous painter John La-Farge, had been a staunch supporter of the Liturgical Arts Society, and the office of chaplain quite naturally fell to him.[118] As an editor of *America* and an influential author of political and religious commentary, LaFarge contributed balance, intelligence, and wit to the Society's work. Although the bylaws had stipulated a three-year term for the chaplain, his successive appointments were virtually automatic until his death on November 23, 1963.[119]

The Benedictine Guild envisioned by many of the Portsmouth Priory retreatants in 1927 and 1928 never materialized, and the lay organization established in its place had certain definite advantages over a monastic establishment. Since the members were working artists and architects rather than monks, the principles of the group were more likely to be translated into actual building projects for a variety of clients. In addition, the flexibility of the organizational scheme and the relative freedom from ecclesiastical strictures allowed the Liturgical Arts Society to pursue a number of creative options in the years to come. One of these options, the publication of a journal, would give a distinctive shape to the Society's future.

24

CHAPTER TWO

The Liturgical Arts Society and *Liturgical Arts* Magazine

THE BEGINNINGS OF *LITURGICAL ARTS*

Once the mechanics of membership, ecclesiastical approbation, and internal organization were settled, the Liturgical Arts Society could consider widening its sphere of influence, and thoughts soon turned to a possible publishing venture. But initiating a new publication, a risky undertaking at any time, was particularly uncertain during the Depression years.[1] Indeed, because of the precarious financial situation (both that of the Society and of the nation as a whole), it had originally been suggested that the Society's literature be associated with an existing journal, such as *The American Ecclesiastical Review*, "which conceivably might be interested to the extent of allowing a number of pages in each issue."[2]

Some members questioned the availability of advertising revenues required for an independent publication. It was believed at first that advertising could not be expected from sources other than those already committed to existing Catholic magazines, "in other words, the firms which have to do with that sort of commercialistic art against which you [the Liturgical Arts Society] are aiming your thunder."[3] Although several charter members, including Lavanoux and Maginnis,[4] seriously opposed an independent journal, by 1930 opposition began to fade. Not surprisingly, John LaFarge, S.J., and Michael Williams, each on the staff of a successful Roman Catholic weekly journal, were most encouraging about the feasibility of such a publication. Their opinion finally prevailed.[5]

Eventually, even Charles Maginnis became convinced; in December, 1930, he described his thinking on the matter:

"I wrote Mr. Harmon [sic] about a year ago, when he invited my opinion in reference to the feasibility of such an organization [as LAS]. I recall at that time I had definite reservations as to the expediency of a journal, feeling that there might be behind this idea too inexperienced a purpose. In talking with Maurice Lavanoux, however, I find that there is a thoroughly intelligent perception of the need of confining this general enterprise to the most modest dimensions."[6]

The belief that an independent publication for the Society was desirable was nearly unanimous, and in December, after a meeting of the New York group, van der Gracht reported:

"All present last night seemed to think that a journal was really the only way to get some national hearing and to achieve anything beyond a few pleasant evenings among ourselves . . . . Fr. LaFarge is convinced it would be easily self-supporting."[7]

Proposals that the journal appear as an annual or a quarterly 16-page leaflet or as a monthly or bi-monthly 24-page brochure were put forward for discussion. The question of costs was deliberated at length, and the matter was referred to the Finance Committee[8] at the December 28, 1930, meeting.[9] But not until a managing editor was hired in late February of 1931 was any concrete action taken toward publication.

THE MANAGING EDITOR

On various occasions since the spring of 1930, Maurice Lavanoux had been approached about moving to New York and taking over the duties of Society secretary, including management of the proposed journal, on a full-time basis.[10] Though he admitted that the work of secretary appealed to him very much, Lavanoux was reluctant to leave Boston. Eventually, it became clear that the New York group had to look elsewhere for a salaried person who could "devote his entire time to the development of the Society's activities." They found the person they were seeking in Henry Lorin Binsse.

Binsse, a 1926 graduate of Harvard University *magna cum laude*, had been connected with the editorial staff of the Oxford University Press and was between jobs when the Society hired him. Van der

Gracht expressed his initial enthusiasm in a letter to Charles Maginnis:

"Through the efforts of Miss [Hildreth] Meiere we have gotten in touch with a Mr. Binsse, a distant cousin of the LaFarges [LaFarge's mother was a member of the Binsse family] and of Mrs. Schuyler Warren. He is highly recommended by Mr. Reginald Townsend, editor of *Country Life*. Mr. Binsse was for several years business manager of the *Living Age* and is now trying to launch a publication of his own for which he is attempting to raise funds . . . . He seems to have all the required background, a very thorough knowledge of all aspects of the publishing game, a keen and wide grasp of our own problem, wide connections socially, financially, and among sources of information of all kinds, and last but not least, a sense of humor."[12]

With the full support of the New York group ("All of us in New York are terribly keen on him and think he is a real find"[13]), 26-year-old Henry Lorin Binsse was confirmed at a meeting of the Board of Directors on April 15, 1931, as the salaried Executive Secretary of the Liturgical Arts Society. [14]

Binsse's job was broadly conceived:

"He will be charged with the routine matters involving memberships, subscriptions to the journal, and canvassing the financial possibilities. He will also inaugurate an editorial program looking toward the publishing of a quarterly, which is the field in which he is exceedingly experienced. He will organize the various bibliographies, information bureau, library, and lists of original source material, as well as compose the lectures which we hope will be given. He will also make a survey of work being done currently— in a word, set the thing in motion."[15]

AN EDITORIAL POLICY

"And set the thing in motion" he did. Binsse was immediately anxious that "some sort of editorial policy be established for his guidance in laying out and collecting the material" for the journal,[16] and an editorial committee was appointed by Maginnis (consisting of Maginnis himself, Riggs, Williams, and Lavanoux). By the time of the meeting of Corporate Members held on May 7, 1931,[17] Binsse had done enough "behind-the-scenes" work on the quarterly that a proposed editorial policy could be thoroughly debated:

Scant assistance in formulating this policy had been afforded by referring to the 1928 Constitution of the Liturgical Arts Society. The bylaws of the Society designated that the editorial committee "shall publish a journal of the Society which shall be an exponent of its aims and ideals, and which shall present authentic and practical information of all kinds relative to the liturgical arts."[18] In the years that had followed the drafting of the Constitution, the members discussed more fully what sort of publication the Society would produce. It was generally thought that the journal should, most simply, be aimed at explaining to clergy "the difference between good and bad, and why they should want the best, and where it is to be gotten . . . ."[19] These early imaginings, undeniably lavish, anticipated a journal:

"including everything from architecture, the arts and crafts, liturgy in understandable language, music, iconography, hagiography, to lessons in good practise [sic] of construction and the theory of proper planning, and even financing. (It's all liturgical in its way, and all grist to our mill!)"[20]

With the hiring of Binsse, however, a more realistic attitude toward the proposed magazine was adopted. He began by consulting respected publishers, editors, and financial experts about the commercial aspects of a journal for the Society.[21] These conversations convinced Binsse that "the Society has a business opportunity in its journal such as I have never before seen, even in a commercial paper."[22] According to his calculations, the market supplied by Catholic church building and decorating was in the area of $100 million a year:

"To the seller of basic materials . . . this is a market of major importance. He at present cannot reach it adequately in any publication. The architectural journals do not reach the clergy and laity who spend the money; the Catholic journals have, from his point of view, a great deal of 'waste' circulation. And there is no Catholic journal published that has standards of content and manufacture high enough for such advertisers to wish to be associated with."[23]

When Binsse reported his findings to the New York group, van der Gracht (who was the chair of a temporary Editorial Committee)[24] drew up a trial editorial policy. According to this policy, which met with general, if informal, approval, the content of the magazine would be divided into six areas:

"1) General discussions of the proper nature of the liturgical arts written by authorities, both American and European, more or less philosophical.

"2) Historical material, including a more or less chronological series on the history of Christian art from the beginning and articles on the historical side of minor arts.

"3) Practical articles on current liturgical matters giving concrete suggestions for the architect, artist, priest, and layman.

"4) Descriptions of good modern work, both in architecture and the minor arts.

"5) Descriptions of rare and important ancient objects in museums or offered for sale, in order to make them available for study or to help restore them to their proper liturgical use.

"6) A regular bibliography of all publications affecting the liturgical arts.[25]"

On the whole, the editorial program was intended to be positive rather than negative. It would encourage the good, proper, functional, and appropriate in art and architecture, not castigate the bad. This general program was adopted by the permanent editorial committee (headed by Charles Maginnis) and approved at the May 7, 1931, meeting of Corporate members.[26] The appropriate "look" of the journal was also a matter of some debate. Many of the members who had originally supported a fairly modest publication were persuaded by Michael Williams and John LaFarge, both experienced in publishing, that "a swanky publication was necessary to put the idea over in this country."[27] The hiring of Binsse was certainly in line with this general approach, familiar as he was with a rather sophisticated sector of the publishing world.

In June, 1931, less than a month after the editorial policy had been finalized, a mock-up of the first issue was produced and taken to a few knowledgeable and influential people for their opinion. One of them was Dom Gaspar Lefebvre, O.S.B., monk of Abbey of St. Andre, Belgium, and founder-editor of *L'artisan liturgique* (later *Art d'eglisé*). On July 1, 1931, Binsse and Maurice Lavanoux (who had not met) traveled separately to Montreal where Dom Lefebvre was staying. At dinner at the Ritz Carleton Hotel that evening, they presented him with the prototype issue for his assessment. Lefebvre had substantial reservations about the proposed project: a lead article on art history (by a professor of fine arts at Princeton) was described as "too Protestant"; the whole magazine stressed too much the "material aspects of the question" and not enough the "fundamental issue of the liturgy"; the entire enterprise was "doomed" because it did not depend on a priory or an abbey; the projected 20,000 subscribers would surely dwindle to 2,000-3,000 within two years; and finally, the publication, if not the movement as a whole, was "premature."[28] A full report of the meeting with Lefebvre was drawn up by Lavanoux (who was badly shaken by the entire episode and described it as "a fiasco") and sent to Charles Maginnis and the Society's other officers and directors.[29]

If there was any renewed uncertainty about the feasibility of a journal on account of the Lefebvre meeting, it was only momentary, and Binsse's confidence in his own assessment of the potential success of the publication carried the day. In response to Lefebvre's final argument against a Liturgical Arts Society journal, Binsse argued:

"Any publication is 'premature.' If one waits until one is absolutely certain of a response one will wait indefinitely . . . and there is always danger that some other group will get a foothold and do badly what we hope to do well."[30]

From the beginning it was acknowledged that the journal was something of a "chicken-and-egg" problem: without financial support no journal would appear; without a journal, no financial support would appear. But Binsse saw the journal as an essential first step to any other work the Society might undertake:

"We have perhaps put the cart before the horse in issuing our publication before commencing our other activities. The purpose of this is to insure our Society sufficient revenues to make possible the activities we contemplate. Our magazine is not only a means of propaganda among the clergy, but also a source of financial support which the Society must have."[31]

Some deprecated the New York group's reliance on "wealthy patrons," but it was just such an individual who turned *Liturgical Arts* Magazine from a dream into a reality. In April of 1931, Charles Maginnis reported that he had been offered the princely sum of $6,000 (equal to Binsse's annual salary) by an anonymous benefactor, to further the Society's aims.[32] With that money in hand, the organization could turn its attention to the more material aspects of publishing a journal.

LITURGICAL ARTS, 1:1: FORMAT AND DISTRIBUTION

Even though it was generally assumed by the membership and directors that the journal would bear the Society's name, the title *Liturgical Arts* did not meet with universal approval. One Sustaining Member wrote:

"The name 'Liturgical Arts' is intelligible to you and me, but I doubt that it would seem so to the general public (or even to some people higher up!) Those words suggest to most people merely the art employed in the actual liturgy itself, vestments, altar, etc., not the arts in general."[33]

But since this concern apparently was not widespread, and since no viable alternative was suggested, the name "Liturgical Arts" seems to have been adopted without any serious discussion.

In late July, 1931, the Liturgical Arts Society signed a contract with the Rumford Press of Concord, New Hampshire, to print a softcover quarterly journal in a 9" by 12" format (9 ¼" by 12½" overall). The choice of the Rumford Press, which had a reputation for producing quality publications, including the *Atlantic Monthly*, is itself evidence of Henry Lorin Binsse's firm commitment to excellence. The first issue of *Liturgical Arts*[34] was to be an impressive piece of work, totaling 56 pages: 24 pages of text, 14 pages of illustrated advertising, 12 pages of black and white photographs, 2 pages of colored illustrations, and several floor plans. It was to be printed on ecru rag paper, with heavily coated stock for the illustrations. The body type was 12-point Baskerville, described by one commentator as "a handsome and most legible type."[35]

By October 24, 1931, the printer was ready to go to press with the first number of *Liturgical Arts*. Publication was delayed, however, in part because there wasn't enough money and in part because Binsse "refused to commit the Society to anything for which it cannot pay cash if necessary."[36] The anonymous donation of $6,000 made the previous May notwithstanding, one -fourth of the projected budget for the journal alone came to $6,600, and this did not include Binsse's salary for the quarter ($1,500) or rent for the Society's New York office.[37] Binsse was confident that money was forthcoming, however, and by the first of November enough advance subscriptions and memberships had been received that he could give Rumford Press permission to proceed.

On November 20, 1931, 20,000 copies of Vol. 1, No. 1 of *Liturgical Arts* were mailed from Concord, New Hampshire. Only a small percentage of these, perhaps as few as 2,000, were sent to paying subscribers. (The initial subscription fee was $2.00 per year.) The rest were sent free of charge to Roman Catholic clergy, ecclesiastical architects and designers, "those whose names were sent in by the various officers and charter members," and rectors and professors of liturgy in Roman Catholic seminaries.[38] Along with the distribution of the first number of *Liturgical Arts*, the Society issued a press release intended for publication in every major newspaper in the United States, secular and Roman Catholic alike. The statement was produced in numerous recensions, each carefully tailored for its intended audience. A given press release might note, for example, local individuals and places related to the Liturgical Arts Society or mentioned in its new journal.[39]

In the end, copies of *Liturgical Arts* were sent not only to Roman Catholic clergy and educators, but to the editors of daily and weekly newspapers throughout the country. These included the editors of publications as diverse as *The Christian Science Monitor*, *The Daily Oklahoman*, and the *New York Evening Post*. Accompanying these complementary copies was a cover letter that indicated that the Society would be gratified by an editorial comment on the magazine, "since this is the first publication in the United States devoted exclusively to the architectural problems of one faith."[40] Several of these papers, including the *Baltimore Evening Sun*, ran favorable editorial opinions of *Liturgical Arts*.[41]

Throughout nearly 40 years of publication, the format established by Henry Lorin Binsse for 1:1 of *Liturgical Arts* remained remarkably stable, despite the oscillation of the Society's fortunes. The page size (9" by 12") never changed, but the number of pages varied considerably, from a maximum of 82 pages (23:3, May, 1955, and 35:1, November, 1966) to a minimum of 22 pages, typical throughout the war years, 1939-1944. The weight and quality of the paper always conformed to the high standard Binsse had originally demanded. The layout of the page likewise remained relatively consistent. In 1939, the magazine went from its original full-page format for the text to a three-column format, which allowed the text to be set on fewer pages. With Vol. 35, 1967, the journal moved to a two-column format for the text, and remained so throughout the rest of its years. For the 30th anniversary issue (31:1, November, 1962), the magazine experimented with an illustrated cover on glossy stock, replacing a plain rag stock cover containing only the name of the magazine, date of issue, and the words "A Quarterly Devoted to the Arts of the Catholic Church." (Very occasionally, and only after 1946, the special emphasis of a particular issue was noted on the cover with a line drawing, map, or brief headline. The illustrated cover gave the magazine a more "contemporary" look, and became a permanent feature in 1963.)

The response to the initial issue was highly favorable. An example of the popular reaction is found in the lead editorial in *America*, December 12, 1931:

"The first issue of the quarterly of the newly formed Liturgical Arts Society, *Liturgical Arts*, comes not merely as a success, but as a sensation. 'How is it possible? We never expected such text, such illustrations, typographical form, wide range of topics from early Christian art to modern California! Now you see what can be done!' These, and similar remarks, according to all available sources of information, have heralded the appearance of the quarterly in every circle where clergy or laity have been gathered together."[42]

Letters to the editor of *Liturgical Arts* and editorials in *The Common-weal*, *Orate Fratres* (6:132), and elsewhere echoed these sentiments, and the continued publication of the Society's journal was assured by long-term contracts for advertising and a number of new subscriptions.

The program of the Liturgical Arts Society through the next decades was clearly dominated by the publication of *Liturgical Arts*. Henry Lorin Binsse, the Society's salaried executive secretary, was in full charge of all aspects of the magazine's production, as well as the mechanics of running the Society until 1932. In September of that year, however, Maurice Lavanoux, the Society's elected Secretary, abandoned his earlier resolve to remain in Boston and moved to New York City. There, he took over some of the day-to-day work at the office, including some of the editorial work.

Maurice Lavanoux's background was very different from that of his privileged, Ivy League-educated fellow founders.[43] Lavanoux was born in New York City on June 10, 1894, the son of French émigré parents, and spent his early years amid the multicultural bustle of turn-of-the-century Greenwich Village. At the age of eight he was sent to live with his grandmother near Orléans (because of what he referred to as "family difficulties") for traditional French primary schooling. He returned to North America in 1907 to continue his education at Institut Mont St. Louis, a Christian Brothers school in Montreal, but was forced to leave before graduation to find a job. Returning to New York, he worked as office boy for an architectural firm until 1917, when he volunteered to serve in a private ambulance corps attached to the French army. In his patriotic enthusiasm, however, he had forgotten that he had never learned to drive, and so on his arrival in France he was found to be of little use to the ambulance corps. He was almost immediately reassigned to an Air Force construction unit as an interpreter, and remained in that position for two years.

Upon his discharge, Lavanoux remained in Paris to study at the Sorbonne, the École des Beaux Arts, and work at an architect's *atelier*. A year later, in 1921, he returned to the United States, and took a succession of jobs as draftsman in New York City and Santa Barbara, California, architectural firms.[44] But his special interest had always been in the area of ecclesiastical architecture, so when he was offered a drafting job in the offices of Maginnis & Walsh, the architectural firm most noted for its Roman Catholic church building, Lavanoux quickly accepted it, and moved to Boston in 1925.

During his years in Boston, Lavanoux met regularly with a group of young architects, artists, and draftsmen who shared his concern with Roman Catholic church art. (Many were individuals soon to become the nucleus of the Liturgical Arts Society.) Lavanoux hoped to become an independent architect and set up an office in Boston, a city he had come to love. Meanwhile, the Liturgical Arts Society, of which he was an Incorporator and first Secretary, became increasingly important to him, and he worked tirelessly to achieve its goals. Facing more and more difficulties for the Society in Boston,[45] he continued to hope that a base of operations would be established there and placed under his leadership. On several occasions before Henry Lorin Binsse was hired, Lavanoux refused requests from the New York group to join them there as the Society's paid executive.[46] But the building industry was particularly hard hit by the Depression, and in March, 1931, Maurice Lavanoux was laid off by Maginnis & Walsh. For over a year he looked for work in Boston, but to no avail, and so, in the fall 1932 he returned to his family's home in New York.

Lavanoux says very little about the events of the next several years. Most of his time seems to have been spent promoting the Society and gathering material for *Liturgical Arts*. In 1937, Henry Lorin Binsse was offered a position on the newly-reorganized editorial staff of *The Commonweal*[47] and Lavanoux assumed more of the editorial and management responsibilities for the Society and *Liturgical Arts*. Binsse continued to oversee the layout and typography of the magazine.

During the next several years, many of the founding members of the Liturgical Arts Society apparently discovered that shifting priorities made it difficult for them to continue active participation in the Society's efforts. In several cases, persons whose names appear over and over again in the materials relating to the Society's founding simply drop out of sight within a few years.[48] Others, however, made a more visible exit. One such was Ides van der Gracht, whose early efforts had ensured that the Society would not simply be a secluded enclave of artistic monks, but a group of people in all walks of life committed to the renewal of Christian art.[49] Soon after *Liturgical Arts* was established, van der Gracht found that his involvement in civil architecture had removed him from the Society's sphere of interest. After working for a year as an architect in the United States Treasury Department (1934-1935) and for a second year as head architect in the War Department, van der Gracht committed himself to government service. Having served his adopted country in the Air Force, he remained in the U.S. Foreign Service from 1947 until his death.[50]

Another individual unable to sustain his commitment to the Society was Michael Williams, who had been profoundly influential in giving the Society's uncertain founders a vision of the possibilities of lay governance and publishing.[51] Williams had provided substantial editorial and financial support to the Society during its early years, but by the mid-1930s his health, always rather fragile, had deteriorated to the point that frequent absences from his duties, at *The Commonweal* and elsewhere, were required.[52] The Depression had taken its toll on the nest egg that Williams had carefully built up for *The Commonweal* during times of prosperity, and the paper's finances were precarious by the beginning of 1937.[53] Complicating matters, Williams had taken an extremely unpopular editorial stance on the Spanish Civil War, and had driven the magazine in a pro-Franco direction against the express wishes of his Board of Directors.[54]

On June 16, 1937, with *The Commonweal* on the brink of financial collapse, the Editorial Council and Board of Directors met privately and drafted a request for Williams' resignation, noting their "distinct misgivings about the rather arbitrary manner of management and the financial situation of *The Commonweal*" among reasons for their action.[55] But Williams negotiated a compromise with the Board and remained titular editor until March of 1938,[56] when *The Commonweal* was reorganized under a coalition of former staff members, including Henry Lorin Binsse.[57]

Saddest of all, however, was the case of Everitt Harman, whose efforts had led to the formation of the Liturgical Arts Society.[58] Quite early on, Harman's rather overzealous approach to the problem of organizing the Society had begun to be seen as something of a liability by those who liked his basic idea.[59] When his original plan for a monastic community was abandoned, Harman was generous enough to step into the background (although he did sign the papers of incorporation), and the Society proceeded along its own path without him. On August 11, 1931, Harman wrote Binsse, explaining that he had to tender his resignation from the Society because financial problems made it impossible for him to pay his dues.[60] Responding on behalf of the Membership Committee, Binsse informed Harman that it had been decided that he could be a non-dues-paying member until he could afford to pay "in view of [his] early interest in the Society."[61]

Harman continued to travel among Benedictine houses throughout the United States until 1949, when he was ordained priest and settled in the diocese of Utah.[62] Although he remained interested in ecclesiastical architecture,[63] he seems to have made no further attempt to become involved with the work of the Society, which he had helped to found. Unlike other founding members, however, the death of Everitt Harman in November, 1967, was not noted in the pages of *Liturgical Arts*.

With the departure of so many of the influential members of the original *Liturgical Arts* group, the few who remained were able to shape *Liturgical Arts* and the day-to-day life of the Society more or less in their own image. Those who had been active since the Society's founding[64] formed a cohesive core of opinion and support for the Society's paid staff. But it was clearly the staff of the Liturgical Arts Society which exerted the most profound influence on the shape and direction of the Society and *Liturgical Arts* over the years. When Henry Lorin Binsse left his full-time work as managing editor of *Liturgical Arts* in 1937 to join the staff at *The Commonweal*, staff,[65] the responsibility of making the Society a viable enterprise fell to Maurice Lavanoux.

In 1947, Henry Lorin Binsse took his mother to her native home in Canada; finding her too ill to be left alone, he was forced to remain there. For the next three years, he supervised the layout of *Liturgical Arts* long-distance. But by 1950 the job had became too difficult, and Binsse severed his connection with *Liturgical Arts* altogether.[66] From then on the magazine was essentially a one-man operation, with Lavanoux functioning as "editor, advertising manager, subscription director, and file clerk."[67] The technical work of layout and typography for *Liturgical Arts* was taken over by Joseph Asherl, a longtime supporter of the Society, who, after serving in World War II, had taken advantage of the G.I. Bill to learn the art of book production.

With the journal successfully launched, the life of the Society took on a more routine aspect, punctuated by annual meetings, financial crises, travel opportunities for the staff, and its full share of successes and failures, rejoicings and disappointments. The Society was gratified that *Liturgical Arts* was received with enthusiasm in those quarters where the liturgy and the material expression of the Christian faith were taken seriously. But the degree of frustration was also high. In their idealistic fervor, the Society had half expected the Roman Catholic world to turn to a more sophisticated way of approaching liturgical art and church architecture. It was soon recognized, however, that much of the Society's future would be a slow and often painful struggle to make itself heard above the din of fakery and pious sentimentalism in ecclesiastical art.

CHAPTER THREE

Indebtedness and Idealism: The Liturgical Arts Society, 1930-1939

MANAGING A FINANCIAL CRISIS

"I believe it is well to state again that it is absolutely necessary for everyone to realize that the work of the Liturgical Arts Society is one of long range and that we need the cooperation, patience, and forbearance of all the present members and subscribers and any other persons deeply interested in furthering the very necessary and practical ideal for which the Society was originally founded. With continued effort we can confidently look to the day when the present difficulties will be seen as the crucible through which all worthwhile achievements must pass."[1]

The work of the Liturgical Arts Society between 1930 and 1939 was shaped by the interplay of two opposing forces: a serious financial crisis on the one hand, and extravagant plans for the Society's program on the other. At first it was hoped that the profit generated by the sale of subscriptions and advertising for *Liturgical Arts* would soon cover the indebtedness incurred in establishing the Society and its projects. Since the second issue of the magazine lost only $3,000, the third exactly paid for itself, and the fourth made a small profit,[2] these projections were not unreasonable. But the original debt of between $5,000 and $6,000 proved more difficult to manage than had been anticipated, and it soon became clear that aggressive measures to bring the debt under control were called for. In September, 1932, the Board of Directors authorized that $5,000 worth of Certificates of Indebtedness be issued (sold in units of $100 and $500, payable in 10 years, and bearing interest at 5% per annum), so that the deficit "might not exist in the form of unpaid bills but would be rather in the term of long-term obligations."[3]

By early 1936, $4,100 of the Certificates of Indebtedness had been sold.[4] But many individuals who had purchased the bonds in good faith, expecting interest to be paid regularly, were beginning to become annoyed with the Society's continued silence on the matter. A. Graham Carey, one of the original Portsmouth Priory group, expressed his annoyance about the interest payments on the certificates in a letter of resignation from the Society:

"I bought a $100 bond, which I was seriously assured would pay regular interest, but the interest was not paid and no reference to the default was made either to me personally, or formally in the Treasurer's annual report."[5]

In his response to Carey,[6] Henry Lorin Binsse admitted that there had been "a great deal of disorder" in the matter. Expressing the Society's deep regret that no interest had been paid on the certificate, Binsse attributed the failure wholly to the Society's "lack of means."

The early months of 1936 were, financially, the bleakest period of the Liturgical Arts Society's existence. In March, the situation was such that the Bankers' Trust Company, where the Society had kept its account for many years, requested that the account be closed because the Society had consistently failed to meet minimum balance requirements. The Society complied, withdrawing its balance of $10.33 on May 19, 1936.[7]

As the year progressed, however, the Society's fortunes began to improve. The magazine *Liturgical Arts* was turning a profit issue after issue, while new opportunities to lower the deficit presented themselves. One opportunity was the special memorial issue of *Liturgical Arts* marking the death of Bishop James Anthony Walsh, founder of the Maryknoll Community, Hawthorne, New York.[8] Fellow bishops and friends of Walsh contributed $400 to underwrite the issue, which allowed more of the magazine's revenues to be applied to reducing the debt.

In the end, calendar year 1936 -1937 would be the turning point in the Liturgical Arts Society's battle against financial ruin. *Liturgical*

Arts reported to its readers in November, 1937, that the Society's operating income for the period "almost exactly balanced" with its operating expenses. "Our only problem at present," the editor acknowledged,[9] "is the deficit which we carry over from the years when the Society was first establishing itself." In spite of this, it was the Society's hope that within the following year it would find its "financial house . . . completely in order."[10] During the rest of the decade, the Society's staff, and particularly Maurice Lavanoux, made further progress against the debt by making extended lecture tours. For $50 per lecture, Lavanoux criss-crossed the country, speaking on behalf of the Society and the cause of revitalizing religious art. Invitations for these lectures came from all quarters: bishops,[11] college presidents, seminary faculties, and organizations of Roman Catholic lay people.[12] Toward the end of the decade, the total liquidation of the original indebtedness seemed to be in sight.

Although hopes for the Society's future were running high, there was still reason for realistic concern. Long-term certificates of indebtedness and private loans remained outstanding, no annual interest on them had been paid, the staff was living on a pittance and working in spartan surroundings, and the political situation in Europe made projections of continued economic stability difficult. In 1939, the Society launched a final effort to consolidate the progress already made against the deficit and to move toward a balanced budget. Clearly, expertise was needed to extricate the organization from its financial predicament, and for this expertise the Society looked to John Moody, a Roman Catholic lay person and president of Moody's Investor's Service (New York). In April 1939, Moody was contacted by the Board of Directors and asked to consider serving as president of the Society. Wrote Maurice Lavanoux on behalf of the board:

"As you know, we have made some progress in the past year in reducing the deficit, but we must work several years more before the Society will be on a solid foundation. The next year will be a particularly important one for us and your assistance and advice would be deeply appreciated."[13]

After considering the matter thoroughly and assessing the Society's financial situation, Moody decided to "accept the presidency for at least a brief period and lend [his] efforts to placing the Society squarely on its feet."[14] He immediately took the situation in hand, lent the Society money to "bridge the gap so that the Society [could] enter the fall with a clean slate,"[15] and made arrangements with creditors for acceptable repayment plans and the cancellation of outstanding debts.[16] By the end of the year, John Moody had made astonishing progress toward turning the Society away from the path of financial ruin. He would serve two terms as president of the Society, and would leave office in 1940 with the knowledge that he had made the extinction of the debt a reasonable goal for the future.

SUBSIDIARY ACTIVITIES

Liturgical Arts was undeniably the centerpiece of the Liturgical Arts Society's program, but achievement awards, exhibits, competitions, an information exchange, a Gregorian choir, and a brokering service for silversmiths were all expected to be a part of the Society's future:

"We have rarely mentioned the activities of the Society which publishes this magazine, since we do not wish to give the impression that this magazine is merely an organ of the Society. The magazine is far more than this, in fact, the Officers and Directors of the Society have always felt that the Society exists principally in order to publish the magazine and if it can fulfill this function, its most important purpose will be achieved.

"But the Liturgical Arts Society has a real existence of its own as well. Its other activities may seem unimportant compared with the publication of *Liturgical Arts*, yet the Society would not wish Catholics to think that it merely existed for the sake of a quarterly publication."[17]

Even though the early projections of financial success soon proved wholly unrealistic, extravagant plans for the Society's program continued largely unchecked. On several occasions this combination of an increasingly empty pocketbook and idealistic over-enthusiasm nearly proved disastrous. But not all of the Society's efforts at a diversified program were unrealized or misguided. In fact one, the Society's *schola cantorum*, stands out as a distinct success.

The Liturgical Arts Schola, an all-male Gregorian choir, was organized early in 1934. Heir to the renewed interest in the restoration of the chant precipitated by the promulgation of Pius X's November 22, 1903, *motu proprio* , *Tra le sollecitudini*,[18] the Schola's 38-year history is, after *Liturgical Arts*, the Society's most durable effort. The roots of the Schola go back to the earliest American attempts to put the principles of *Tra le sollecitudini* into effect. In 1918 the Pius X School of Liturgical Song (later the Pius X School of Liturgical Music) had been founded at the Manhattanville College and Convent of the Sacred Heart, (Manhattanville, New York) by Miss Justine Ward and Mother Georgia Stevens, S.S.C. (1870-1946). The school enjoyed a reputation within the American church for its extraordinary commitment to the restoration of the chant.

Among the school's many patrons was Lady Vivian Gabriel of Mt. Kisco, New York, a recent Anglican convert to Roman Catholicism.[19] In addition to her patronage of the Pius X School, Lady Gabriel was also one of the earliest life members of the Liturgical Arts Society and, in the interest of bringing together her commitment to both Roman Catholic Church art and Church music, she worked to make a Gregorian choir a part of the Society's program. To that end, she arranged at her country home a meeting between the Society's chaplain, Fr. John LaFarge, S.J. , and one of the period's leading lights in American liturgical music, Dr. H. Becket Gibbs.[20]

Harold Becket Gibbs was born on August 2, 1868, at Rustington, Sussex, England. At the age of 10 he was sent to the St. Nicholas Choir School, Arundel, where he studied for six years and became a leading chorister. Soon his talent took him to London, where he was accepted for study at the Royal College and Academy of Music and as an assistant organist at All Saints', Margaret Street, one of the most fashionable of the city's churches and parish of members of the Royal Family. In 1897, at the age of 30, Becket Gibbs became principal of Nottingham College of Music, a position he held for eight years. Although he had once considered becoming an Anglican priest, he converted to Roman Catholicism while at Nottingham.

It was *Tra le sollecitudini* that indirectly drew Becket Gibbs to the

United States. To accompany the promulgation of his *motu proprio* on Church music, Pius X planned to have experts in the field of liturgical music serve as "missionaries" of the reform of the chant throughout the world. In search of such men, he consulted with the Abbot of Solemnes, who recommended Becket Gibbs, a sometime lecturer at the Abbey, to serve in this capacity. In 1905, Gibbs traveled to the United States and began his labors for the reform of the Church's music at the Cathedral at Covington, Kentucky. He founded the Gregorian Congregation there and served as its first president. In Kentucky, and later at St. Peter's Cathedral in Cincinnati, Gibbs worked tirelessly for the restoration of Gregorian chant as the most appropriate musical expression of the Church's faith. When he met Fr. John LaFarge at the home of Lady Gabriel, Becket Gibbs, then 65 years old, had established himself in New York City, teaching at Union Theological Seminary, lecturing around the country, and serving as foreign examiner for American applicants to the Royal School of Church Music, London. He was looking, it seems, for an outlet for his practical experience directing Gregorian chant.

One of the major obstacles to the formation of a Gregorian choir was the problem of finding a cohesive and stable group of singers, and it was here that the Liturgical Arts Society connection was made. The many New York members of the Society formed the perfect nucleus for such a group. The "Quilisma Club," as the Liturgical Arts Schola came to be known, met weekly from September to June for rehearsal, dinner, and often a brief lecture at various places around the city.[21] Throughout its 39-year history, the Schola offered its talents for special services at churches in and around New York City, sang the mass for the Society's annual meeting, as well as special requiem masses for deceased members of the Society.[22] At each occasion, members were attired in cassock and surplice "according to the ancient tradition."[23] The Liturgical Arts Schola saw its purpose to "praise God, [and] to give some example to the Catholic people as to how the chant could be performed, and to try to bring out some of the beauties which had been neglected."[24] John LaFarge called the Schola "a special and deadly weapon against the monster of mediocrity."[25]

In 1946, at the age of 78, Becket Gibbs retired to Wynnewood, Pennsylvania,[28] where he lived out the last 10 years of his life. In 1954.

he received the Society of St. Gregory of America's liturgical music award "in recognition of his many years of tireless effort . . . promoting and encouraging due regard for the legislation of Holy Mother Church in behalf of appropriate music for the celebration of her sublime mysteries and sacred offices."[27] On November 5, 1956, the Liturgical Arts Schola sang a Solemn Requiem Mass for Dr. Harold Becket Gibbs. Becket Gibbs's place as the head of the Quilisma Club was taken by Fr. Joseph R. Foley, C.S.P., director of the Paulist choristers in New York City. Fr. Foley guided the Schola for its final 26 years .

THE CRAFTSMEN'S SERVICE AND THE BUILDING INFORMATION SERVICE

Not all of the Liturgical Arts Society's attempts at a well-rounded program were as successful as the Quilisma Club. Many such efforts suffered from poor management and from an unrealistic assessment of the needs of the Society's constituency. One of the programs that had particular difficulties was the Craftsmen's Service (also known as the "Silversmiths' Service"). In January, 1933, the Society issued a prospectus in which the service was described:

"Pursuant to its policy of making available to the American Catholic Clergy those liturgical appurtenances not readily obtainable elsewhere, the Liturgical Arts Society announces its Craftsmen's Service for the making of correct and worthy Sacred Vessels. . . .The Society will be glad to receive communications from anyone desiring work of this kind, particularly at moderate prices, and to superintend, at no cost to the client, the making of any Sacred Vessels." [28]

In response to this advertisement numerous inquiries came in from clergy and seminaries, as well as from lay people who sought appropriate gifts for friends and pastors. Requests for chalices, patens, and croziers were referred to craftspeople for whom the Society had agreed to act as broker. But as the year 1933 went on, delays in the delivery of promised items angered clients, and letters of apology from the Society multiplied. The silversmiths who did the work for the Society were not always reliable, and added costs for such things as polishing and shipping increasingly created the impression that the Society could not deliver on promises made. Moreover, certain items were marked by poor workmanship, further tarnishing the Society's reputation.[29] In the end, it was admitted that the service had not been adequately organized when it was announced.[30]

By 1934, the advertising of the Craftsmen's Service had become slightly less expansive:

"The Society, for the time being, continues to act as agent for a small group of silversmiths. It is hoped that eventually these men will form a selling association, or 'guild,' of their own which will help solve the problems of the individual craftsman in precious metals."[31]

Finally, in July of 1935, the Society abandoned its Craftsmen's Service "for a number of reasons, chiefly because of the temperamental natures of the silversmiths."[32] The balance of that year was spent arranging for the repair of objects that had been badly made, mending relations with angry clients,[33] and referring new requests for altarware to outside agents.[34]

The Liturgical Arts Society's Building and Information Service fared slightly better than its Craftsmen's Service. A part of the earliest deliberations for the Society's program, the Service was considered again once *Liturgical Arts* was safely launched. In late 1932, a meeting between Charles Maginnis and Henry Lorin Binsse resulted in a renewed effort to set the Building Information Service on course. "The idea is that our Society should act as a clearinghouse for *correct* information concerning Catholic building projects, particularly when they are not in an advanced stage."[35] In December of 1932, the Building Information Service was officially announced, and Maurice Lavanoux was asked to manage it in exchange for a $25 per week stipend.[36]

In its inaugural year, a remarkable volume and variety of inquiries came into the Building Information Service. Requests for information on such matters as the making of a "tabernacle safe to be as liturgical as possible,"[37] the proper method of laying a cornerstone,[38] and the appropriate dimensions of the mensa[39] were common.

In addition, requests for information on the liturgy itself were also addressed to the Service. One lay person who had been studying the Church's worship asked if the Society would "please interpret

46

... the meaning of 'a white garment' in the baptismal rite."[40] And finally, there were more general requests for architectural information: "How can we make our little church more liturgical?"[41] and "How can we alter a Baptist Church to make it fit for Roman practice?"[42]

Though there was no lack of requests for information, Lavanoux was hampered in responding by a "lack of funds and lack of a research library."[43] More and more questions on various topics were referred to outside authorities. Despite the difficulties, as the decade went on the Building Information Service continued to thrive, having established a reliable network of consultants who cheerfully addressed questions of all kinds. By 1935, however, the Service had lost its independent identity within the Society's program and had simply dissolved into the day-to-day operation of the office.

EXHIBITIONS AND COMPETITIONS

"One of the principal purposes of the Liturgical Arts Society is to hold exhibitions which will stimulate interest in and concern for correct and beautiful objects of art and architecture for the Catholic Church . . . .It has now become possible to organize the first exhibition, and plans have been underway for some time to make this exhibition an important and fundamental contribution to the progress of the arts in the Church in the United States."[44]

The Society's maiden voyage into the world of exhibitions and competitions was not altogether smooth. Twenty-nine objects, including statues, stained glass, and altarware, were selected by the jury[45] to be placed in the Liturgical Arts Society Small Church Exhibition to be held May 13-June 15, 1933, at the New York Architectural League, 115 East 40th Street, New York City. Preparations for the exhibition were elaborate and generally conformed with the social style of the wealthier segment of the Church, of which the Society then felt itself apart. A formal cocktail reception was held, with members of the press invited to preview the exhibition before it opened to the general public.[46]

The exhibition itself was reasonably well-attended, and favorable notices appeared in the Catholic press and architectural trade journals.[47] It had been planned that the exhibit would be stored for the summer after its month-long New York City debut, and then it would travel, spending one month in each of a number of major American cities for the next year in order to "extend [the Society's] national influence."[48]

But this plan was never realized, largely because of the prohibitive cost of transporting the exhibit from city to city[49] and partly because the individuals who had purchased objects of art displayed at the exhibition were not inclined to wait a full year for delivery.[50] The Society considered the whole experience a marginal success, however, and confidently announced the details of its first competition.

The Liturgical Arts Society's Competition for Remodeled Churches was not destined to be even as remotely smooth as the Small Church Exhibition. Originally announced in the pages of *Liturgical Arts* in the fall of 1934,[51] the final judging did not take place until November 19, 1936, over two years later. The delay was said to be due to the fact that "because of economic conditions, very few churches were submitted to [the Society] for this award."[52] In the end, the Society's financial difficulties made it necessary to substitute a certificate in lieu of the promised medal for the competition's winner, and there was general dissatisfaction with the handling of the entire matter.

Undaunted, the Society announced a second competition shortly thereafter (December, 1936). In this case, the competition was for the best painting representing the 40 saints mentioned in the canon of the Mass. But lessons had been learned from the previous experience, and participants were included primarily by invitation.[53] The entries were exhibited at the Passedort Gallery, 22 East 60th Street, New York City, beginning May 31, 1937, and the winning works were featured in *Liturgical Arts*.

It had originally been thought that competitions and exhibitions would be a staple item on the agenda of the Liturgical Arts Society. But the limited success of the early ventures led to the Society proceeded with more caution as the years went by, thereby avoiding more serious blunders.

"At the annual meeting of the Society held in the Spring of 1933, it was decided that the Society should award a gold medal to some person, clerical or lay, who has contributed notably to arousing popular interest in the liturgy, particularly in its spiritual aspect."[54]

The annual gold medal was intended as the Liturgical Arts Society's token of respect to those who had helped to provide a theological and spiritual foundation for its work. It was to be awarded to someone who has "labored in the interest of the liturgy, either through writing, or merely by example."[55] The rationale for the award was explained to an influential member in this way:

"We have always felt the necessity of the internal approach to liturgy . . . .And we have always thought of our work as the practical work to those who clearly have the desire which arises only from internal devotion."[56]

Because of this, the terms of the award were such that it could not be given to any artist or architect, "unless that person likewise devoted himself to the inner meaning of the liturgy," wrote Henry Binsse, adding that "the medal [would] never be given for 'externals.' "[57]

The individual proposed as the recipient for the first (and, as it would turn out, the only) Liturgical Arts Society Gold Medal was Rev. Cornelius C. Clifford, then pastor of the (Roman Catholic) Church of Our Lady of Mercy, Whippany, New Jersey.[58] Born in New York on August 24, 1859, Clifford had studied at Fordham University before entering the Society of Jesus in 1879 and completing his theological studies at Woodstock. In 1899, he left the Jesuits with permission and taught scholastic philosophy for one year in England and Wales. Returning to the United States in 1900, Clifford edited the Providence, Rhode Island diocesan newspaper *The Visitor*, lectured at Columbia University, and served as parish priest in Morristown, New Jersey.[59]

The Society's Gold Medal to Clifford was in special recognition of his two books on the liturgy, *The Burden of Our Time* and *Introibo* (1903), the latter a series of essays on the introits for every Sunday of the year. In its selection of Clifford, the Liturgical Arts Society noted that these two books were written "many years before any definite liturgical movement came into existence."[60] It was admitted that Father Clifford was not a liturgical expert or student of ancient texts but rather was "concerned with the spiritual and mystical power of the public worship of the Church."[61]

Because of the Society's precarious financial situation during the middle years of the decade, the question of a second annual Gold Medal did not resurface until the spring of 1938. At that time H. Becket Gibbs, director of the Society's *schola cantorum*, was proposed to the directors as the second recipient of the award.[62] The directors, however, rejected the idea of honoring Gibbs by an overwhelming majority. Many echoed the sentiments of one (a bishop) who wrote:

"Dr. Gibbs's present position as director of the Episcopal ('high') Church of St. Ignatius of Antioch in New York City and at Union Seminary . . . practically excludes him from consideration for the award.

"I cannot see how the award would fail to be misunderstood by many of those whose good will the Society actually stands in need of, nor can I see any advantage that compensates for the gratuitous assumption of the burden by all of the explanations that would have to be made, and probably could not be made effectively."[63]

Lavanoux hastily replied to the directors that the matter of awarding the Liturgical Arts Society Gold Medal to Becket Gibbs would be dropped at once.[64] This discussion seems, however, to have somehow derailed the entire issue of an annual award, and a second gold medal was never conferred.

MISCELLANEOUS ACTIVITIES

Most of the life of the Liturgical Arts Society between 1930 and 1940 was made up not of great crises and great victories, but of small disappointments and small accomplishments. These episodes, though not major moments in its history, shaped the Society in subtle but important ways. The disappointments served to narrow the focus of its work and give it direction for the future. The accomplishments, on the other hand, provided the Society with much-needed energy to see it through this period of financial difficulty. Elaborate plans for retreats, [65] regional centers for the Society in major American cities,[66] and participation in the National Eucharistic Congress (Cleveland, Ohio, 1935)[67] were never activated. Some of these failed ambitions were merely embarrassing to the Society; others were more costly. (In one case, photographs requested from abroad in the attempt to give the pages of *Liturgical Arts* a more international scope arrived, much to the editor's surprise, with an exorbitant bill attached along with an angry demand for immediate payment.[68]) The failure of these efforts was largely due to misguided enthusiasm and an overestimation of influence and the needs of its constituency. But the Society learned valuable lessons about its own limitations and the degree to which it could profitably expand its program.

One area, however, in which the organization could boast a moderate success was in arousing the interest of the Roman Catholic hierarchy in its work. After the bitter experience with Cardinal O'Connell in Boston during the days of the Society's founding,[69] expectations of episcopal support had been somewhat dampened. But by the fall of 1934, 34 bishops had become members of the Society[70] and Maurice Lavanoux believed it not unreasonable to hope that the day would come when the membership would "include sixty—or even more—members of the American hierarchy."[71]

Several of these bishops proved tireless supporters of the Liturgical Arts Society and its work, applying both episcopal influence and financial resources to the cause of religious art and architecture. Archbishops John T. McNicholas of Cincinnati and Edward Mooney of Detroit, and Bishop Thomas J. Walsh (brother of James A. Walsh, the founder of Maryknoll), were members of the Society's directorate during this period, and several bishop members made visits to the Society's office while on business in New York.[72] Bishop James E. Cassidy of Fall River, Massachusetts, who had supported the Society from the beginning, wrote in 1932 that "it would be a tragedy if anything should interfere with [the Society's] continued prosperity;" for his own part, he offered a challenge grant of $1,000 to the Society on the condition that $2,000 be raised to match it.[73]

As the financial situation began to improve toward the end of the decade, it was believed that some more public show of episcopal support for the Liturgical Arts Society and its activities would be beneficial. As a result, in February of 1939, Lavanoux requested a letter of endorsement from Bishop Hugh C. Boyle of Pittsburgh, a longtime advocate of the Society's aims. In his response, Boyle affirmed the work of the Society and the importance of *Liturgical Arts* to the life of the Church:

"The publication of the Liturgical Arts Society, which has gone on in spite of many difficulties, makes a valuable contribution to the life of the Church in this country.

"I want to congratulate all of you upon having done a difficult job very well, and to wish you a continuing success. I wonder if the group responsible for the magazine knows how much good has come of its publication, and how priests everywhere are accustomed to consult it, and to allege it as an authority in the building of churches and the furnishing and adornment of the interior, especially the sanctuary. I send you my congratulations and my blessing."[74]

Lavanoux sent copies of this letter to the 33 bishops, then to members of the Society for their personal endorsement. In all, 23 of the 33 (70%) responded that they were entirely willing to have their names attached to the letter. Eight of the bishops made no response and two declined, but for reasons of propriety rather than disagreement with the intent of Boyle's letter.[75] The letter, along with the list of those bishops endorsing it, was published in the May, 1939, issue of *Liturgical Arts* (7:3, page 35).

Some progress was also made during the period 1930-1940 to give *Liturgical Arts* and the Liturgical Arts Society a wider international reputation. In early November, 1933, Monsignor (later Cardinal) Eugenio Tisserant, then Pro-Prefect of the Vatican Library, visited the Society's offices in New York. In the course of conversation, Lavanoux expressed the hope that a volume of *Liturgical Arts* might be presented to Pope Pius XI, and Tisserant offered to do this on his return to Rome.[76] On December 1, 1933, Tisserant reported to the Society:

"I presented to the Pope the first volume of *Liturgical Arts* and told [him] that you would like to have some letter of encouragement . . . .His

Holiness did not promise anything, but I hope he will give an order for writing the letter you wish."[77]

Throughout this period, Tisserant served as the point of contact between the Liturgical Arts Society and the Holy See. On April 29, 1935, he presented the second volume of Liturgical Arts to the Pope,[78] and on September 11, 1935, the third.[79] On each occasion, Tisserant conveyed to the Society news of the words and actions with which the Pope received the magazine.[80] Although the Society's request for an autographed letter or photograph was denied,[81] the Pope did instruct Tisserant on several occasions to convey to the Society his blessing on its work.

DETERMINING THE LIMITS OF THE SOCIETY'S PROGRAM
The Society's youthful enthusiasm during its first full decade of existence occasionally pushed it outside the boundaries it had originally set for its work, and in several instances this resulted in severe criticism from its constituency. Shortly before Christmas 1933, the Liturgical Arts Society was asked by the drama critic of *The Commonweal* to cooperate with playwright Eugene O'Neill in the design of a crucifix for the stage set of his play "Days Without End." O'Neill had voiced the desire that the play express "the necessity of a return to Christianity, and particularly Catholicism," and that it not "run the risk of a crucifix that would offend because of its grotesqueness or lack of feeling."[82]

The Society complied with O'Neill's request and supervised the making of a crucifix carved by Adam Dambrowski. Early in the new year, the resulting work was pictured in *Liturgical Arts*,[83] along with O'Neill's appreciative letter to the Society for its help in the project.

Almost immediately, there was a cry of outrage from some of the Society's more influential members. William Busch, an early pioneer of the liturgical movement, wrote a vehement letter of protest to the Society:

"I write simply to tell you of the unfavorable impression upon me of the solemn deference which you showed a play called "Days Without End" and its author. Apart from the merits or demerits of the carving which you reproduce, I think that the approval of said

53

play does no credit to *Liturgical Arts* and is apt to cause people to lose interest in your publication . . . .It seems that 'Days Without End' is an unfortunate affair and I am sorry that *Liturgical Arts* has seen fit to give it such a favorable notice."[84]

Busch added that the whole matter made him wonder if the Society had a clearly defined purpose and standards.[85]

Maurice Lavanoux and Henry Lorin Binsse immediately wrote letters to all who expressed such concern, explaining to them that it was only the excellence of the crucifix itself which had led them to include mention of it in *Liturgical Arts*. But nothing further appeared in print in *Liturgical Arts* either by way of criticism or defense of the Society's part in the matter, and the whole incident was, it seems, soon forgotten. However, it was the first serious objection to the editorial policy of *Liturgical Arts* and to decisions regarding the Society's proper sphere of responsibility. As a result, it would be a very long time before the leadership of the Liturgical Arts Society would involve the group in "secular matters."

It was perhaps this episode that added to the caution with which the Liturgical Arts Society approached a suggestion made a few years later by Michael Williams, editor of *The Commonweal*. Lavanoux described the proposal in a letter to the Society's Board of Directors:

"At the annual meeting of our Society, Mr. Michael Williams of *The Commonweal* proposed from the floor that the Society join with him in sponsoring a meeting to be held in Carnegie Hall some time at the end of June at which meeting Mr. Williams will express his views on the situation in Spain . . . .His proposal was that we share with him in the proceeds."[86]

Lavanoux went on to say that all of the directors present at the annual meeting were "strongly opposed" to the Society's participation in the enterprise, and had expressed the general opinion that the "Liturgical Arts Society has no connection with the present Spanish conflict and that there is no reason why we should become involved in this controversial matter."[87] The directors polled by mail unanimously concurred in this opinion and Williams' request was denied.

54

For the major part of the next three decades, *Liturgical Arts* and the Society would maintain a decidedly neutral stance in the area of world and national politics. Even as the storm clouds gathered over Europe in the last years of the decade, *Liturgical Arts* maintained almost total silence on the subject of the war.[88]

The journey through the decade of the 1930s was a most arduous one for the Liturgical Arts Society. The entire period was overshadowed by the threat of financial ruin, and each day brought special challenges to the new organization's stability. After an initial period of strong leadership during the four terms of president Charles Maginnis, the job of guiding the Society fell to less able men,[89] who saw the presidency more a matter of status than responsibility. Finally, in the last years of the decade, with the Society close to bankruptcy, the directors were forced to abandon the idea that the office of president was simply a reward for distinguished service in the field of architecture, and sought instead a president who would set it on sound financial footing.

The announcement by the Benedictine Liturgical Conference of the first National Liturgical Week in 1940 came as a breath of fresh air to those who had labored to keep the Society afloat. As the Liturgical Week would herald an increased vigor to the liturgical movement, so too would it give renewed confidence for a fresh beginning for the Liturgical Arts Society, a "second spring," as Lavanoux described it. [90]

CHAPTER FOUR

"Second Spring":
The Liturgical Arts Society, 1940-1949

The expectation of a "second spring"[1] in the life of the Liturgical Arts Society was realized, in large measure, during the decade from 1940-1949. Having survived financial hardship, naive leadership, and misguided enthusiasm, the Society began to rebuild on its foundations. During the war and postwar period, the Liturgical Arts Society struggled to find a place for itself, both in the world of religious art and architecture, and in the Roman Catholic Church.

CONTAINING THE DEFICIT

Putting the Society's financial house in order had been largely accomplished during the previous decade.[2] As of November 30, 1937, the Society had debts of $22,982.92 and assets of $659.64, leaving a deficit of $22,323.28.[3] Less than three years later, in July of 1940, this deficit had been reduced by more than half, to $10,163.29.[4]

In order to continue the progress in deficit reduction, in November of 1940 the Society launched a special appeal with the hope of raising an additional $5,000. Within a few months, negotiations with a longtime friend of the Society, Miss Justine Ward, had resulted in her pledge of $1,000 on the condition that it be matched by $4,000 from other sources.[5] By the end of the next year, the matching funds had come in, thus reducing the total debt to just over $4,000.[6] A second such campaign in 1944 elicited donations of $660, reducing the Society's indebtedness still further.[7] It was, however, the generosity of Bishop James Cassidy of Fall River, Massachusetts, that would make the Liturgical Arts Society's deficit a thing of the past. In November of 1944, Bishop Cassidy made a substantial gift to the Society, with the stipulation that it be applied directly to the final liquidation of the debt.[8] "This last operation," reported Maurice Lavanoux, "ends the deficit of the Society (our little mascot for so many years) and the financial statement — up to the end of September — shows that we have a balance in our favor of about $264."[9] Almost unbelievably, the Liturgical Arts Society began the year 1945 with no red ink on its ledgers. "I had given up hope of such a day!" wrote Charles Maginnis, first president of the Society, upon hearing the news. [10]

As the decade went on, additional money from unexpected sources would become available for the funding of special projects, thus enabling the Society to expand its sphere of influence. In 1946 Gerald Carroll, longtime friend of the Society and legal counsel to the William Grace family and Grace Steamship Lines, convinced his employers to support the work of the Liturgical Arts Society. For the next 20 years, an annual donation of $2,000 from the Michael P. Grace II Fund was added to the Society's coffers.[11]

Much of this astonishing reversal in the fortunes of the Liturgical Arts Society can be credited to the strong leadership of persons well-versed in business methods. John Dooley and Gerald Carroll, corporate attorneys, John Moody, investment counselor, and Otto Spaeth, industrialist, each a successful and astute businessman, contributed their time and expertise to setting the Society on its financial feet. By crafting a sound management strategy for the Society, these men completely eradicated a debt of more than $22,000 in less than seven years. Although the Society would never be prosperous, without the constant threat of bankruptcy, it could go forward confidently with its program.

The successful liquidation of the Society's deficit is even more remarkable when one considers that it was accomplished during the war years, a period of general uncertainty and restraint on the part of potential donors. The exigencies of war also presented certain opportunities for the Society to make an artistic contribution to the nation. In the fall of 1942, for example, the Citizens' Committee for the Army and Navy devised a plan whereby portable triptychs for use in armed forces chapels in the field would be crafted and donated to the war effort. Painters and sculptors were to contribute their time and talent to the project.[12] Upon hearing of this plan, Lavanoux expressed to the Committee the Society's concern with the quality of the final designs and was chosen as a member of the jury of selection for the triptychs. In this capacity he was able to promote both the values of the Society and the work of first-rate sculptors. By the winter of 1944, more than 300 panels had been commissioned and were installed in armed services' chapels.[13]

INCREASING PRESTIGE

Particularly gratifying to the Liturgical Arts Society during this period was the increase in its prestige within the American Roman Catholic Church. In February, 1942, Archbishop (later Cardinal) Francis Spellman of New York, under whose patronage the Society functioned, attended the Solemn Mass celebrated at the 12th annual meeting of the Society at St. Ignatius Loyola Church. Lavanoux reported that:

"The Archbishop was also present at the meeting which followed . . . . From all accounts, everybody was much pleased, and we now feel that Liturgical Arts has come of age in this archdiocese."[14]

The Society's ecclesiastical backing was not confined solely to the New York archdiocese, however. Several American bishops continued their interest in the Society, and a number of new bishop-members were added to the Board of Directors.[15] It was reported that Bishop Francis O'Hara, archbishop of Kansas City, had remarked "that it was unheard of that a Society that had only been established for 10 years could have won the approbation of the hierarchy to such an extent as Lit. Arts [sic]."[16] In addition, the Liturgical Arts Society continued to receive encouragement from Rome for its work during this period, with Jacques Maritain and, later, Monsignor Giovanni Montini[17] serving as liaisons between the Society and the Vatican.[18]

An occasional vote of confidence for the work of the Society came from the secular world of art and architecture. George Lober, Executive Secretary of the Art Commission for the City of New York, wrote to Spellman:

"For a number of years , it has been my pleasure to observe the work being carried on by the magazine *Liturgical Arts*, under your patronage.

"This magazine has greatly influenced architects, painters, and sculptors in producing better designs for Catholic Churches throughout the country. Much credit must be given to its managing editor, Maurice Lavanoux, for his broad understanding of liturgical art and the interesting manner in which its material is presented."[19]

THE FRUITS OF SUCCESS

A growing local, national, and international[20] reputation brought to the Liturgical Arts Society further opportunities to disseminate its ideas. Increasingly, Lavanoux, the Society's secretary and editor of *Liturgical Arts*, was asked to serve on competition juries, to organize exhibitions, and to speak at a variety of academic and ecclesiastical gatherings. In 1941, Lavanoux was the first lay person to be invited to participate in teaching sessions of the St. Mary of the Lake Seminary (Mundelein, Illinois) Summer School on the Liturgy for Priests, "the only exception . . . made in four years of summer schools."[21] Lavanoux began to be regarded as an expert on ecclesiastical art and architecture outside the Roman Catholic Church as well. When the director of the Boston Museum of Modern Art began planning its Exhibition of Religious Art and Architecture Today (January 13-February 12, 1944), he sought out Lavanoux's advice, having been told that he "knew more about Catholic Church art than anybody in the country."[22]

During this period, the magazine *Liturgical Arts* also received a certain amount of attention within the field of architecture. The prestigious *Bulletin of the American Institute of Architects* published a "Bibliography on the Church Building" in July 1948, in which were cited 49 references to articles and illustrations which had appeared in *Liturgical Arts* in the previous eight years.[23] The following year, a special reprint publication, "An Account of Calligraphy in the 16th Century," which had originally appeared as an article in *Liturgical Arts*, was winner of the Printing for Commerce Exhibition Prize sponsored by the American Institute of Graphic Arts.[24] Another of the Society's reprint publications, "Notes on Building Maintenance," had wide distribution within the Roman Catholic Church. Originally requested by Monsignor James Gaffney for use in the diocese of New York, this reprint pamphlet went through numerous printings as several other diocesan offices asked for copies.[25]

Toward the end of the decade, Lavanoux's writing and radio broadcasts on the "NBC Catholic Hour" further spread the influence of the Society and made its name and work more widely familiar.[26] His monthly column, "Art by the Way," appeared in *Tidings*, the Los Angeles (California) diocesan newspaper, beginning in March, 1944.[27] At the Academic Convocation held in connection with the centennial celebration of St. Vincent's College (Latrobe, Pennsylvania), Lavanoux was awarded the honorary degree of Doctor of Laws for his presence as a "dynamic force in the American field of religious arts and crafts."[28]

THE NATIONAL CATHOLIC WELFARE CONFERENCE STATUE COMPETITION

The Liturgical Arts Society was naturally hesitant about resuming the conduct of its own competitions, having experienced only marginal success in this enterprise during the previous decade.[29] But when an outside group asked the Society to oversee a competition, there seemed to be little risk in accepting the commission. In October of 1936, *Our Sunday Visitor* had launched a campaign to raise funds for a new headquarters for the National Catholic Welfare Council, and by 1940, readers of the *Visitor* had contributed more than $90,000 to this cause.[30] Soon after, reports began to surface about the way in which these funds were to be spent, reports that included architectural drawings of the proposed building. The design, by architect Frederic V. Murphy, included a larger-than-life-size statue of "Christ the Light of the World" to be placed in a niche in the facade of the building. When the drawings of the proposed statue were made public, there was an immediate outcry from a number of members of the Roman Catholic clergy concerned with the state of religious art. One longtime friend of the Liturgical Arts Society, the Rev. Thomas Coakley, rector of Sacred Heart Church, Pittsburgh, Pennsylvania, wrote a two-page critique of the proposed statue and of the process by which it was designed. He concluded by suggesting that a national competition was the ideal way for selecting a design for "such an ambitious project," because it would "attract the attention of the best sculptural brains in the country."[31] Coakley's letter aroused the interest of a number of influential bishops in the process by which the NCWC statue was to be designed,[32] and during the following year, they worked with the NCWC toward a more open competition for the design of the statue.

Their efforts proved successful, and in the spring of 1941, the NCWC announced a competition for a statue of "Christ the Light of the World" to be placed in the central niche of the facade of its new headquarters building. This competition was to be conducted under the supervision of a bishops' advisory committee.[33] To its surprise and pleasure, the Liturgical Arts Society was entrusted with the practical details of the statue competition.[34]

The circumstances of the Liturgical Arts Society's involvement seemed almost ideal. The Society was to be given a substantial fee for conducting the competition,[35] and the program was to be prepared by the Society in collaboration with the Program Committee of the National Sculpture Society.[36] Acting on behalf of the bishops' advisory committee, the Society was to be wholly responsible for the selection of the jurors,[37] who would be paid daily fees and expenses for their work. Most significant, under the terms of the competition, the decision of the jury was to be final.

The jury[38] began its work and in the fall of 1941 invited 67 contestants to prepare models for a statue of "Christ the Light of the World".[39] "After two days of competition,"[40] Lavanoux reported, "the jury found that it could not award a first prize, so they decided to award three preliminary first prizes and then asked these three contestants to recompete for first, second and third prizes."[41] All three winners (George Kratina, Suzanne Nicholas, and Robert Koepnick) agreed to this arrangement[42] and submitted new designs based upon new guidelines devised by the bishops' advisory committee.[43] Although this second set of jury deliberations[44] was attended by representatives of the NCWC[45] and the opinion of the jury was unanimous in favor of George Kratina's dynamic and somewhat impressionistic design, difficulties immediately arose:

"The committee of bishops in charge of the project viewed the models of the finalists . . . and considered the verdict of the jury. This committee, however, concluded that 'the present model of the winner in the competition could not be accepted for several reasons but principally because it could not be identified with Christ, whether under the title Light of the World or any other title.' "[46]

This was indeed a blow to a jury whose decision, it had been promised, was to be final.[47] Up to that time, hopes had been running high within the Society, not only for a competent piece of sculpture for the new NCWC headquarters building but also for a decisive change in the way decisions in such matters were made in the Roman Catholic Church. Very early in the process, Lavanoux expressed his delight in the fact that "a committee of bishops entrusted the conduct of this competition to the Liturgical Arts Society, representing quite a departure in affairs of this sort in the Church and an indication of what will be done."[48] But in the end, in spite of all assurances that the decision of the jury would be final, the bishops reasserted their authority and effectively derailed the process of selection. The final model submitted by George Kratina, although respectable, lacked the evocative power of the original. But the Liturgical Arts Society was not entirely discouraged by the episode.[49] It had conducted the NCWC competition fairly and economically, and in the end, Lavanoux confided to a friend that he "would not have missed it for the world."[50]

THE STATUE PROJECT

At the end of the decade, the Liturgical Arts Society returned to a concern that had been uppermost in the minds of many at the Portsmouth Priory meetings in 1927-1928: the power of the religious goods catalog sales companies to control the state of religious art and architecture by mass-producing and selling products of deplorable quality. It was lamented, for example, that the average parish had only two options when choosing sculpture. If the parish was unable to pay a large sum of money for a private commission, it was forced to turn to the church goods houses and be served up mass-produced statuary. *Liturgical Arts* reported that:

"It had often been the hope of the officers and directors of the Society that means might be found to do something constructive to solve this problem, but here again, the difficulty has been lack of funds. Finally, early in 1947, a member of the Society broached the subject and, more important, offered to defray the expense involved in commissioning a number of sculptors to make models of statues which might eventually lead to a solution."[51]

The solution was to combine the cost-effectiveness of mass production techniques with the high standards and fine design available in individually commissioned works of art. Fifteen sculptors were invited to participate in what was to be known as the "Statue Project,"[52] and each received $500 for producing a 30-inch plaster model. Ten of these 15 were chosen to go on to make a five-foot plaster model of the same subject,[53] and received an additional $1,500. Everything proceeded as planned, and the models by the 10 finalists[54] were illustrated in *Liturgical Arts* and exhibited at the Demotte Gallery, New York City,[55] and at the Dayton (Ohio) Art Institute from January 17 to February 15, 1950.[56] As a result of this exposure, a number of orders for the statues came in from parishes around the country.

But the Liturgical Arts Statue Project did not go very far toward stemming the tide of "Barclay Street" products flowing into Roman Catholic churches. No commercial manufacturer was interested in the designs, which, if made according to the Society's specifications, would reduce the manufacturer's profit. In the end, the Society found that if it were to maintain its own integrity, there could be no compromise with the merchants of mass-produced art.

SUMMARY

During the decade 1940-1949, the Liturgical Arts Society managed to get its financial house in order, to focus its energies on the essentials in its program, and to gain a certain degree of respect within the world of ecclesiastical art and architecture. In 1949, the Society was described by an onlooker as one which:

"like a young David . . . continues to do battle with its giant adversary, in this case a very real Philistine. No single pebble can bring him low. It is an unending campaign, but in its course, a tangible victory can sometimes be counted. The battles must be fought in precisely this desert of indifference that stretches wastefully between the vigorous contemporary artist and the equally vigorous religious interests of today. Until the Church and artist can be reconciled, or at least persuaded into some form of healthy collaboration, both must suffer subtle impairment of their energies."[57]

But in spite of the "desert of indifference," the Liturgical Arts Society's energies were running high at the end of the decade. In a sense, it shared the same positive outlook that possessed the country as a whole in the years after World War II. The future beckoned, and the Society faced it with optimism; the past was viewed not as failure but as a firm foundation for that future. Between the years 1940 and 1949, the Liturgical Arts Society had had first-hand experience with ecclesiastical power at work, and it could no longer be naive about its chances of emerging triumphant in a battle of wills with the Roman Catholic hierarchy. But it had also caught a glimpse of the difference its work could make if the proper climate could be developed and had become increasingly convinced of the best ways to create that climate. In general, the Church was becoming more and more accepting of the Society's liturgical agenda; the Liturgical Movement as a whole was gaining in strength and influence, with larger numbers of American bishops supporting its goals.[58] The American pioneers of that movement viewed the work of the Society as a necessary adjunct of their own, and there were growing opportunities for the Society to communicate its ideas. On the whole, the promise that the 1940s would be a "second spring" for the Society had been fulfilled, and that spring would result in a fruitful summer in the decades that followed.

CHAPTER FIVE

Growth, Maturity, and Decline:
The Liturgical Arts Society, 1950-1972

BROADENING HORIZONS, 1950-1960

By the year 1950, with more than a score of years of struggle and uncertainty, trial and error behind it, the Liturgical Arts Society had gained a great deal of strength and confidence. Described by Maurice Lavanoux as the period of "maturity,"[1] the years from 1950 to 1970 saw the Society grow to become a dominant force in religious art and architecture, not only in the United States but in the Church at large.

Several factors were responsible for this increasing prestige. The quarterly *Liturgical Arts* continued to be, as one onlooker expressed it, "the envy of other art magazines,"[2] and most of the Society's energies had come to be devoted to its production. In addition, many persons who had been supporters of the Society since the very beginning had now reached the peak of their careers and acquired sufficient standing in the architectural profession to make the Society's ideals more widely known.[3] The financial situation was also more favorable to the Society's growth. Between 1950 and 1960, two private foundations[4] supported several special projects and contributed to the Society's operating budget. With approximately 75% of its annual budget underwritten in this way, no great financial crisis threatened the well-being of the Liturgical Arts Society during this decade, and it could conduct its business without the constant threat of bankruptcy.[5]

MAURICE LAVANOUX: A PREDOMINANT ROLE

During the first two decades of the Society's existence, several forces had worked together to give Maurice Lavanoux substantial power over policy and program. This process was brought to completion in the early years of the 1950s, and Lavanoux clearly dominated the life of the Liturgical Arts Society from then on. There was no trace of sinister power politics in all of this, however. By 1950, those individuals whom Lavanoux referred to as "tired enthusiasms" had fallen by the wayside and, because no one volunteered to do the work necessary to keep the organization afloat, it all fell to Lavanoux, the Society's only paid staff member. Two decades of financial difficulty had made it impossible to hire additional staff,[6] and by this time, Lavanoux was quite simply indispensable, having allowed more and more of his own life and work to be absorbed by the life and work of the Society.

In 1953, the last architect-president of the Liturgical Arts Society was elected to office,[7] and internal controversies about Society policy and its liturgical and artistic foundations largely disappeared. From then on, corporate attorney Gerald Carroll[8] guided the Society as president, and the Society as a whole began to function primarily, if not exclusively, as a vehicle for financial and moral support for *Liturgical Arts* and its one-man staff. For all intents and purposes, by the mid-1950s, Lavanoux, the Liturgical Arts Society, and *Liturgical Arts* were one and the same.

HONORS AND AWARDS

The year 1950 was undeniably the high-water mark for the Liturgical Arts Society and Lavanoux. During that year, designated a Holy Year by Pope Pius XII, Lavanoux began to widen the Society's sphere of vision and influence, a process that would continue throughout the next two decades. At the same time, the Society and its leadership made important international contacts and began to gain a measure of recognition outside the American Church.

On June 15, 1950, in a small private ceremony at Cardinal Spellman's New York residence, Lavanoux received the Papal *Benemerenti* medal.[9] Awarded in recognition of his "devoted and effective efforts toward the advancement of the arts of the Church,"[10] the *Benemerenti* gave the Society a measure of confidence in the direction it had been traveling since its founding. "The medal," Lavanoux explained, "will help to prove that Liturgical Arts and its secretary are not too dangerous."[11] (Lavanoux himself wore the honor lightly, however, remarking to a friend that it simply meant that he had "been a good boy for the past 20 years."[12]) That same year, Lavanoux was appointed to the United States delegation of the First International Congress of Catholic Artists.[13] The Congress, sponsored by Pax Romana (Mouvement International des Intellectuels Catholiques) and the Unione Cattolica Artisti,[14] was to meet in Rome on September 1-5, 1950.[15] Even though a trip to Rome in order to attend the Congress seemed an extravagant dream for Lavanoux and the less-than-affluent Liturgical Arts Society, it was suggested[16] that a private foundation might be enlisted for support. Lavanoux explained that:

"The deciding factor might be whether I could have an important spot on the program to present our point of view and also to impress on the Roman authorities, in art circles at any rate, that the United States is on the map and not merely a colony of the Roman Empire!"[17]

When Lavanoux was assured by the organizers of the Congress that he would be allowed to make a 40-minute presentation as part of the proceedings,[18] the Michael P. Grace II Fund (of which long-time friend of the Society Gerald Carroll was co-trustee) agreed not only to pay for the trip to Rome, but also for visits to France, Switzerland, and Great Britain to gather material for *Liturgical Arts*.[19] At the Congress, Lavanoux was chosen chairman of the United States delegation, and his speech, delivered both in French and English, made a significant impact on the deliberations of the Congress.[20]

WORLD TRAVELS

The Rome trip confirmed Lavanoux's growing conviction of the need for a wider scope to the work of the Liturgical Arts Society, and throughout the rest of the decade , it became his passion to make the Society and *Liturgical Arts* an international endeavor. For a number of years, he had been corresponding with Roman Catholic missionaries in Japan about the role of the arts within non-Western Catholicism,[21] and in the winter of 1951, he requested a second grant from the Grace Fund to finance a trip to Japan, "during which he would attend a forum on Japanese art and architecture."[22] The trustees of the Fund obliged, and in June, 1952, Lavanoux began an around-the-world tour that took him to Japan, Thailand, India, Palestine, Southern Europe, and Great Britain.[23] Further trips, all financed by the Grace Fund, to Mexico and the Caribbean (1954), Africa (1956), and Northern Europe (1958) consolidated *Liturgical Arts'* editorial connections abroad. Lavanoux explained that:

"The idea of all these dreams of mine (and some of my friends here feel that all I need to do is take care of home matters) is to give Lit. Arts [sic] a sort of "universal" prestige and knowledge; then we can more easily come down to local developments."[24]

But in December, 1960, the Michael P. Grace II Fund, which had played fairy godmother to Lavanoux for more than a decade, had exhausted its resources, and the period of international travel abruptly ended.[25] With one last voyage to Ireland to attend the International Eucharistic Congress[26] and to represent the United States at the Munich, Germany, meeting of the International Congress of Catholic Artists,[27] Lavanoux returned to New York to devote his attention to the work of "mending editorial fences" in the United States. But his wide travels during the previous 10 years had gained him a host of editorial consultants whose contributions of information, articles, and photographs kept the editor of *Liturgical Arts* and its readers abreast of current events in the field of religious art and architecture throughout the world.

INCREASING PRESTIGE IN THE UNITED STATES AND IN ROME
A growing international reputation for the Society, and Lavanoux's own increasing reputation within the world of religious art at home, served to increase the number of opportunities for the Society to exercise influence. During this period, Lavanoux continued to be appointed to juries[28] and consulting and editorial boards[29] and to lecture at colleges, universities, and professional gatherings around the United States and Canada. His articles appeared in numerous journals and books,[30] and twice he appeared on the CBS television program "Look Up and Live."[31] In 1953, Lavanoux was called upon by the U.S. State Department to organize a traveling exhibit on "The Church in America."[32] In spite of all of this activity, the 1950s did not bring substantial advances in the economic fortunes of the Society in the form of increased membership or subscriptions to *Liturgical Arts*.[33]

The decade from 1950 to 1960 was also a period of the Liturgical Arts Society's gradual disengagement from its reliance on the American Roman Catholic hierarchy, which had, with a few notable exceptions, generally manifested indifference toward its work. The Society seemed less inclined to ask the bishops' approval of its work than it had been in previous years and less likely to assume that encouragement would be gratuitously offered. At the same time, however, in his search for other sources of support and encouragement, Lavanoux was able to make firm connections between the Society and the Vatican. Volumes of *Liturgical Arts* had been presented to the Pope since the first issue appeared in 1931, and having received the Apostolic Blessing on the Society's work, Lavanoux now desired a more emphatic statement of papal approval. In September, 1959, Lavanoux traveled to Rome and was included in a group of 12 for an audience with Pope John XXIII,[34] and the Vatican publicly congratulated the Society for its contribution to "bringing about a normal and healthy evolution of all the arts in the service of the Church Universal, according to the principles laid down by the Sacred Congregation of the Holy Office."[35] The 1960s would present new challenges to the work of the Liturgical Arts Society, and its international reputation would prove important in meeting those challenges.

CONSOLIDATING GAINS, 1960-1970

Most of the decade between 1960 and 1970 was spent attending to matters closer to home, primarily because of lack of travel subsidy but also because of a decline in Lavanoux's energies; he was then in his mid-seventies. In 1962 , the death of the Rev. Gerald Ellard severed one of the Society's last links with the foundations of the American liturgical movement.[36] John LaFarge, chaplain of the Liturgical Arts Society since its founding, died the following year at the age of 83,[37] and the loss of these two great friends left a painful void in the life of the Society. At a meeting of the Society's Board of Directors, December 11, 1963, Clement J. McNaspy, S.J., was appointed to the chaplaincy "to replace our dear friend Uncle John."[38] Although Lavanoux had slowed his previously breathtaking pace, he continued to write and lecture, and to garner, with the usual humility, honors and awards from the worlds of both architecture and Church. On March 22, 1961, he received the Conover Award of the

National Conference on Church Architecture, the first Roman Catholic so honored.[39] Three years later, on June 8, 1964, he was given the honorary degree of Doctor of Humane Letters by Georgetown University.[40] The Catholic Action medal from St. Bonaventure University[41] and a prestigious honorary membership in the American Institute of Architects were both awarded Lavanoux in 1968.[42]

THE LITURGICAL ARTS SOCIETY AND VATICAN COUNCIL II

On January 25, 1959, Pope John XXIII called an ecumenical council to be convened at Rome the following year. Lavanoux was convinced that the Liturgical Arts Society could play a role in the forging of a positive statement concerning the arts of the Church, a statement that might be eventually included in the proceedings of the Council. "I feel," he wrote, "we could consider it a vindication of Liturgical Arts' long fight for sanity in the matter."[43]

Fortuitously, a longtime friend of the Society, Monsignor Joachim Nabuco of Rio de Janiero, Brazil, was appointed moderator of the subcommittee on sacred art for the liturgy commission of the Council.[44] In May, 1961, Nabuco sent Lavanoux a draft of the document that the sacred art subcommittee had prepared for submission to the commission.[45] In response, Lavanoux compiled a set of relevant materials to be included in the subcommittee dossier,[46] and he was appointed as a "technical adviser" to the committee.[47] At the same time, Lavanoux sent copies of *Liturgical Arts* to members of the subcommittee and certain other "key persons in Rome."[48] Having offered their services to those preparing for Vatican II, Lavanoux and the Liturgical Arts Society patiently waited for results. During the years the Council was in session, *Liturgical Arts* occasionally expressed cautious optimism that Vatican II would result in a revitalized climate for the arts. But generally, the Society attended to work at home between 1960 and 1963, preparing the ground for the postconciliar era.[49]

A NEW FINANCIAL CRISIS

By 1964, the Liturgical Arts Society had once again accumulated a debt sizable enough to require yet another major fund-raising campaign. But at the same time, it was beginning to be clear that *Liturgical Arts* and the Society could not thrive without some sort of ongoing subsidy. "But that issue," Lavanoux lamented, "is something all seem to want to 'push under the rug.'"[50]

A plan for a group of supporters to be called "Friends of Liturgical Arts" was one of the numerous abortive (and generally misguided) attempts at a rescue operation.[51] Further suggestions were made that the Society move to an "austerity" program.[52] (It is not surprising that these suggestions were met with a certain amount of frustration on the part of Lavanoux, who had been running the entire operation single-handed, without even a typist, for 20 years in return for a salary that finally averaged $50 per week.) In 1963, Lavanoux had made a full report on the status of the Society and its future needs to John LaFarge and the board of directors, but nothing concrete ever came of the suggestions it contained. As in the past, loans, gifts, minor fund-raising appeals, and indulgent creditors were the life-support systems of the Society during the turbulent decade of the 1960s. But it seemed that the enthusiasm of many of the supporters of the Society was becoming gradually diluted by the many diverse demands the decade placed on them, and when, in 1968, more than 800 bishops, clergy, and laity were asked to contribute to keeping the Society alive, only 58 responded with cash donations.[53]

Even the ever-optimistic Lavanoux was beginning to become discouraged. He lamented that:

"There is usually so much talk, many suggestions of what *we* should do, etc., etc. — then, next morning, I sit in the office, alone, with all the problems. At the moment, we have only 71 corporate members. We lost quite a few by death, and to get more means, again, more paperwork for me . . . . My great puzzle has been the lack of support from those few who really have means, but they seem to lack the spirit of adventure, generosity, vision, imagination."[54]

On the other hand, however, he still feared the consequences of the involvement of wealthy investors. "Please don't urge anyone to 'buy into' Liturgical Arts. I value my independence too much to have any wealthy person with a hand in the pie."[55]

At long last, Gerald Carroll and others began to realize that Lavanoux would not be able to continue indefinitely in his job as editor of *Liturgical Arts* and secretary of the Society. Having established an impressive network of volunteer "editorial assistants" in all parts of the world, material for *Liturgical Arts* was in adequate supply. But Lavanoux was beginning to lose some of his boundless energy, and hearing impairment had curtailed his willingness to accept speaking engagements which, in the past, had given the Liturgical Arts Society wide exposure and which had also brought in a certain amount of operating capital.[56] There seemed, however, a reluctance on the part of the Directors to deal with the practical difficulties of planning for the Society's future.

In 1967, Lavanoux expressed his impatience with the situation in a letter to a close friend:

"The question of continuity and a trained replacement for me has come up repeatedly in the past five years, but those who really could do something positive have little vision, imagination, and generosity. Perhaps what is now the Liturgical Arts Society and its quarterly is fated to become something different, etc. In the meantime, I am doing my job and enjoying it."[57]

But despite his uncertainty over the Society's future, Lavanoux ventured into the 1970s with the same curiosity, wit, and enthusiasm which had been the mainstays of the Liturgical Arts Society and *Liturgical Arts* for nearly 40 years. "The job," he wrote, "is a never-ending source of enjoyment and never a dull moment . . . I look forward to the coming decades with equal enthusiasm and interest."[58]

"The END OF A GREAT ADVENTURE," 1970-1974

Lavanoux's effort to keep the fires burning under *Liturgical Arts* and the Liturgical Arts Society had become an increasingly solitary one as the years went by. In 1965, annual meetings of the Society membership had been suspended due to lack of interest, and even the Quilisma Club, long a gathering of the Society's staunchest supporters, was in difficulty.[59] The files of the Society for this period are littered with the obituary notices of friends who had shared their lives with that of the Society through 40 years of high times and low. In addition, the turn of the decade had seen the collapse of periodicals from other countries whose interest in religious art had run parallel to that of *Liturgical Arts*. In the year 1970 alone, France's *L'Art Sacre* and *L'Art Chretien* and Italy's *Fede e Arte* and *Chiese e Quartiere* all ceased publication.[60]

In 1970, there came the possibility of a way to insure the survival of *Liturgical Arts*. In March of that year, the Liturgical Arts Society received a letter from a publishing syndicate in which was outlined a plan to buy out *Liturgical Arts*, along with other arts publications, and to contract for cheap printing for the lot in order to make a profit.[61] But to Lavanoux , this seemed a solution without honor for a periodical that had strived, above all, for the highest in production standards. "All design, layout, positioning of ads would be keyed and geared to making money fast," a friend knowledgeable about the publishing business advised,[62] and Lavanoux declined the offer.[63] And so, as the Liturgical Arts Society entered its fifth decade, the question of its continued survival and continuity of leadership went unanswered. It had occurred to Lavanoux that "perhaps what is now the Liturgical Arts Society and its quarterly is fated to become something different,"[64] and he went on quietly making plans for the day when he would no longer be able to keep the failing Society alive.

THE FINAL CRISIS: THE LITURGICAL ARTS SOCIETY DISBANDS

In November, 1971, *Liturgical Arts* marked its 40th anniversary, an occasion for celebrating, as Lavanoux put it, the "reality of dreams."[65] But neither reality nor dream could preserve the Society through its 41st year. The debt to Rumford Press had become wholly unmanageable, and the printer had decided that all costs related to the production of previous issues were to be paid before another issue was put to press.[66] Although a former director of the Society offered more than $10,000 to be applied to the printing bill,[67] $2,800 remained outstanding, and no one came forward with the extra sum. Subscriptions to *Liturgical Arts* and membership in the Society were down, and there was no money for a campaign to solicit more. Most important, no replacement for Lavanoux had been sought, and it was extremely unlikely that anyone could be found to take the job for less than $15,000 to $20,000 per year (as opposed to the approximately $3,640 that Lavanoux had been paid during his final year as secretary). To think of promising a replacement adequate compensation for the work Lavanoux had been doing was simply impossible.

One of Lavanoux's special concerns throughout this period was that the 40-year saga of the Liturgical Arts Society and its work would not be entirely forgotten. In 1971 , he wrote to the archivist at Portsmouth Priory, suggesting that, should the Society be unable to continue, its files might find a home at the Priory, "the place of the Society's origin."[68] The Priory declined the offer, but the following year, another possibility for housing the Society's records presented itself. Later that year, Lavanoux reported:

"I happened to meet Fr. James Burtchaell, Provost of the University of Notre Dame, and as I knew that there was a department of history and a center for liturgical studies at the university, it occurred to me to ask whether, when the time came, the archives of the Liturgical Arts Society could find a home there."[69]

After some deliberation, the University agreed to accept the Liturgical Arts Society archives.

Clearly, the idea that the Society's papers would not be simply discarded was a great comfort to Lavanoux. In a sense, his life and the life of *Liturgical Arts* had become virtually indistinguishable and, although he sensibly planned for the end of both, he continued to work as if both would go on forever. A third honorary degree (from Loyola University, New Orleans, Louisiana),[70] a retrospective exhibit of the life of *Liturgical Arts*,[71] and an annual award given in his honor and bearing his name[72] were further testimony to a faithful career in service of a society and its quarterly, of a Church, and of quality in religious art and architecture.

On September 6, 1972, at a quiet lunch at a downtown New York restaurant, the Liturgical Arts Society breathed its last. Reports of the meeting are sketchy, but it is clear that by the time the lunch had ended Society president Gerald Carroll, Lavanoux, and former Director John Dooley had concluded that the use of extraordinary measures to keep the Society alive was futile.[73] During the following weeks letters informing members of the demise of the Society and the end of *Liturgical Arts* were mailed out,[74] loose ends, financial and otherwise, were tied up, and arrangements were finalized for the disposing of the Society's archives.[75]

PUBLIC REACTION TO THE DEMISE OF THE LITURGICAL ARTS SOCIETY

Throughout this period, Lavanoux fought to control his bitterness and disappointment over the situation. He sincerely believed that if those individuals who:

". . .had talked endlessly about what *should* be done had actually *done* something (and they certainly had the means to do so) *Liturgical Arts* would be alive and well today! In all of this I have lost a very precious thing—my faith in human nature. Generally, I do not believe many [people] anymore."[76]

Even as the last of the Society's debts were liquidated[77] and files were packed, Lavanoux continued to hope that the public would demand and support the revival of *Liturgical Arts*. But as the weeks went by and the public remained silent, it became apparent that Lavanoux would have to turn elsewhere for help. Since the Society had enjoyed a measure of recognition from the Vatican, and had thereby, it was surmised, brought honor to the archdiocese which it called home, it seemed reasonable to look to the New York hierarchy for the restoration of the Society's fortunes. On October 31, 1972, representatives of the Society called on archdiocesan executives to explain the situation and to propose that Cardinal Cooke put his financial and episcopal weight behind the revival of *Liturgical Arts*. The Cardinal's secretary listened, and the Cardinal promised to call a committee together to discuss the fate of the Society and a possible means of rescue.[78] The results were, to say the least, disappointing. The Cardinal's Director of Communications wrote to Gerald Carroll:

"Cardinal Cooke spoke to a number of key people regarding the state of Liturgical Arts, and met with a committee of three Cardinals and three Bishops. All of them had available to them the information you gave me and they gave considerable time to the question.

"It was the resolution of the committee that they were all concerned with the survival of *Liturgical Arts*, but they could not make an immediate practical recommendation at this time."[79]

It had also been suggested at the meeting between the Liturgical Arts group and the Cardinal that he carry to the upcoming Conference of United States Catholic Bishops a request for a statement of episcopal support for the Society. The Cardinal's representative reported that there was "no device available to make a public expression of approval for *Liturgical Arts*."[80] Having failed to arouse the interest of the bishops in the revival of the Society and its quarterly, Lavanoux had hoped that the religious press would take up the cause. But only a handful of brief notices appeared.[81] It was later suggested that the Liturgical Arts Society was simply another victim of the turbulence in the post-Conciliar Church, and that if any of the 2,000 subscribers to *Liturgical Arts* cried out, they could not be heard over the din of change. In any event, the passing of the Liturgical Arts Society and *Liturgical Arts* caused hardly a stir in the Church it had sought to serve for more than 40 years.

And so it seemed that the final door had closed on the Liturgical Arts Society and *Liturgical Arts*. On December 11, 1972 , a North American Van Lines truck pulled up to 521 Fifth Avenue and carried away "13 cardboard boxes, 10 metal filing cabinets, and one large carton":[82] the 44-year life story of the Liturgical Arts Society. "I feel a bit sad and empty," Lavanoux wrote to a longtime friend.[83]

THE AFTERMATH OF THE SOCIETY'S DEMISE

Lavanoux's despair was not long-lasting, and his buoyant spirit soon took over. He accepted the editorship of the magazine *Stained Glass*[84] and wrote a monthly "Visual Arts" column for *Liturgy*, the journal of the Liturgical Conference.[85] On May 12, 1973, The Catholic University of America bestowed upon Lavanoux his fourth honorary degree.[86] Lavanoux also served as president of the Society for the Renewal of Christian Art, Inc., which he saw as the legitimate heir to the Liturgical Arts Society (although it outlived the latter by only six years).[87] On the presumption that this group would eventually find the means to revive *Liturgical Arts*, Lavanoux continued to seek material on religious arts from all over the world, referring to himself as an "editor without venue."[88] "It is hard to accept the fact," he wrote, "that I am now without the means to make known the work of talented architects and of the many artists who can be found in all parts of this land."[89] On October 21, 1974, Lavanoux was entertaining a visitor in the tiny Queens apartment in which he had lived and worked for half a century. "Sorry I don't have all my old pep!" he said to his companion and died quietly in his armchair.[90]

"This is the end of a beautiful adventure!" Lavanoux had written to a friend just before his death.[91] The adventure had taken the Liturgical Arts Society through the establishment of a liturgical renewal movement and through the massive changes it produced in the Roman Catholic Church. It had survived ecclesiastical indifference, financial hardship, and the assaults of commercialism. Since its demise in 1972, no real successor to the Liturgical Arts Society has risen up. Although a number of religious arts periodicals, sponsored by various denominational and professional organizations,[92] have been established, none has lasted more than a few years. Certainly none has had the visual, stylistic, and intellectual impact of *Liturgical Arts*.

The complexion of the Liturgical Arts Society underwent several profound changes over the 44 years of its existence. In the beginning, the Society was a band of young idealists seeking to serve the Church as the arbiters of artistic and architectural good taste. In the end it was basically a magazine and its readership, held together by a charismatic and energetic 80-year-old editor. During its lifespan, the Society had witnessed remarkable changes in the Roman Catholic Church, of which it saw itself a part. It is a tribute to the creativity and flexibility of the organization that it could respond to these changes without compromising its basic ideals. In the following chapters, the theological and liturgical principles that underlay the work of the Liturgical Arts Society will be investigated, along with the ecclesiastical context within which it operated.

CHAPTER SIX

The Liturgical Arts Society and the Liturgy

It is clear that the founding of the Liturgical Arts Society coincided with the heightening of liturgical interest in the United States commonly referred to as the "American Liturgical Movement."[1] Whether or not the Society's founding was a direct *result* of that interest is more difficult to determine. The very presence of the word "liturgical" in the name of the group is significant (especially at a time when liturgical concerns were generally relegated to the margins of Roman Catholic religious thought), but it does not necessarily prove that the Society consistently pursued the principles and goals of the liturgical movement. However, there is other evidence that both the European effort for liturgical renewal and its American counterpart had significant impact on the Society's founding and future development and that the Society saw itself as a full participant in the liturgical apostolate.

Maurice Lavanoux had had immediate contact with the European liturgical movement as early as 1920 and often spoke of his first introduction to the liturgical revival through pioneer ecumenist Désiré Joseph Cardinal Mercier:

"... my 1920 conversation with him [Mercier] and his hope that I might meet Dom Lambert Beauduin was my *first* step in my ever-deep interest in church planning, based not on frozen norms but on an awareness of a living liturgy."[2]

Although he missed meeting Beauduin by half an hour,[3] Lavanoux's encounter with Mercier inspired him to further study of the sources of the liturgical renewal. He returned to Belgium in 1925 to spend three days at Mont Cesar[4] and kept up with his reading in the early classics of liturgical scholarship.[5]

Were other members of the Portsmouth Priory group acquainted with the European liturgical movement? Everitt Harman[6] had spent time in the mid-1920s touring some of the monastic centers in which the European liturgical renewal had been born, but it seems to have been the spirit of reformed monasticism, rather than the spirit of liturgical reform, that captured his imagination. The documents which Harman authored for the founding meetings of the Society show little evidence of liturgical awareness: His proposed "Constitution and By-Laws for a Benedictine Oblate Guild of Artists, Architects, and Craftsmen" never once mentions the liturgy.[7] Another of the more influential of the founding members, who as a Dutch national might have had some contact with European sources, was Ides van der Gracht.[8] But once again, his numerous proposals for the future of the Liturgical Arts Society show little evidence of concern for liturgical renewal.[9] As for the other founders, especially John W. Wood, John Howard Benson, Donald Wood, and A. Graham Carey, concern for the restoration of a sound philosophy of art seems to have been at the forefront of their thinking.[10]

It seems, then, that only Lavanoux had a deep appreciation for and commitment to the principles of the European liturgical movement.[11] But in the end, because of Lavanoux's continuing influence on the Society, his familiarity with the roots of liturgical renewal in Europe would have a profound impact on the direction the Society would take. It was Lavanoux who made contact with Abbot Ildefons Herwegen of Maria Laach, persuaded him to serve as advisor to the Liturgical Arts Society in its infancy,[12] and kept discussions of the liturgy at the center of the founding deliberations.

Lavanoux also seems to have had early contact with American liturgical pioneer Virgil Michel and his work at St. John's Abbey, Collegeville, Minnesota, and often said that Michel's writings had "always been of great help" to him.[13] An article by Lavanoux entitled "An Architect's Dilemma" appeared in *Orate Fratres* in 1929,[14] only three years after it began publication. As soon as word of the formation of the Liturgical Arts Society was announced in *The Commonweal* (November 30, 1930), in *America* (November 19, 1930), and in *Orate Fratres* (January 25, 1931), a number of the American liturgical pioneers wrote to express their congratulations and hopes for the success of the new enterprise. Gerald Ellard and William Busch, both close collaborators with Virgil Michel, clearly saw the Liturgical Arts Society as a vital link in their own efforts for liturgical renewal in the United States.[15] With the appointment of John LaFarge, S.J., as chaplain to the new Liturgical Arts Society in 1930, its liturgical foundation was made even more solid. In his work as editor of *America*, LaFarge had a wide acquaintance with both the American and European efforts at liturgical renewal.[16]

The Society sought for itself a dual role within the liturgical movement. First, it wanted to provide accurate liturgical information to a segment of the Church's population — artists, craftspeople, and architects — who might not otherwise have access to it. Second, it hoped to be the voice of those involved with the planning and designing of the setting for the liturgy, continually calling the larger liturgical movement to take their special concerns seriously. In developing its program and in setting editorial policy for *Liturgical Arts*, the Society sought to serve as intermediary between these two distinct, but related, constituencies.[17]

THE DEVELOPMENT OF THE LITURGICAL ARTS SOCIETY'S LITURGICAL UNDERSTANDING

In order to locate the Liturgical Arts Society more precisely within the American liturgical movement as a whole, it is necessary to analyze the Society's own liturgical agenda. Much of the evidence for the Society's early understanding of the liturgy is found in proposals made for presentation at the Portsmouth Priory retreats, 1927-1928,[18] especially proposed constitutions and by-laws, as well as in correspondence among the founding members. In addition, by looking at the explicitly liturgical material in *Liturgical Arts* we can piece together the liturgical "world" that the Liturgical Arts Society wished to lay before its constituency.[19] Articles on the history and theology of the liturgy, the editorial pages, and after 1951, the "Editor's Diary"[20] served as a forum for the Society's views on the contemporary scene, advocating and chronicling liturgical reform and functioning as a window on the world of the liturgical apostolate. Although *Liturgical Arts* was never intended as a coherent body of theological material, it gives a reasonably clear picture of the development of the Liturgical Arts Society's understanding of the place of the liturgy in the life of the Roman Catholic Church over forty years.

THE LITURGY AS ART FORM

During the earliest period of deliberations over what would eventually become the Liturgical Arts Society, several views of the liturgy of the Roman Catholic Church were held. For one segment of the Society's founding group (represented most fully in the proposals made by Ides van der Gracht) the liturgy is seen primarily as one of the "treasures of the Church,"[21] one facet of the great Roman Catholic cultural heritage. This group understood the liturgy as one of the arts, which, like all arts, had a "spiritual value"[22] for the individual Christian. As an art-form, the Roman Catholic liturgy stood alongside sculpture, painting, music, and architecture both as "spiritual food" for the starving Roman Catholic intellectual and as one element in the Church's cultural contribution to society as a whole. But because of the fear and suspicion with which the Church was regarded in the United States, and because the Church was identified with the "lower cultural and social status" of the immigrant population, the infinite beauties of the Roman Catholic liturgy were unable to exert proper influence in contemporary American culture.[23] One of the stated goals of this group of founders for the new organization was to make the flowering of the Church's cultural heritage, including the liturgy, "more effective and fertile" in the "modern intellectual and artistic life" of the United States.[24]

Even though, in the end, this understanding of the liturgy was found to be deficient in theological substance, some of the language of the liturgy-as-art-form point of view was carried over into the Society's published prospectus which was sent to potential members between 1931 and 1938. There, under the heading "Ideals and Purpose," it is stated that "the official, public worship of the Catholic Church has ... a unique and majestic beauty."[25] But in the paragraph that follows, something of a disclaimer is made, when the Society asserts that it has "no sympathy with a merely aesthetic approach to religion. It is not devoted to 'arty' matters."[26] On balance, the concept of the liturgy as one of the arts of the Church had a rela-

81

tively short life in the Society's thinking, and by the time the founding group had begun to disintegrate (that is, shortly after 1930), it was difficult to detect any but the most rudimentary remains of this view.

THE ROMANTIC: NEO-MEDIEVALISM AND MONASTIC REVIVAL

The restoration of European monasticism, the reliance on Thomistic theology, and a desire to wipe away what were seen to be the unfortunate results of the Reformation and of Renaissance humanism were all central elements within the earliest period of the 20th-century liturgical renewal. To some degree or another, each of these elements contributed to a certain measure of "medieval nostalgia" among the liturgical pioneers, both in Europe and in the United States. In believing that the faith of medieval Christianity was of a purer form than that of later periods, and in believing that the liturgy of the Middle Ages somehow both reflected and reinforced that faith, the Liturgical Arts Society was not out of step with the liturgical movement as a whole during that same period.

A second segment of the Society's founding members[27] looked to the renewal of monastic life and of the medieval guild system as inspiration for their work. These members advocated the formation of a Guild of Benedictine Oblates, whose life together would inspire and inform their art. Working and living under the *Regula* of St. Benedict, this "Benedictine Oblate Guild of Architects, Artists, and Craftsmen" was to serve to integrate the lives of artists with the "Source of their inspiration."[28] It might be presumed that the renewal of the liturgy begun by European Benedictines would contribute to this bond between oblate artists and the "source of their inspiration." But this connection is never made in the constitution and by-laws proposed by this segment of the Society's founding group.[29]

While the plan of an oblate guild under the Rule of St. Benedict failed to win the support of any but a few of the Society's founders, the monastic and medieval romanticism that it reflected did have a certain impact on the Society's early program and on its understanding of the liturgy. Book reviews and articles on medieval church history (including a six-part series on the liturgical directions of St. Charles Borromeo[30]) appeared with some regularity in the early numbers of *Liturgical Arts,* along with numerous photographic reproductions of medieval art and architecture. Much of this medievalist sentiment is crystalized in *Liturgical Arts'* tribute to Augustus Welby Northmore Pugin,[31] whose efforts to "return to the Great Age of Faith" made him the high priest of the Gothic revival. The *Liturgical Arts* reprint of Pugin's "An Earnest Appeal for the Revival of Ancient Plain Song"[32] set the agenda for the Liturgical Arts Society's own commitment to the restoration of Gregorian chant as the single most appropriate music for the liturgy.

A fuller expression of the medieval ideal is to be found four years later, in 1937, in an article entitled "The Importance of the Liturgy" by Cardinal Villeneuve. "The Middle Ages," he contends, was a time during which:

". . . the people, although illiterate, were accustomed to attend long liturgical functions and thus acquired a thorough knowledge of the whole theology of Christianity. . . How did the barbarous nations of Northern Europe become the Admirable Christendom of the Middle Ages? Was it not by making them attend the services of the Church. . . ?"[33]

The sense here is that not only is the medieval period the golden age of the faith, but it is the Church's liturgy that stands at the center of that age, keeping the forces of chaos and barbarism from tearing it asunder.

LITURGICAL LAW AND THE "SPIRIT OF THE LITURGY"
A number of those associated with the founding of the Liturgical Arts Society thought it was not sufficient to view the liturgy simply as one art form among many or to reduce it to a bit of ecclesiastical nostalgia. Upon circulating his proposal for making "catholic spirit, culture, and liturgy more effective and fertile," Ides van der Gracht received the criticism that:

"One fundamental thing is lacking: an illuminating exposition of the deep benefit that Catholic liturgy can procure for the human soul by expanding the aspects of spiritual life and sanctifying the individual. This means: Liturgy as the profound and mysterious expression of the innermost of the Faith, as *Lex orandi,* is the bridge to eternity, and being at the same time *Lex credendi,* offers moral guidance and partnership with our Saviour, through Holy Mother Church."[34]

Having absorbed much of the liturgical movement's liturgical agenda, Maurice Lavanoux was also concerned that the Liturgical Arts Society seek a deeper understanding of the inner dynamics of the liturgy and the rubrics and canons that guide it. The first concrete evidence of Lavanoux's liturgical stance is found in his article "An Architect's Dilemma," which appeared in *Orate Fratres* in 1929.[35] There he criticized those who build churches without inquiring into the "spirit of the liturgy," a practice that, he alleged, "has caused a great deal of mischief" and necessitated "a reform in liturgical observance which is, at present, limited to a few . . . abbeys and a few rare parishes."[36] Lavanoux then proceeds to give examples from recent church building and renovation projects in which "an amazing disregard for the decisions of the Sacred Congregation of Rites" is displayed.[37] It is clearly liturgical law, both canon and rubric, as well as the authority of the liturgy itself, that is at the heart of Lavanoux's concern.

Interest in the "proper liturgical observance"[38] is further manifested in the documents under which the Liturgical Arts Society was incorporated in 1928. By-Laws, Article I, Section 2 ("Standards") stated that "strict conformity to the Liturgical Laws of the Catholic Church is expected of the Society's members."[39] In addition, according to the Society's brochure, the purpose of the organization is to "devise ways and means for improving the standards of taste, craftsmanship, and *liturgical correctness*" (italics ours).[40] Phrases such as "proper observance," "liturgical requirement," and "liturgical correctness" are liberally distributed throughout the Society's early materials, including the pages of *Liturgical Arts*. There, we find in the early numbers several articles outlining the canonical requirements of the Sacred Congregation of Rites,[41] pastoral letters from American bishops chancery directives,[42] and expositions by canon lawyers on liturgical matters.[43]

Although Lavanoux and others would come to regret the days when "rubrics masqueraded as liturgy,"[44] the Liturgical Arts Society's early emphasis on correct liturgical observance was not simply a manifestation of fastidious rubricism. In stressing the importance of the canons and rubrics governing the liturgy, the Society was participating in the conviction of the American and European liturgical pioneers that careful attention to the liturgy itself, and particularly to the liturgy of the Mass, rather than to the myriad accretions and extra-liturgical devotions, would enable the Church to return to a purer state.

Careful attention to the letter of the law could not, in principle, be separated from what had been called (initially by Romano Guardini) the "spirit of the liturgy," and the development of this connection between the internal dynamic of the Church's liturgical life and its external manifestations would occupy much of the Society's attention during the years that followed. The most fully-developed explication of the Society's understanding of how the balance between the spirit of the liturgy and the letter of the law was to be achieved is found in Gerald Ellard's article "The Liturgy and Catholic Life,"[45] which appeared in *Liturgical Arts* in 1934. There, Ellard describes the plight of the modern human being:

"baffled and confused, he finds no resting place . . . disillusioned, despairing, drifting . . . and forced in on himself, more and more our modern man wrestles in vain with the philosophic riddle of why physics should be opposed to, or should have conquered, metaphysics and closed even the refuge of thought."[46]

After outlining the history of the decline of Christian worship from Trent to the late-nineteenth century, Ellard describes the stirrings of the liturgical movement in Europe, its advancement by Pope Pius X, and its manifestation in the United States. Finally, Ellard explains the ways in which the liturgy, properly understood, will "arrest this progressive deterioration inexorably sapping our civilization, a process that set in when the Renaissance man made himself — and not God — the measure of all things," by returning human beings to "spiritual solidarity."[47]

Ellard's thesis might be looked upon as simply an expansion of the van der Gracht[48] notion of the liturgy as a part of the Church's contribution to Western culture, but clearly it has considerably more theological substance. The liturgy has an inner reality opposed to everything that works to fracture society and estrange human beings from one another. This article also marks an important development in the Liturgical Arts Society's liturgical understanding in that it backs away, to a substantial degree, from attention to liturgical externals, and places the primary emphasis on the "spirit of the liturgy." Throughout its 40-year history, the Society stressed the organic unity between the liturgy and the life of the Roman Catholic Church. Although proper observance would never be disregarded, the Society clearly believed that "if, in liturgical matters, the 'internal' is looked out for, the externals will take care of themselves."[49]

THE MYSTICAL BODY OF CHRIST MOTIF

In addition to its attention to the inner reality of the liturgy, this article by Gerald Ellard is important to the development of the Liturgical Arts Society's understanding of the liturgy for another reason. "The Liturgy and Catholic Life" is *Liturgical Arts'* first attempt at a full explication of the doctrine of the Mystical Body of Christ and of its relation to the liturgical life of the Church and the transformation of society. It stands as a classic statement of Mystical-Body theology as interpreted by the American liturgical movement. In the encyclical *Mystici Corporis Christi* (promulgated June 29, 1943)[50] the goals and principles of the liturgical movement received specific attention from Pius XII. In saying that the Mystical Body was an appropriate definition of the Church and a proper source of liturgical and theological reflection, *Mystici Corporis* affirmed that the foundations of the liturgical movement were sound and that it had been generally traveling in the right direction. In "The Liturgy and Catholic Life," Ellard makes a strong case for the claim of the Mystical-Body motif on those who would seek a deep understanding of the liturgy:

"None but the most superficial idea of the Liturgical Movement and its relation to Catholic life is possible without a grasp of the doctrine of the mystic body of Christ [which is] . . . 'the sign and seal of modern Christianity.'"[51]

For Ellard, it is the re-establishment of the Mystical Body as a central theme in Roman Catholic theology that has returned the Church to a fuller understanding of the word liturgy, i.e., a corporate act wherein the whole Christ, head and members, unites to offer worship to God the Father.

With this liturgical foundation firmly in place, Ellard then sets out the implications of the Mystical-Body doctrine for society as a whole, describing the fruits of the "Christ-life," which is born out of "active and intelligent participation in the Liturgy."[52] He presents a vision of a reunified society, transformed by individuals who can claim as their own St. Paul's dictum: "It is no longer I that live, it is Christ that liveth in me."[53] For Ellard, as for his fellow pioneers in the American liturgical movement, the Mystical Body of Christ, the worship of the Mystical Body, head and members, and the resulting sanctification of all of life taken together form a coherent theological framework.

The Liturgical Arts Society underlined its own commitment to the connection made by Ellard between the liturgy and social action in an editorial comment that appeared in *Liturgical Arts* a few years later:

"The liturgy is the Mystical Body at prayer, and Catholic Action is the Mystical Body in action upon the world; therefore active participation in the Liturgy and Catholic action are vitally connected."[54]

Further articles by Gerald Ellard[55] and others[56] re-emphasized the importance of and implications of the doctrine of the Mystical Body. Over and over, in the pages of *Liturgical Arts,* it was asserted that with a firm understanding of the Mystical Body, the observance of liturgical norms would follow as a natural result.[57]

But despite this commitment to the primacy of a liturgical spirituality with important connections to social action, it took a certain amount of editorial energy during the first decade of *Liturgical Arts* to keep these matters at the forefront of the Society's consciousness. Since many of the members, as architects and artists, were *indeed* interested primarily in the "externals" of worship, its visible manifestation, there was always a certain amount of tension. "Properly understood," the Society stated in an attempt to put the whole matter to rest:

"the liturgy is *both* the internal homage of the soul *and* its outward bodily expression by means of words, chant, ceremonies, etc., in the forms ordained by the Church for her . . . public worship! The aims of the Liturgical Arts Society have always stressed these two aspects of the liturgy without which what has become known as the Liturgical Movement might well be mere aesthetic speculation or an unbalanced insistence on externals without corresponding spiritual foundation."[58]

In a very real sense, the special nature of the Liturgical Arts Society gave particular urgency to the question of the balance between the "outward and visible" and the "inward and spiritual" aspects of the liturgy. Made up as it was by those especially concerned with the material side of Christian worship, the Society could very well have fallen into excessive fussiness over ceremonial details. But with constant support and encouragement from the mainstream of the American liturgical movement, and especially with the interjection of the Mystical-Body motif and its relation to social action, the Liturgical Arts Society was able to resist that temptation, and to move into the Church's liturgical future with a solid foundation.

THE QUESTION OF LITURGICAL CHANGE

Out of this interest in the relationship between inherited liturgical forms and the ever-new "spirit of the liturgy" grew a concern with the place of tradition in Christian worship. By the end of its first decade, the Liturgical Arts Society was beginning to whisper the questions "Could the liturgy change?" and, if so, "Under what circumstances?" In 1937, Society chaplain John LaFarge suggested that for particularly "urgent missionary or apostolic reasons," changes in certain elements might be authorized in order to prevent the "liturgical spirit [from being] seriously impeded."[59] However, during the first decade of its existence , the Society (like the liturgical movement as a whole) believed that it was not Christian worship that was in need of transformation but rather Christian worshipers. Thus liturgy, according to one article in *Liturgical Arts:*,

"is the way religious human beings integrate past, present, and future . . . It is not necessary for us to speak new words to God but only to maintain the objectively adequate, 'valid' word in the prayer of the Church and to participate in it always more deeply and originally."[60]

Many early articles in *Liturgical Arts* develop the theme of the eternal permanence of the Roman liturgy, its beauty, harmony, fitness, objectivity, and truth. Partaking, "in a certain limited way, of the immutability of God . . . the external forms of the Liturgy correspond in perfect harmony with the Divine Things which they reveal and at the same time conceal."[61]

At the same time the Liturgical Arts Society was beginning to sense that the liturgy of the Church was part of a living stream of Christian tradition, "imbued with the dynamism of life and not archeology."[62] Certain articles in *Liturgical Arts* , which dealt with the liturgy, had already made it plain that at certain times in the history of the Church, the liturgy had, indeed, undergone change,[63] and it was almost inevitable that this would call into question many of the Society's presuppositions about the "eternal permanence" of the liturgy. Although during the Society's first decade, "The Church is a living organism"[64] became a recurring refrain, the matter of liturgical change was never given sustained treatment.

MEDIATOR DEI

For those involved in the liturgical movement, the promulgation of *Mediator Dei et Hominum* (November 20, 1947)[65] was further affirmation of the importance of the liturgy within the life of the Roman Catholic Church. Although it gave serious attention to curbing errors and innovations in liturgical practice, it was viewed by many as the charter of the liturgical movement.[66] Since the contents of *Mediator Dei* pertained so directly to the work of the Liturgical Arts Society, Lavanoux, as the Society's secretary, wrote to the Apostolic Delegate to the United States requesting a copy of the encyclical before it was available to the general public.[67] When the Latin text arrived, Lavanoux sent it to Gerald Ellard for his translation and his opinion on its impact on the work of the Society. "I have read the Latin," Ellard reported, "and can tell you that there is nothing there . . . that you have not been saying all along."[68]

For the Liturgical Arts Society, *Mediator Dei* was viewed as an "epoch-making event throughout the entire world."[69] The Society, for its part, saw the encyclical as a very real vote of confidence for its own work as well. "To us," John LaFarge reported to the readers of *Liturgical Arts* , "[*Mediator Dei*] is a general consolation for two reasons:

"first, that it places the seal of the highest authority of the Church on the great reform for which we have been laboring from the foundation of our Society and, secondly, a particular consolation in that errors against which the Pope raises a warning voice are those we believe we have studied to avoid."[70]

In addition, LaFarge pointed out, the Society takes *Mediator Dei* as the occasion for further development of the idea that evolution of liturgical forms is part of a dynamic ecclesiastical tradition. "The Church," John LaFarge continued in his editorial on the encyclical:

"is a living organism and therefore the sacred liturgy keeps the integrity of its teaching: but the Church increases and develops and conforms the liturgy to all circumstances and exigencies, which vary according to the times, while being cautious about new customs or the revival of those which have fallen into disuse ... [Thus], the door is left open for possible changes as long as they are made with the permission of the Holy See."[71]

Although a minimum of formal attention is given to the contents of *Mediator Dei* after the initial commentary in *Liturgical Arts*, the Society viewed many elements within the document as giving a papal seal of approval to the liturgical direction in which the Society had been traveling for the previous 19 years. There is also the implication that the Society was willing to take a rather elastic view of *Mediator Dei*. In his editorial commentary on the document, John LaFarge emphasized that "the Papal pronouncements [within the encyclical] are to be taken not merely word for word as they stand but in relation to the entire context of the utterance as a whole."[72] In short, then, *Mediator Dei* served more to confirm, than to guide the liturgical views of the Liturgical Arts Society in the years that were to follow.

THE IMPACT OF SYSTEMATIC THEOLOGY

It would be a mistake to see the Liturgical Arts Society as standing in the vanguard of creative theology or to see *Liturgical Arts* as a periodical of great theological depth. Outside sources were culled and distilled for those elements that would prove useful to the Society's work, and both the Society and its periodical tended to follow in the theological wake of the general liturgical movement. But during the 10 years that followed the promulgation of *Mediator Dei*, the Liturgical Arts Society seemed less certain about its theological approach to the liturgy. In many ways, the old theological sources had ceased to be wholly adequate to assessing the liturgy's relationship to art and architecture, and new sources had not yet been established. The Mystical-Body theme, which had sustained the liturgical movement during its earliest phase, had been largely abandoned,[73] and *Mediator Dei* had provided no strong, new theological direction.

By 1957, however, the Liturgical Arts Society was ready to experiment with alternate theological approaches. In a brief, but important, article entitled "The Dynamics of the Liturgy,"[74] the Most Rev. Ettore Cunial (identified as "second vice-regent of the diocese of Rome") explored the relationship between incarnational theology and the liturgy. For Cunial, creation itself is "a liturgy used by God to manifest himself to man."[75] Although creation is a constantly renewing manifestation of God's revelation, the fullness of God's "liturgy" is the word made flesh. In the incarnation, Cunial says, God is put in touch with humankind in a way that is, at the same time:

"real, supernatural, universal, and personal, and which has its beginning in this world and will be completed only in the heavenly liturgy. Jesus Christ is the liturgical axis . . . the living soul of all liturgical expression."[76]

Like others in the theological world of the 1950s, the Liturgical Arts Society located the liturgy within the framework of a theology of creation. The implications of this incarnational concept were developed and reached a certain amplitude by 1961, as the Liturgical Arts Society sought to present its ideas to those preparing the Constitution of the Sacred Liturgy:

"It would help to clear the air if we could agree that we are on earth *here and now* and that the grace of God is operative now as it has been through the ages. We could also avoid the smokescreen of inveterate prejudice by pointing out that tradition is, by definition, a dynamic element and surely not a static encumbrance. It can be compared to a golden chain to which each generation must add its own link. The strength of this golden chain then resides in the strength of each link through the acceptance of the conditions which caused its fashioning in the unfolding of God's grace in the soul of man at all periods in history. It is that dynamism which should inform our understanding of the value of tradition — a value that points the way forward and is based on the distillation of accumulated knowledge."[77]

The Liturgical Arts Society did not pursue all of the liturgical implications of this incarnational theology. But by simply considering the possibilities, it had offered the readers of *Liturgical Arts* the vision of a Church possessed of a dynamism that would inevitably propel it into a future marked by liturgical change. During the next several years, the relationship between past forms, present realities, and future aspirations became a frequent topic of discussion. "We look with hope to the future," Lavanoux said in an editorial six months after the appearance of Cunial's article:

"but we can only do so in the present. We can look to the past for guidance, but only in the present moment. Jacques Maritain has characterized the desire of many to return to some past age as actually a blasphemy against God's government of history."[78]

THE *CONSTITUTION ON THE SACRED LITURGY* AND ITS AFTERMATH

The promulgation of the *Constitution on the Sacred Liturgy* was the cause of great joy to the Liturgical Arts Society. It marked the advent of "an era of new life"[79] for the Roman Catholic Church and gave support and renewed energy to the liturgical understanding that had been developing within the Society over the past two decades. Editorially, *Liturgical Arts* did little to conceal its enthusiasm for the Council documents and for the depth of change that they implied. "By 'renewal,'" *Liturgical Arts* said:

"the Council does not mean a break with the past, nor does it mean something merely formal and nominal. It means a real renewal with a number of practical and external changes and with a *true conversion of heart but by way of organic development that brings new life* to the *whole body*."[80]

The perceived elasticity of the directives of the Constitution on the Sacred Liturgy marked, for the Liturgical Arts Society, the definitive end of the period during which "rubrics masqueraded as liturgy."[81]

The liturgy had been freed from "rubrical niceties and [had] achieved a dynamism of its own."[82] Over and over, *Liturgical Arts* re-echoed this theme: "All the people of God can sing a fervent Hosanna," the editor exclaimed, "and rejoice that they are freed from the accumulation of rules which had long lost their initial meaning and vigor. They were like barnacles on the barque of Peter!"[83]

The Society did see certain potential difficulties with this "newly acquired freedom."[84] It demanded a high degree of "common sense and liturgical intuition"[85] lest liturgical innovation, introduced strictly for the sake of novelty, become the norm. At the other extreme, the Liturgical Arts Society was concerned that the initial enthusiasm over the Council might give way to a general complacency about the liturgy and that the work of the liturgical movement and its theological foundations might be entirely forgotten. "The promulgation of the *Constitution on the Sacred Liturgy*," warned *Liturgical Arts*:

". . . might tempt us to believe that what has been called the 'Liturgical Movement' these past thirty years or more has now run its course and we can settle down to a long night of comfortable and unimaginative *status quo*."[86]

The effort to find a middle course between undisciplined liturgical experimentation on the one hand and the unreasoned fear of liturgical freedom on the other occupied *Liturgical Arts* and the Liturgical Arts Society throughout the final years of their existence. "The *Constitution on the Sacred Liturgy* demands an entirely new approach," *Liturgical Arts* admonished its readers. "The intransigence of the Latin diehard and the extreme experimentation of the liturgical 'hippie' can only cloud issues that are basically simple."[87] The "issue," for the Society at least, was the full and rapid implementation of the directives of the *Constitution*, unhindered by the "obtuseness of timidity."[88]

Accordingly, the catchword in this period became "sensible evolution."[89] New liturgical forms were to develop naturally, born out of the dynamism of a living ecclesiastical tradition and nourished and guided by Vatican Council II documents. But at the 1967 Liturgical Week held in Kansas City, Missouri, liturgical events occurred that, from the Society's point of view, seemed to deviate from this principle of "sensible evolution." Describing the experimental worship at the Kansas City meeting as "arrogant nonsense,"[90] *Liturgical Arts* went on to express its views on liturgical individualism, quoting from a press release issued by the archdiocese of Kansas City shortly after the Liturgical Week:

"By definition, the liturgy is not simply a private affair, not only in its implication but in its expression as well. Therefore, it cannot be reduced to private symbols or expressions, however publicly they are performed. This means that national liturgical associations must not only encourage diverse experimentation, but somehow must coordinate this activity to achieve a pluralistic unity . . . The liturgy is too important to be identified with one segment only of man's life in contemporary society."[91]

"Patience and time can do more than impatience!" Lavanoux added, "Not as glamerous [sic], perhaps, as more ephemeral 'happenings,' but of more lasting value."[92]

But on the whole, the Liturgical Arts Society's view was that liturgical experimentation (however undisciplined) was less dangerous to the Church than was liturgical archaism. As Lavanoux argued in a 1968 editorial:

"The excesses of the progressives are easier to take than those of the 'diehards.' The argument of the progressives at least offers the possibility of indignant rebuttal. With the diehards, however, any rebuttal meets, head on, the dead mass of a pile of sand—the sand of inertia, of unreasoned nostalgia, of complacent inactivity, of death."[93]

Despite the "liturgical shenanigans"[94] that seemed to pervade the Church in the period after the Council, the Society believed that the changes in the liturgy were a part of the Church's "normal evolution." In one sense, to be sure, the Council had left something of a vacuum, which those who had always relied on rules and structures sought to fill with more of the same. The freedom engendered by the Council placed great responsibility on those involved in the liturgical life of the Church, although there would always be some who would seek to "shirk [that] responsibility and hide behind the screen of unquestioned authority."[95]

94

The problems of liturgical freedom versus liturgical responsibility, evolution versus stasis, tradition versus innovation had not been fully resolved by the time the Liturgical Arts Society shut its doors in 1972. In retrospect, the Society believed that its own liturgical understanding had flowed naturally from its openness to the guidance of the liturgy, the liturgical movement, and later, the Council. "In a way," *Liturgical Arts* reflected:

"the work of the Liturgical Arts Society has come full circle. The initial enthusiasm which stemmed from the writings of Dom Lambert Beauduin, Romano Guardini, and Dom Virgil Michel is now replaced by enthusiasm generated by the directives of Vatican Council II."[96]

In the end, Lavanoux would reach back to the very origins of the Society and of his own interest in the liturgy for a synthesis of the Society's understanding of the liturgy. Many times in the course of its publication, *Liturgical Arts* had referred to Romano Guardini's *The Spirit of the Liturgy* (1918) as "required reading" for those who wished for an intimate understanding of the Church at prayer. One particular passage was seen to have special significance, and was quoted as something of a crystalization of the Liturgical Arts Society's overall view of the liturgy:

"It cannot be denied that great difficulties lie in the question of the adaptation of the liturgy to every individual, and more especially to the modern man . . . More than one would be willing to sacrifice the most beautiful liturgical prayer if in exchange he might meet Christ face to face and speak to Him from the bottom of his heart. The liturgy wishes to teach but not by means of an artificial system of aim-conscious educational influences; it simply creates an entire world in which the soul can live according to the requirements of its nature."[97]

LITURGICAL REFORM AND THE LITURGICAL ARTS SOCIETY

Although liturgical matters were of the utmost consequence to the Liturgical Arts Society, the actual reform of the liturgy was never a primary focus of the Society's work but rather a by-product of its interest in the reform of Roman Catholic liturgical art. And yet, over the 40 years of the publication of *Liturgical Arts*, the Society took a stand, both in editorials and in the choice of articles printed, on one side or another of several important issues related to the reformation of the liturgy. As a rule, the reform agenda of the liturgical movement as a whole set the Society's course in these matters, but there are certainly exceptions to that rule. The "dialog Mass," which was so dear to the hearts of a number of the pioneers of the American liturgical movement (and especially H. A. Reinhold[98]) , received almost no attention from the Society, even though it had clear implications for the design of church interiors. Over the years, a few passing references were made to such things as the primacy of the liturgy of the Mass over private devotions,[99] the return to a Christological focus in the Church year,[100] the celebration of the Mass *versus populum*,[101] the deep connections between the liturgy and social justice,[102] and the role of ecumenism in liturgical reform. But there was no sustained treatment of any of these themes. It was as if each of these was taken for granted rather than viewed as unimportant.

A number of specific reforms, however, did receive sustained and developed treatment in the pages of *Liturgical Arts*. The Society gave continuing attention to arguments for the restoration of Gregorian chant, active lay participation in the liturgy, the use of the vernacular, and the adaptation of liturgical forms to indigenous situations. Since many of the pioneers of the liturgical movement saw *Liturgical Arts* as an important forum for their views, the Society was never far behind the front lines on the issues it chose to address.

DEEP ENGAGEMENT WITH THE SPIRIT OF THE LITURGY

The founding of the Liturgical Arts Society in 1928 coincided with the American liturgical movement's renewed interest in returning the liturgy, and especially the liturgy of the Mass, to the center of Roman Catholic life. In order to fulfill this function, the liturgy would have to be performed in strict conformity with the rubrics and canonical directives and stripped of centuries' worth of accretions. It is not surprising, then, that *Liturgical Arts'* earliest reform initiative involved calling the attention of its readers to those sources that governed the celebration of the liturgy. In its first brochure, the Liturgical Arts Society described one of its aims as "placing particular emphasis on the integrity of the incidentals of worship and observance of the rubrics."[103] To this end, the early numbers of *Liturgical Arts* often carried notice of special restrictions that the hierarchy placed upon liturgical observance.[104]

But soon the pages of *Liturgical Arts* began to reflect the Society's growing understanding of the need for deep engagement with the liturgy itself rather than simple attention to the rubrics and canons which governed it. In 1939, the Society's chaplain, John LaFarge, wrote an article that the editor called "a sort of platform on which our work is based."[105] "Devotion to the liturgy is devotion to the Person of Christ," LaFarge declared.[106] Although such devotion would naturally inspire strict observance of "the rules and prescriptions which the Church makes for [the individual's] welfare," the more important result would be the "holy joy" inspired in the individual. To the extent that the Christian enters into the official liturgical life of the Church, "lives of worship [will become] outwardly an expression of that *inward* reality which is life in Christ."[107]

This first phase of the Society's liturgical reform agenda, then, involved the renewal of *persons* and not of the liturgy itself. The Society saw the liturgy as the "inner life of the Church," handing down in each generation "the newness of life in God."[108] In advocating a deeper engagement with the liturgy, the Society was calling on each individual worshiper to exercise a form of Christian responsibility, not only for the sake of the individual soul but for the transformation of the world as well.

ACTIVE AND INTELLIGENT PARTICIPATION OF THE LAITY

In order for this transformation to take place, however, an "active and intelligent"[109] participation on the part of the laity was a prerequisite. This active lay participation in the liturgy (often regarded as the cornerstone of the liturgical movement's reform agenda) was seen by one influential member of the Society as:

"a revolt from the lamentable state of things, which has tended to make the layman little more than a passive spectator in the public worship of God, in favor of a return to the corporate congregational worship of the Primitive Church."[110]

Many in the Church, however, saw the increased participation of the laity in public worship as a serious threat. In response to criticism that lay participation was a form of "Protestantism,"[111] the Society answered that it was actually proposing "a return to the life that existed prior to the Reformation and not [engaging in] an attempt to foist upon the Church practices or beliefs which have come into existence since the Reformation."[112]

The Society saw clearly that the prerequisite for more active lay participation was a Church that understood the laity as a fit *subject* for participation in the Mass. Had this fitness been more readily accepted, and had "the intelligence and willingness of the layman ... not been generally underestimated,"[113] active and thoughtful participation on the part of all Church members might have been an accomplished fact. In later years, the Liturgical Arts Society even criticized the Liturgical Conference for a lack of aggressiveness in promoting lay participation: "We hope," *Liturgical Arts* suggested after the Sixth Liturgical Week:

"that next year the program committee [of the Liturgical Week might] consider the possibility of having more laymen take an active part. Why not, for example, have a layman alternate with a priest at each session? There are laymen who are competent to treat of subjects which may be deemed fitting next year and the participation of such laymen might help to ... make the liturgical revival more intelligible to the majority."[114]

THE RESTORATION OF GREGORIAN CHANT

In the early years of the Liturgical Arts Society, a substantial amount of attention was devoted to the restoration of Gregorian Chant according to the principles set out in Pius X's 1903 *motu proprio* , *Tra le sollecitudini.*[115] Both in its own program and in the pages of *Liturgical Arts*, the chant was promoted as a vital weapon

in the battle to return to the laity an important liturgical ministry it had exercised in the Middle Ages. "During the golden days of plain song," the Society argued, "the people sang all the responses and all the common parts of the mass and it is the hope that people will desire to return to such active participation in Divine Worship."[116]

The publication of Augustus Welby Northmore Pugin's "An Earnest Appeal for the Revival of Ancient Plain Song"[117] was *Liturgical*

Arts' initial volley in the campaign for the re-establishment of Gregorian Chant. In this article, originally written in 1850, Pugin argued that if the chant were to be "taught in every school, and inculcated in every Catholic family," then:

". . . our churches would soon present the cheering, inspiring spectacle of a mass of people united not only in heart but in voice in the worship of their Creator; and this not in modern and unhallowed sounds but in the very words sung by the angels in heaven when the Redeemer was born; and in the words which the old vaults, raised to God centuries ago, have often re-echoed with the returning festivals; and in words which, protected by Catholic authority, will descend by tradition to ages yet unborn."[118]

Throughout more than a decade and a half, *Liturgical Arts* continued to offer suggestions whereby Pugin's vision might be realized. This involved advocating specific methods for teaching Gregorian Chant[119] and strict enforcement of the norms established by the *motu proprio*, especially with regard to the composition of parish choirs. "The parish can help matters," the readers of *Liturgical Arts* were advised:

"by appealing to male members of the parish and by pointing out to the enthusiastic ladies that their place is in the pews as members of the congregation. The members of the parish can also help by forgoing the desire to indulge in sentimental hymns which do little to enhance divine service. We can all do something along these lines if only we will realize that we all have a place in church. The trick is to find out where we rightly belong and be satisfied with what we are to do to worship Our Lord."[120]

The restoration of Gregorian Chant, then, would have various benefits. The first, and most important, was that it would allow the laity to exercise a liturgical ministry by singing the Ordinary of the Mass in simple and easily learned melodies. Second, the re-establishment of the chant would restore to the Church music worthy of Divine Service. And finally, the chant would link the contemporary Church with the Great Age of Faith, when all of society mirrored a Christian conception of human ordering and divine authority.

Growing out of the Liturgical Arts Society's interest in increased liturgical participation on the part of the laity, was concern for the language of the liturgy. As might be supposed, the earliest suggestions were to the effect that "since the liturgy is in Latin, its meaning ought to be part of the curriculum of all schools and colleges."[121] Articles in *Liturgical Arts* reported great success in the efforts of lay persons to learn liturgical Latin. Having puchased a Latin/English missal, one layman wrote of the "thrill of reading along with the priest the prayers of the Mass" and the great spiritual value he received thereby. "Certainly," he continued, "I am getting more out of attending Mass this way than by saying my rosary; this is *real* participation . . . . I am instantly lifted out of my individualism into a 'social act.'"[122]

But quite early, there were scattered suggestions in *Liturgical Arts* that Latin might not be an absolutely permanent feature of the liturgical life of the Church. In his article "The Social Mission of the Liturgy,"[123] Society chaplain, John LaFarge, S.J., reported that:

"Various European liturgists are urging that the Latin language is one of the major obstacles to the spread of the liturgical spirit in the non-Latin peoples of Europe and other continents. The difficulty of the Latin liturgy, they maintain, is many times increased in certain mission countries like China, whose manner of thought and expression is radically different from that of the Western world."[124]

Writing as he was in 1937, LaFarge approached the question of the vernacular with extreme caution but without actually foreclosing the possibility.

"While the gravest kind of objections would militate against departing from the use of the Latin in the parts of the Mass or other services which are recited more or less privately by the priest, such as the prayers of the Canon, or in the formulae of the sacraments, it has been suggested that certain concessions made for historical reasons to some East European countries with regard to the use of the vernacular, might be extended and not for historical but for urgent missionary, or apostolic, reasons to other nations that find the liturgical spirit seriously impeded by the Latin language."[125]

Clearly, LaFarge saw the possibility that these "urgent missionary, or apostolic, reasons" might also apply to the ecclesiastical situation in the United States. At the end of his article, LaFarge suggested that had the language not been a problem, Gregorian Chant itself might have won wider and more rapid acceptance since "nine-tenths of the trouble in achieving congregational participation in the Church's chant would disappear."[126]

In 1947, the cause of vernacular liturgy received a certain degree of official recognition with the promulgation of *Mediator Dei*,[127] and the Liturgical Arts Society took this as an opportunity to strengthen its own calls for reform. In "The Ritual Is an Unfinished Book,"[128] liturgist Gerald Ellard described the progress that had been made in "unlocking by translation the treasures formerly hidden in the Latin of the Missal, the Breviary, the Ritual, and the Pontifical."[129] In addition to English translations of the liturgy for use by the laity, Ellard reported that there was growing evidence, especially in France[130] and in Germany,[131] of the use of vernacular in the liturgical celebration itself. This, Ellard said, "marks a new phase for the liturgical apostolate," a phase during which, "with Papal permission, in one country after another, [the Ritual] is now beginning to cut away from the Latin, in whole or in part, in performing its rites."[132]

Liturgical Arts' s quest for a vernacular liturgy continued unabated for the next 10 years. By 1954, only seven years after reporting the rather tentative statements of *Mediator Dei* on the value of the vernacular, there was little ambiguity in the Society's rhetoric. In case after case, "intelligibility" seemed to be the Society's criterion for judging the adequacy of liturgical celebration, and this intelligibility was almost always equated with the use of the vernacular.[133] One argument for the vernacular, which *Liturgical Arts* often employed, was to describe in its articles and editorials liturgical "success stories," such as the experience of using the *Collectio Rituum* in the diocese of Burlington, Vermont.[134] In all of this, the Liturgical Arts Society "looked toward the day when the vernacular would be permitted in the administration of the sacraments" as well as in other parts of the mass.[135]

After Vatican Council II, even the Liturgical Arts Schola finally felt the impact of the vernacular movement. As the Society itself was promoting the value of vernacular liturgy, there had been those who had strongly advocated the continuance of Latin chant as the sole repertoire for the Schola, partly because of its value as an "art form."[136] But by 1968, all of the members of the *schola* had become convinced that Gregorian Chant had reached the end of its useful life, and the group began to be "devoted to the vernacular."[137]

With the attention given by Vatican Council II to the place of the vernacular in the Roman Catholic liturgy, the Society's goals in this matter had been largely accomplished. The only item left on the agenda for discussion was the provision of English translations adequate to the worship of the Church. In exploring the possibilities, the Society turned to the experience of the Church of England and the compilers of the various editions of the Book of Common Prayer, 1549-1662, for guidelines in translating the Latin of the mass into English.[138] What was needed for this task, according to an article which appeared in 1966, was the talents of Christian *poets* rather than theologians or historians. Where, in the past, mass texts had been "prosaic, pedestrian, verbose, stilted, and unclear,"[139] the Church of the present must seek a vernacular liturgical language possessed of "clarity, nobility, simplicity, and pregnancy of style."[140]

INDIGENIZATION OF THE LITURGY

In addition to the introduction of the vernacular into the liturgical life of the Roman Catholic Church, the adaptation of the liturgy to local forms and customs was an important item on the Liturgical Arts Society's reform agenda, especially after 1950. In that year, Maurice Lavanoux had visited Rome and seen an exhibition devoted to the Church in mission lands that made a profound impression on him.[141] In the years that followed, Lavanoux traveled to Asia, India, and Africa and, as editor of *Liturgical Arts*, transmitted to his readers his own increasing commitment to the indigenization of the Church and its liturgy. In 1954, *Liturgical Arts* reproduced catechetical materials that had been adapted for the speakers of African Pidgin English: a "Hail Maria," Ten Commandments, and a passage entitled "What Be Angels?"[142] There followed several articles dealing with the place of the liturgical revival in third world missions[143] and the adaptation of the liturgy to ecclesiastical communities in places as different as Japan and Ireland.[144] In the end, even the question of adaptation of the liturgy to possible extraterrestrial civilizations was considered.[145]

Two problems seem to recur in the Liturgical Arts Society's thinking about the cultural adaptation of the liturgy. The first is the adequacy of the term "adaptation," and the possibility of finding a more suitable term. In an issue of *Liturgical Arts* devoted entirely to the situation in Africa, Lavanoux considered the possibilities:

"In the semantic battle where words lose their meaning or have unfortunate connotations, I wonder whether or not a change might be wise: for example, *adaptation* now really means a superficial veneer, a compromise, so why not use the word *assimilation*, which means more nearly co-penetration, a merger in which both sides — the indigenous and the European — contribute a like share."[146]

The second problem to which *Liturgical Arts* devoted considerable attention was how the adaptation of the liturgy to indigenous peoples might affect the liturgical situation in the United States. As it sought an answer to this question, the Society came to understand that liturgical adaptation in missionary situations could offer hope for the future of American liturgical renewal:

"If we dream of the adaptation of the liturgy in mission lands, we can dream of its adaptation at home and realize our own deficiencies . . . We would then realize that the difficulties in the preparing for *active participation* are the same the world over and the papal direction in *Mediator Dei* and *Musicae Sacrae Disciplina* are applicable everywhere."[147]

FREEDOM WITH RESPONSIBILITY

In a very real sense, the Constitution on the Sacred Liturgy's call for "full, conscious, and active participation"[148] in the liturgy was a summary of all that the Liturgical Arts Society had been advocating by way of liturgical reform since 1928. Attention to the rubrics, engagement with the "spirit of the liturgy," a deep liturgical understanding, the encouragement of lay participation through the use of the vernacular, and liturgical adaptation to diverse circumstances were goals that were, the Society believed, fulfilled and perfected in the liturgical directives of Vatican Council II. But at the same time,

103

the Society's sense of the dynamism of ecclesiastical tradition made it aware that the Council was a milestone, but not a terminus, in the Church's liturgical journey. *Liturgical Arts* also frequently remarked on the elasticity of the Council's directives:

"[The guidelines of the Council] are not a petrified framework intended to replace the equally petrified practices of past centuries. They can be understood as suggestions, which can be carried out within a framework of disciplined elasticity, shorn of stubborn prejudice or lethargic nostalgia."[149]

As the Liturgical Arts Society carried its reform agenda into its final years, the implications of this elasticity for the liturgical life of the Church would be of special concern:

"It is no longer possible, or even desirable, to imprison our liturgical life in a web of picayune rules, which may well be inoperative in certain areas of the world. A reasonable elasticity, based on common sense and liturgical intuition, is the obvious concomitant of our newfound freedom."[150]

And so, in the "ecclesiastical tug-of-war" between overzealous liturgical experimentation on the one hand and intransigent opposition to liturgical change on the other, the Liturgical Arts Society called for a new reform: a move to *balance*, to what would be referred to as "freedom with responsibility."[151]

In the hope of encouraging its constituents to find this balance between freedom and responsibility for themselves, the Liturgical Arts Society itself engaged in writing some experimental liturgies, especially after the Vatican Council II. Several proposed rites appeared in the pages of *Liturgical Arts*, among them a service to "Commemorate the Moon Walk,"[152] a mass for the second Sunday after Easter,[153] and a fantasized "Moon People's Liturgy."[154] All of these were accompanied by some sort of disclaimer, however, such as the one that attended the moon-walk liturgy: "No Roman decree can justify such a Mass, which should rather be understood in the light of the Liturgical Movement as a whole."[155]

In spite of these creative endeavors, the Society believed that the Church as a whole was handicapped in restructuring its liturgical life by centuries of reliance on externally imposed norms and regulations which had allowed it to "shirk its responsibilities . . . and hide behind the screen of unquestioned authority."[156] The Society admitted that these were indeed disturbing times but that they also contained "the seeds of a healthy renewal for all involved."[157] But it would be only through careful attention to the liturgy itself and "reasoned interpretation" of the Vatican directives that the Church would keep its balance.[158]

For the Liturgical Arts Society, a 40-year odyssey through the Roman Catholic liturgical movement came to an end in the safe harbor of the *Constitution on the Sacred Liturgy*. Throughout each phase of the journey, the primacy of the liturgy had served as the Society's compass, keeping it always on course as the ecclesiastical winds blew around it. The Society could rest in the knowledge that the conciliar decrees had affirmed its vision of the role of the liturgy within the life of the Church. More important, by having presented the challenge of liturgical reform to its own constituency, the Liturgical Arts Society could claim a share of responsibility for the Church's liturgical future.

CHAPTER SEVEN

Art, Liturgical Art, and the Liturgical Arts Society

If the founding members of the Liturgical Arts Society held diverse views on the place of liturgical matters in the agenda of the new organization, there was no such diversity with regard to the arts and architecture. Those who attended the Society's founding meetings in 1927 and 1928 had been drawn together by a common interest in art. In addition, as sculptors, muralists, silversmiths, architects, and draftsmen, they also shared a common understanding of the difficulties faced by working artists who wished to serve the Church. It soon became evident, however, that underlying the founding members' common interest in the arts was a plurality of views on the meaning of the word "art" and on the part philosophical and theological discussions would play in the Society's work.

THE SOCIETY'S PHILOSOPHY OF ART

Several opinions on the essential nature of art and architecture were expressed at the founding meetings of the Liturgical Arts Society held at Portsmouth (Rhode Island) Priory in 1927 and 1928. Everitt Harman's call for those who, like himself, wished to "flood the world with beauty"[1] had struck a responsive chord in several of the founding members, but Harman never made any attempt to explicate the inner relationships between "beauty" and "art." The assumption seems always to have been that where there is beauty, art will be found, and vice versa.[2] Others of the founding group were more explicit about their understanding of the nature of art, if not more profound. As one might suppose, those of the founding members who understood the liturgy as one element in the flowering of Roman Catholic culture[3] viewed art and architecture in the very same light. For Ides van der Gracht, the spokesman of that group,

106

the "beauty" of Roman Catholicism had its "physical manifestation [in] the artistic expression of the Church."[4] The arts, however, are clearly the province of those with an "extraordinary level of culture and 'Weltkenntniss,'"[5] and it is their responsibility to bring this "urge for esthetic expression" to "those whose intellectual and esthetic demands are simple."[6] Despite claims of intellectual superiority, the members of this group were not inclined to plunge themselves more deeply into a philosophy or theology of art. Just as they had equated liturgy with beauty,[7] so, too, they equated art with beauty, both of which, although clearly recognized by the "cultured few," could not otherwise be defined.

Others of the founding group believed this approach to be too simplistic to serve as a firm foundation for the Society's program. For Maurice Lavanoux, the idea that there were indeed rich theological and philosophical resources available for an understanding of the nature of art and architecture had been nourished by reading Jacques Maritain's *Art et Scolastique*[8] in 1924. (Lavanoux would always rank this book with Romano Guardini's *The Spirit of the Liturgy* as required reading for anyone interested in art for the Church.) With Léon Bloy, Charles Péguy, François Mauriac, and Paul Claudel, Jacques Maritain had worked to broaden the intellectual base of Roman Catholicism and, by the time the Liturgical Arts Society was founded in 1928, was at the forefront of the neo-Thomist revival. In *Art et Scolastique*, Maritain described the relationship between art and Christianity, between the making of things and the artist who makes them, and between the substance of art and the Being of God. Maritain's reading of Aquinas and of the Middle Ages would provide at least a few of the founding members of the Liturgical Arts Society with a firm theological and philosophical basis on which to establish the group's program. But for Lavanoux and those of the founding members who agreed with him,[9] Maritain's Thomist philosophy of art was to be only a foundation for the Society's work, remaining below ground and never given formal exposition.

But at least two of the founding members were convinced that simply to undergird the work of the Liturgical Arts Society with a philosophical framework was insufficient and that the entire effort should be aimed at spreading within the Church an understanding of the aesthetic principles on which art could be evaluated. For the first few years of the Society's existence, John Howard Benson, silversmith and carver, and Arthur Graham Carey, philosopher of art and Benson's partner in a Newport, Rhode Island, craft shop, attempted to reform the organization from within. Carey, especially, saw the possibility of using *Liturgical Arts* as a forum for a brand of philosophy of art based on the work of Jacques Maritain, and refined and adapted by Eric Gill, Ananda K. Coomarswamy, and Carey himself. Blending socialist political philosophy, craftsmanship (or "right making") as the basis for artistic judgment, and an organic Thomism in which art flowed logically from the structure of creation, Carey's philosophy of art aimed at the formation of a guild system (what Eric Gill would call a "cell of good living") in which men and women seek the truth about the nature of things and craft useful, beautiful objects.[10]

Although several influential members of the Society (in particular, Lavanoux and Henry Lorin Binsse) appreciated the desire to set the work of the Society on a firm philosophical foundation, they had in mind an organization, serving a more practical purpose than simply expounding art theory. As Lavanoux would later describe the difference between the two points of view, "they [the Benson-Carey group] seemed to be more interested in 'philosophy of art,' while we were more interested in the practical relations between the artist and the potential client." In matters of art and architecture, Lavanoux and others saw the *product*, rather than the process, as of primary importance and the use of that product by living persons and communities as the ultimate goal of the Society's work. This practical emphasis on art and architecture was carried over into the editorial policy of *Liturgical Arts*.

In the end, Benson and Carey did not find the program of the Liturgical Arts Society and *Liturgical Arts* elastic enough to accommodate their philosophical approach, and in 1936 they both resigned from the organization which they had worked so hard to establish. "I no longer feel the work of the Society is constructive," Carey wrote to Binsse by way of explanation:

"The L.A.S. has never succeeded in making perfectly clear to its readers 1) what Art is, 2) why all Christians are obliged to be good artists, or 3) what analytical framework they must build upon to in order to be good artists. These things should have been emphasized and reiterated over and over again. Instead, the readers of *L.A.* have been fed on 'Good Taste' . . . 'Good Taste' is apparently what the editors of L.A. have but ordinary Americans have not . . . Emphasis on the Liturgical requirements does very little good, if the artist and his patron are not instructed in *how* they are to follow these requirements *intellectually.*"[12]

In response to this critique, Binsse suggested that Benson and Carey had been "laboring under a misapprehension concerning the Society" and that there was "no advantage to be gained by discussing the artistic conception which [they have] set up for *Liturgical Arts*, [since] the officers and directors have never had such a conception and certainly never will."[13] As added emphasis, Binsse concluded that "*In fine, Liturgical Arts* is *not* an art magazine."[14]

Lavanoux's concern about maintaining depth and balance for the program of the Liturgical Arts Society meant that the departure of Carey and Benson did not result in the utter abandonment of attention to art theory. Although the organization would never be exclusively, or even primarily, interested in questions of the philosophy of art and architecture, such matters were occasionally presented in the pages of *Liturgical Arts* during its 40 years of publication. Before he resigned from the Society, Carey himself had already provided *Liturgical Arts* with several articles as his contribution to broadening its readers' understanding of art and architecture, and even after his departure, other contributions appeared.

In the first of these, "The Craftsmanship of Sacred Vessels," Carey defined art as "the business of making things with skill"[15] and "the best work of God's best work [i.e., the human being]."[16] Expanding on these themes in "The Word Art," Carey went on to stress that the goal of art is not the service of the artist, but "the service of God and of neighbor."[17] Finally, in "Some Notes on the Design of Struck Medals," which appeared in 1948, Carey presented a fairly well-developed synthesis of his own understanding of the nature of art and of the process by which it is produced:

"Art is the power by which human beings make things. Perfect artificial things are made with much art, less perfect things are made with little art . . . . They are well made when they are designed and executed according to right reason, and this is just as true of hammers, saucepans, and automobiles as it is of landscapes, novels, and symphonies."[18]

The impact of this philosophy of art on the Liturgical Arts Society is difficult to assess. Although Carey's style was invariably articulate and persuasive and he worked from a thorough knowledge of Thomistic philosophy, his articles in *Liturgical Arts* provoked a great deal of severe criticism from readers because, as Binsse put it, "they relate only indirectly to what [the Society] is trying to do."[19] More favorably received were articles that had a more distinctly theological content and approach.

THE THEOLOGY OF ART IN *LITURGICAL ARTS*
In the early years, some of the theological material in *Liturgical Arts* seems to have been influenced by the scholastic philosophy found in Carey's art theory.[20] In *Liturgical Arts'* opening presentation of the theological underpinnings of art and architecture, Abbot Ildefons Herwegen identified art as "a flower from the tree of the Cross, a beam from the transfigured countenance of the victorious Christ." Art, for Herwegen, flows from God, and reflects the Beauty of God, which "rests in all His works. " If, Herwegen concluded, "we must seek this *splendor ordinis*, as St. Augustine defines beauty, it is in ecclesiastical art where everything should speak of God."[21] In successive treatments of the relationship between art and theology, however, writers for *Liturgical Arts* tended to fall back on a theory that equated beauty with good taste — the very theory which the founders of *Liturgical Arts* had tried to transcend. "By art," one writer explained, "I mean the product of man's attempt to produce beauty in the various media through which his senses may be reached and according to the canons of taste and with the available materials of his own particular time and place."[22]

Greater attention was given to the purpose of art and architecture within the divine plan. For many, art is always to be a theophany and an "expression of the Incarnate God's presence in our midst."[23] For others, art has a distinctly catechetical function, "expounding the truths of salvation to mankind,"[24] or serves as a channel "to take us from the visible to the spiritual, from the temporal to the eternal, from the creature to the Creator."[25] One of the more profound statements on the nature of the relationship between art and theology is to be found in the proceedings of the 21st annual meeting of the Liturgical Arts Society (1951). There, sculptor Josep Nicholas linked the human creative instinct to the ultimate transformation of all creation:

"God delights in having his creatures do some creating of their own, and that is why it says in Genesis: 'He created man in His own image.' Here is a man's greatest nobility, and all human activities can be rated to the extent to which they contribute to the perpetual recreation of the world."[26]

Graham Carey had been suspicious of human emotion as a measure of the value of art because it left individuals prey to manipulation by greedy merchants.[27] But as the decade of the 1960s opened, the Liturgical Arts Society's understanding of the nature of art had moved in a decidedly psychological and sociological direction. Art was no longer *defined* objectively as *"recta ratio factibilium"* — right thinking applied to the making of things — but rather was *recognized* by the *effect* it produced in human beings and communities:

"Art is a uniquely humanizing experience. The esthetic experience enlarges the whole man and involves all one's faculties, senses, emotion, intellect, and will. Art is an integrating experience, enriching the personality."[28]

In addition to discussions in *Liturgical Arts* of the theological nature of the arts in general, there is also some clarification of the specific marks of religious art. For many writers, art is religious when it "speaks the language of the truths of life, of time, and eternity, of the mysteries of Christianity."[29] It is religious *content*, then, that transforms art into religious art. A more developed analysis of religious art as distinct from art in general is found in "An Open Letter to an Indian Christian Artist:"[30]

"Every work of art is an expression of beauty, and God is the source of all beauty; in consequence, any work of art links us up with the supreme, and any spectator contemplating any artistic work can soar up to God through the created light of that artistic production. If *ontologically* any art is religious — for there is nothing outside of or independent of God — *intentionally* a work of art can be religious if it conveys *objectively* the sense of connection (*religatio*) with God."

In this case, all art was religious by nature, but its specific manifestation is religious to the extent that it is self-conscious of its own religious character.

For a group that devoted more than 40 years to the various manifestations of ecclesiastical art and architecture, questions surrounding the inner nature of the arts and the sources and goals of artistic expression, receive remarkably little attention from the Liturgical Arts Society. In addition, the few discussions that appear in *Liturgical Arts* do not reflect a great deal of depth or profundity. (Such insubstantial statements as "Art must be understood as art and the approach to this lies in training that develops artistic perception" are to be found all too frequently in the pages of *Liturgical Arts*.) Overall, there seems to be the presumption that all involved in the work of the Liturgical Arts Society are of the same mind about art and architecture and that no thoroughgoing discussion is necessary. When one attempts to connect the fragments of evidence on the subject, what is revealed is a rather disjointed picture, marked neither by consistency nor sophistication. More sustained treatment is given to the more explicit subject of the Society's concern: liturgical art.

THE MEANING OF THE TERM "LITURGICAL ART"

The term "liturgical art" was not new with the Liturgical Arts Society, but neither was it in wide use when the founding meetings were taking place in 1927 and 1928. It is found with some frequency in the early numbers of *Orate Fratres* , alongside "liturgical movement," "liturgical prayer," "liturgical music," and "liturgical education." (And, of course, the publishing house founded by Virgil Michel at St. John's Abbey was The Liturgical Press, and *Orate Fratres* was subtitled "A Review Devoted to the Liturgical Apostolate."[31]) The editor of *Orate Fratres* , admitted, however, that liturgical art was "one of the many aspects of the liturgy which cannot receive extensive treatment at present. But, he added, "the mere mention of it opens up wide vistas of forgotten lore and beauty, of spiritual treasure, for which, among the many, almost all understanding has been lost."[32]

In the sixth number of *Orate Fratres*,[33] however, an initial attempt was made to explicate the term "liturgical art." This attempt is worth taking seriously by anyone who is interested in the Liturgical Arts Society, since it was made by Eric Gill,[34] who profoundly influenced several of the Society's founding members.[35] Although the statement is not in itself remarkable,[36] the very notion of making a "distinction between liturgical art and the other arts" must have been persuasive to those who were devoted followers of Gill's thought.

In the earliest layer of the Liturgical Arts Society's prehistory, there seems to be very little attention paid to "liturgical art" as a distinct entity. Founding member Everitt Harman's original proposal[37] never once uses the term, nor does he identify the relationship between art and the liturgy as a separate category of concern. Indeed, when Ides van der Gracht and others suggested that it was liturgical art that was the real subject of the Society's work, Harman expressed strong reservations:

"In the term 'liturgical art' it is very possible that someone opposed to us might say there is no such thing — as the liturgy does not proscribe many things of art in bad taste and many things in good taste are not required by the liturgy . . . . I think that it would not be open to question if you say 'spiritual value of liturgical and artistic expression' instead of liturgical art."[38]

Clearly, for Harman what is central is artistic "good taste," and those elements in the liturgy that do not serve the cause of good taste should be downplayed. But the other founding members of the Society were not convinced by Harman's purely arbitrary connection between the liturgy and art, and his position was firmly overruled.

In all of the documents under which the Liturgical Arts Society was incorporated in October of 1928, the term "liturgical art" has a prominent place. The Society's constitution states that the "object of the Society is to increase the interest of its members in the spiritual value of the liturgical arts."[39] And the by-laws are even more explicit in stating that "the Society devotes itself to Liturgical art as distinct from secular Christian art. It aims to promote the study and practice of the arts and crafts relating directly to the worship of the

Catholic Church."[40] Later documents further specify the content of the category liturgical art, which is said to concern:

". . . the planning, building, and decoration of churches and all ancillary structures, the renovation and remodeling of existing buildings; the design and execution of sacred vessels, vestments, sculpture, and painting; also . . . music and other matters which are subject to liturgical usage."[41]

Once the term liturgical art had been agreed upon, the Society went on to explore the dynamics of the relationship between art and the liturgy and the ways in which that relationship resulted in a new reality called liturgical art. As one might suspect, the Society's concept of a specifically liturgical art depended upon an understanding of the nature of the liturgy itself.

LITURGICAL ART AND THE BEAUTY OF THE LITURGY

In the early years of the Liturgical Arts Society, those founding members who had focused on the "unique and majestic beauty" of the liturgy[42] tended to understand liturgical art as an extension of that beauty, as a necessary component of the liturgy as art form. Liturgical art as a distinct reality is that art which "adorns the House of God,"[43] which embellishes the setting in which the "majestic beauty" of the liturgy unfolds.[44] On a somewhat deeper level, many of the founding members believed that the "infinite spiritual value"[45] of the liturgy made special demands on art for the church. The church is "not merely the room where the faithful assemble," Abbot Ildefons Herwegen wrote in the first number of *Liturgical Arts*:

"it is also a royal palace—*basilica*—in which the transfigured Saviour renews His redeeming sacrifice, in which He lives and reigns in the Holy Eucharist . . . . Therefore, the House of God properly calls for structure and ornament that conform with its exalted purpose."[46]

The idea that the presence of Christ in the liturgy necessitates proper adornment of the liturgical setting appears, in various guises, over and over again in the pages of *Liturgical Arts* during the first 15 years of its publication. Stated most simply: "The House of God should be made as beautiful as possible because God is worthy of the most beautiful things we can create."[47]

Those in the Liturgical Arts Society who believed that the beauty of the liturgy and the majesty of God necessitated the proper adornment of the liturgical setting also saw liturgical art as having deep spiritual benefits for participants in the liturgy. "We have need," continued Abbot Herwegen:

"for a place set apart from the hurly-burly of the world — for an environment which brings home sensibly to the Christian on his knees God's presence in God's house. The art of the sanctuary, therefore, does not exist for its own sake, but is purposive. Through its achievements — architecture, painting, sculpture, music — it aims to transport the faithful from what is sinful or profane or tinged with the cares of everyday life to what is pure, blessed, divinely joyous."[48]

The function of liturgical art, then, in the words of founding member Everitt Harman, is to "help lead the world to God."[49]

LITURGICAL ART AS RUBRICAL ART

More significant in the overall thinking of the Liturgical Arts Society in these early years was the definition of liturgical art as art that follows exactly the rubrics and canons guiding the liturgy of the Roman Catholic Church. To varying degrees, all of the founding members at Portsmouth Priory could agree that the Society was most concerned with "devising ways and means for improving the standards of . . . liturgical correctness current in the practice of Catholic art in the United States."[50] This concern was manifested in many of the Society's programs. A major portion of *Liturgical Arts'* editorials was to be devoted to "practical and detailed expositions of liturgical requirements governing the construction and decoration of Churches,"[51] and the Information Service promised well-researched answers to artists and architects who wished to produce works that conformed to the rubrics.[52] "The liturgy demands," stated the Society's earliest brochure:

"that the products of artistic endeavor used in the service of the Church be in accord with, and regulated by, norms and canons based on the requirements of the rules and ceremonies of the liturgy as embodied in directions and instructions laid down by the various Roman Congregations."[53]

This position posed certain difficulties for the Society, however. As Everitt Harman had pointed out,[54] careful attention to liturgical norms would not insure art of quality, nor would it eliminate the tasteless. In other words, art and architecture fulfilling his definition as "liturgical" might have no other merit whatsoever.

LITURGICAL ART AND LITURGICAL SPIRITUALITY

As the Society became more and more convinced of the importance of deep engagement with the worship of the Church, it revised its definition of liturgical art and avoided many of the problems of a more legalistic approach. In this new understanding, art was liturgical when it was imbued with the spirit of the liturgy. Liturgical art was seen as the result of a "deep and honest understanding of the liturgy"[55] and the "application of the theology and philosophy of the Church to the arts."[56] It is, in short, "the visual flowering of the liturgy."[57] The most complete explication of this definition of liturgical art is found in chaplain John LaFarge's retrospective on the occasion of the Society's 25th anniversary. Liturgical art, said LaFarge, is more than simply art serving the liturgy of the Church:

"The very term liturgy indicates that the spirit of art, which the Society encourages, should reflect, by its very nature, not only rubrical correctness but the spirit of that official worship itself, the spirit of the Church praying. Thus, the liturgical art movement is an expression of love for the Church, which, if properly understood, is love for Christ Himself; love for the Heavenly Father, for whose honor and glory our Savior founded the Church, and love for the Holy Spirit, who proclaims the Father's glory within the Church unto the end of time."[58]

This understanding that it is the spirit of the liturgy rather than the letter of the law that makes art liturgical had several advantages. First, it allowed the Society to speak of liturgical art as something intrinsic to the life of the Church, more than simply a decorative veneer that, while pleasing, had no substantial connection to Christian life and worship. Second, it allowed the Society to speak of those who participated in the renewal of ecclesiastical art and architecture as "liturgists"[59] and "theologians,"[60] as persons who were involved in the ongoing recreation of the Church and of the world.[61] This definition of liturgical art would serve the Society well throughout its 44-year history, acting as a standard check against excessive rubricism on the one hand and irresponsibility on the other.

OTHER DEFINITIONS OF LITURGICAL ART

Over the years, the Liturgical Arts Society occasionally experimented with other ways of conceptualizing the nature of a specifically liturgical art. For example, in several articles in *Liturgical Arts* we find the concept of "ikon" offered as the paradigm for all liturgical art. As ikon, liturgical art is seen as a vehicle for human prayer and divine communication, a "real symbol of transcendent reality":

"The intention of an ikon is not to please, not even to express beauty, but to fix our attention, to quiet our senses in order to convey our prayer to that which the ikon represents and to bring it down in a very special way."[62]

But aside from occasional allusions to the importance of "praying on beauty,"[63] the implications of this concept were never drawn out. Scattered throughout the pages of *Liturgical Arts* were also references to liturgical art as "servant" of the Church,[64] "interpreter of the community's religious tradition,"[65] "teacher,"[66] and "apostle,"[67] but again, none of these ideas received sustained attention.

Greater attention was given to the idea of liturgical art as part of the whole complex of sacramental activity. The first intimations of the idea that some of the same dynamics are operative in liturgical art as in the sacramental life of the Church are found as early as 1936, when *Liturgical Arts* called liturgical art the "living embodiment of the spiritual ideals of the Christian life."[68] In an article published later in the same year, Albert Hammestaede, O.S.B., gave this idea a more sophisticated treatment:

"[Liturgical art] does not stop at representing the highest ideas: the true, the good, the beautiful; but in the liturgical *Mysterion*, to whose end liturgical art is ordered and without which it would not exist, it brings about objectively and in our very midst the highest form of reality, the *summum pulchrum*, God himself."[69]

117

A more nuanced (and more poetic) treatment of this same theme is found 20 years later in an article on the nature of the liturgy by Ettore Cunial.[70] Taking as his starting point the incarnation as a "living canticle" to God the Father, Cunial spoke of the way in which liturgical art participates in the sacramental life of Jesus for the Church. It is through liturgical art, he said, that "men unite themselves to the joy and sadness of human colloquies with God and vibrate to the stimulating influence of Christ in their lives . . . [and are enabled to] sing a divine canticle."

The strength of the idea that liturgical art was primarily marked by its liturgical inspiration seriously impeded the development of any of these themes. But the Society's constituency seems never to have demanded sophisticated expositions of the subject, and few such expositions were attempted in the pages of *Liturgical Arts*.Because of this, the Liturgical Arts Society did not contribute substantially to the theological and philosophical discourse about the nature of art in general and its relationship to the liturgy.

CHAPTER EIGHT

Who Should Decide Matters of Liturgical Art?

The question "Who should decide matters of liturgical art and architecture?" had a central place in the life and work of the Liturgical Arts Society. From a purely practical standpoint, the answer to this question determined, in large measure, the way in which the Society planned and executed its programs for the reform of ecclesiastical art. But the question "Who decides?" was also a theological question and, more specifically, an ecclesiological question. Thus, to chart the progress of the Society's thinking about ecclesiastical authority is also to trace its understanding of the nature of the Church and of ministry.

If there was any one thing on which those gathered at Portsmouth Priory in 1927 and 1928 could agree, it was that decisions about Roman Catholic liturgical art were being made by the wrong persons. The causes of that situation were variously attributed,[1] but in any case, the unfortunate result had been a liturgical art marked by "banalities and exhibitions of bad taste bordering on the irreverent."[2] In its 40-year quest to correct this situation, the Liturgical Arts Society operated on the presupposition that the answer to the question "What liturgical art is appropriate for the Roman Catholic Church?" was inextricably bound to the question "Who decides what liturgical art is appropriate for the Roman Catholic Church?" Although the Society's primary concern was to find an answer to the first of these two questions, the second also received considerable, if less direct, attention.

WHO WAS DECIDING IN 1927-1928?

If the founding members of the Liturgical Arts Society agreed that the wrong people were deciding matters of liturgical art, there was some diversity of opinion on who these people were and why the power of decision-making had fallen to them. For Ides van der Gracht, "the root of the matter [was] essentially a social very much more than a religious question."[3] The task of transmitting the great intellectual and cultural heritage of Roman Catholicism to the American environment had been left to immigrant Roman Catholics and the clergy who served them, those who were "generally of low social and cultural status."[4] At the same time, persons of higher sociocultural standing in the American Church were "frowned upon as pretentious by the overeager converts to a somewhat misconceived democracy."[5] This condition had proven disastrous, not only for the state of liturgical art but for the perceived status of the Roman Catholic Church within "modern intellectual and artistic life." Since American society tended to judge the Roman Catholic Church by its most visible members, it was not surprising that an unsympathetic and often uninformed public should think that its aesthetic standards should be judged on the same basis.[6]

The idea that those who had been making the Church's artistic decisions were not culturally, socially, or economically equipped to do so seems to have had wide acceptance among the Society's founding members, and appears over and over again in the pages of *Liturgical Arts* until the early 1950s.[7] But many of the founders believed that another group, equally ill-equipped for its task (and perhaps with the added motivation of personal gain) was also an important co-conspirator in the decline of Roman Catholic liturgical art. This group was referred to as the "church goods fraternity": the commercial producers of religious art who dominated the business of church furnishing and decorating at the time when the Liturgical Arts Society was founded. The reaction against church goods houses was often due to aesthetic shock at the volume of items devoid of quality workmanship or artistic integrity that issued from them. But there were objections on important philosophical grounds as well.

For A. Graham Carey, John Howard Benson, and others of the founding members who had been influenced by such writers as Ananda K. Coomarswamy, A. W. N. Pugin, John Ruskin, and Eric Gill,[8] commercial and industrial methods of production and distribution were the very antithesis of everything that art, and perhaps especially art for the Church, demanded. Art required human intelligence, will, and moral and aesthetic judgment. Because machines were seen to be in utter conflict with the essence of humanity, machine-made, mass-produced statues, altarware, and vestments were objectively outside of the category "art." "You cannot have things made by machinery and pretend with success that they are made by human beings," wrote Eric Gill on this subject.[9]

The manufacturer's profit motive, the degradation of the worker, and the enslavement of the underclasses in factories also made commercial art unsuitable for a Church concerned with social justice.[10] In other words, machine-made "art" was basically immoral, since its goal was not the greater glory of God but the greater profit of the merchant class; not the "expression of human sensibilities" but the subjugation of the human spirit.[11] Even those of the founding members who did not believe that philosophy of art should play a major role in the Society's program[12] were convinced that commercial firms, motivated by profit and aided by machinery, should have no part in deciding on the form of appropriate liturgical art for the Roman Catholic Church. Editorials and articles in *Liturgical Arts* repeatedly revile the manufacturers of church goods and give little evidence of real hope of their reformation.[13]

Van der Gracht's social critique and Benson and Carey's philosophical analysis of current artistic trends were understood by the founding members as complementary, rather than contrary, to one another. And so there was almost unanimous agreement on the reasons behind the deplorable state of ecclesiastical art. Because immigrant clergy and laity had such low standards against which to measure art for the Church, unscrupulous church goods houses could sell them inferior products with impunity. The Liturgical Arts Society sought to have the power of decision-making in matters of art for worship wrested away from these elements and given over to those more suited to the task. Because of this commitment, the questions "Who will be the new decision-makers?" and "What role will they play?" echoed throughout the 40-year history of the Society.

It is not surprising that the Liturgical Arts Society, founded and led almost exclusively by lay people,[14] would take it for granted that one of the appropriate participants in the conversation about suitable forms of liturgical art was the laity. The founding members had rather quickly abandoned as impracticable Everitt Harman's idea that membership in the group be limited to "Religious, Oblates, and Guildsmen,"[15] and all of the documents under which the Society was incorporated make no practical distinction between clergy, religious, and laity.[16] Membership in the Society was to "embrace all those competent and interested in the arts of the Church"[17] and was open to "architects, artists, and craftsmen, scholars, educators, and interested laymen."[18] Furthermore, it is made clear that lay persons have some authoritive contribution to make to the "improvement of the standards of taste, craftsmanship, and liturgical correctness" in the arts of the Church.[19] It was advertised that the editorial content of *Liturgical Arts* would include information on "the relation of the arts to the worship of the Church as elucidated by leading authorities, clerical and lay."[20] Although some of the early correspondence among the founding members indicates that there was to be a division of labor between clergy and lay members (with competent lay people providing "architectural and professional information" and clergy "liturgical and educational"[21]), the Society prospectus is clear that one of the functions of lay experts is to educate clergy.[22]

But the group of lay founders had been warned (mostly by clergy) that without ecclesiastical approbation their effort was doomed to failure. As a result, the early documents of the Society were quick to point out that although control of the organization rests in the hands of lay persons, "in order to insure the soundness of its policies, as well as the success of its efforts, [the Society] is seeking the patronage of the Hierarchy."[23] (On occasion, later documents undertook to rewrite the history of the Society's founding, stating that it was "under the guidance of various members of the clergy [that] the initial group organized itself."[24]) As the years went by, the Society began to reflect on its role as a lay organization in the Church, and on the dialogue between the freedom and responsibility of lay experts:

"It is a *sine qua non* that the work of an organization such as ours should develop and grow under the watchful eye of our Ordinary and of the hierarchy. It is true that as laymen interested in the building of the physical fabric of the Church and the embellishment of our sanctuaries, we are allowed wide liberty of action in the fields in which we may claim some competence. We are not, however, free to disregard the pronouncements and regulations of the Church insofar as they relate to the construction of altars and the proper interpretation of the 'Instruction on Sacred Music.' In the observance of an intelligent balance in these matters lies the fundamental policy of the Liturgical Arts Society in its relation to our ecclesiastical superiors."[25]

But within this balance, there was recognized a priority of Church authority over lay experts. "In applying the principles of contemporary architecture to this task," this *Liturgical Arts* editorial continued, "[we] must be guided first by the pronouncements of the authorities of the Church and then by [our] own thorough understanding of the spirit of the liturgy."[26] But as the years went by, this idealistic equilibrium was impaired, as over and over again the Society's offers of help in matters of liturgical art were rejected by members of the Roman Catholic hierarchy on the grounds that they came from lay people.[27] In his advice to a friend who was contemplating serving as a lay member of an episcopal commission, Lavanoux shared his experience as a lay participant in the Church's decision-making processes:

"I realize that there are excellent men in such religious groups, but they are not free agents . . . [which] takes away from them any liberty which they need in such matters. I also realize that we can meet with similar opposition and misunderstanding with lay groups; however, in a showdown, you can deal with lay people and really say what you have in mind; with a religious group, you at once come up against crozier and mitre, and any serious discussion becomes one-sided."[28]

Still later, as developments in the field of ecclesiology emphasized a theology of the laity, Lavanoux was encouraged that the direction in which the Society had been traveling in these matters had been appropriate.[29] One quotation that struck a particularly responsive chord with Lavanoux came from Jean Guitton, who had been the first lay auditor at the sessions of Vatican II. "The wise layman must go foreward," Guitton wrote in the Italian newspaper *L'Avvenire d'Italia:*[30]

"He must not always ask for permission but occasionally accept the risk of being wrong . . . . Without this risk, there is no sacrifice. If there is a conflict between the layman and authority, the layman knows that it is he who will have to give in. In the Catholic Church, it is the prophet who obeys the priest.

"How effective can the layman be? The layman is most effective if he is at [once] independent and submissive. He is not merely a docile son, nor only the man who rebels. He is a synthesis."[31]

(In Lavanoux's editorial comment on this quotation, he added that although Guitton's view is "true enough, . . . the *authority* has the *responsibility* of being right, or at least in the right direction."[32])

Certainly, in the beginning, the Society was not interested in asserting the right of lay persons in general to take part in the Church's decision-making on matters of liturgical art, but rather in asserting the right of a certain *class* of lay persons to do so. Most of the founding members agreed with Ides van der Gracht that the "direction of so high and difficult a mission" rightfully belongs to the "more enlightened elements" of the laity.[33] It was these "cultured Catholics" who must "lead in restoring [the Church's] full inspirational and guiding qualities, not only that she may be the more effective within but that she may manifest to all her full beauty and wisdom and take her rightful place in the cultural life of the nation."[34] As the organization matured, this elitist stance was softened somewhat. Lavanoux, who as the son of immigrants did not fit the pattern set by his wealthy, Ivy-League-educated fellow founders, had exercised considerable influence in the drafting of the documents under which the Society was incorporated and had considerably underplayed their elitist bias. But in a sense, Lavanoux encouraged the replacement of one elite class with another: the class of Roman Catholic artists.

Most of the Liturgical Arts Society's founding members seem to have taken it for granted that Roman Catholic artists were best suited to the task of transforming liturgical art and architecture. Ides van der Gracht was emphatic that "the full beauty of the Church's expression requires the intimate union between the Church and the artist."[35] During the early deliberations, it was thought that this "intimate union" could be best achieved by settling artists in a monastic community, one "ordered toward helping the artist achieve a more profound realization of the spiritual life of the Church in order that it may find a correct and richer expression in their work."[36] Although the idea of a monastic community did not survive, the constitution and bylaws under which the Liturgical Arts Society was incorporated in October, 1928 manifest the supposition that Roman Catholic artists were best qualified to guide "the standards of taste, craftsmanship, and liturgical correctness"[37] of ecclesiastical art. The highest category of membership in the Society, corporate membership, was limited to "Catholics" who had rendered "honorable service" in the "study and practice of the arts connected with the worship of the Catholic Church."[38] More important, corporate membership was a prerequisite to serving as an officer in the Society,[39] on the Board of Directors, or as a member of any of the three Standing Committees.[40]

As it had been with the understanding of the liturgy[41] and with art,[42] the Liturgical Arts Society's early understanding of the Roman Catholic artist was colored by a certain amount of medieval romanticism. Roman Catholic artists were somehow closer to the medieval ideal than were ordinary persons. Like their medieval counterparts, Roman Catholic artists were seen to be especially in touch with the faith, their art mirroring Roman Catholic culture and modes of thinking.[43] In order to nourish and deepen their artistic abilities, artists were encouraged by the Society to return to the medieval guild system of production and distribution and to apply the principles of Scholasticism and its emphasis on "right reason" to their work.[44] It seems that for the Liturgical Arts Society in its early period, the Roman Catholic artist was best suited to making decisions about liturgical art because he or she was the true link to the Great Age of Faith in the midst of the secularism of the modern world.

But gradually, and especially after World War II, the Society began to recognize that it was unrealistic to expect 20th-century artists to return to a medieval womb and that other qualities made them the appropriate arbiters of ecclesiastical good taste. During this period, an emphasis on what might be termed Roman Catholic spirituality came to the surface. Although part of this spirituality involved the willing acceptance of liturgical law, it is because a Roman Catholic artist "thinks as the Church thinks in matters liturgical [that] he can, and often does, anticipate the law without always knowing what it is."[45] It is the "spiritual effort which perfects the work of art."[46] Like prophets, apostles, evangelists, pastors, and doctors of the Church, Roman Catholic artists are "gifted agents to build up the Body of Christ."[47] In a very real sense, the special nature of the task demanded this deep engagement with the spiritual life of the Church. As one Roman Catholic architect put it:

"The client [in the furnishing and decorating of a church] is the Mystical Body of Christ, and if an architect is to provide a place in which such a client can identify Itself, he must understand it fully. His theological and liturgical understanding must be more than just a passing acquaintance with the ritual form of ceremonies or the history of the church building. He must understand the Mass through its origin. He must try to know God. This is the first and basic determinant [of Roman Catholic Church building] and the key to understanding all the others."[48]

During this period, then, the suitability of the Roman Catholic artist for the task of deciding on matters of liturgical art did not rest on doctrinal assent so much as on assent to the *spirit* of Roman Catholicism and the ability to convey that spirit "in terms of form and function."[49] Still later, the Society came to believe that it was the artist's assent to the community — the *ecclesia* — that was primary. According to an article by a Roman Catholic architect, as artists come to value participation in the community of faith as a source of artistic inspiration, "we will see more and more works which will be the occasion for people to discover the beauty of their experience and — more importantly — that of others in the community."[50] In the final analysis, the Roman Catholic artist has legitimate authority in matters of liturgical art because he or she works for the "praise of God rather than self-praise."[51]

Inevitably, discussion arose about the relationship between the artist's responsibility to the discipline of the Church and the artist's freedom to follow the creative spirit. The Liturgical Arts Society observed that many Roman Catholic artists were not exercising their influence on liturgical art because they believed that working for the Church necessarily restricted the free exercise of their creativity. For this reason, "the Church has suffered from a lack of cooperation from so many talented artists and has been, in effect, at the mercy of second-string practitioners."[52] In *Liturgical Arts*, the subject of the freedom and authority of the Roman Catholic artist appeared with some frequency, and several articles were devoted exclusively to the matter. In "Freedom and the Artist," Gerald Phelan lamented that a misunderstanding of the nature of law has inhibited artists from applying their gifts to the betterment of liturgical art. Law, he claimed, is not an impediment to the artist who values creative freedom but a necessity, since "where law is absent, anarchy prevails, and freedom cannot live in anarchy."[53] It is precisely because the most creative artists faithfully follow the laws of their medium, of nature, and of aesthetics that they can "make beauty flourish."[54] The same is true for artists who follow the laws of the Church; they must be aware of the purpose that the artistic product is to serve and aware as well of the spiritual needs of those who will use it.[55] Over and over again, articles and editorials in *Liturgical Arts* return to this theme. Spiritual discipline, attention to canons and rubrics, and love and knowledge of the liturgical life of the Church are benefits to the Roman Catholic artist rather than hindrances, and the refusal to acknowledge them has serious consequences:

"The Catholic architect or artist . . . enjoys the inestimable advantage of a past and a present based on sound tradition; a discipline which by its very nature frees him for a full flowering of his genius. To evade this discipline, to forego the normal evolution of his creative prerogative, is, to put it bluntly, a prostitution."[56]

Increasingly, and especially after 1950, the Liturgical Arts Society devoted its time to the discussion of the *product* of responsible artistic liberty rather than the person who produces it. (Indeed, the label "Roman Catholic" as a qualifier before artist or architect virtually dropped out of *Liturgical Arts'* vocabulary.) Comments on Vatican Council II and art gave primary attention to the marks of appropriate ecclesiastical art and ways in which the Church could nourish it.[57] In 1964, *Liturgical Arts* printed the full text of an address to members of the Italian Union of Artists, in which Pope Paul VI acknowledged that the Church had not always allowed artists to use their God-given talents and pledged change. "We must ask of you all the possibilities which the Lord has given you," he said. "Then, within the ambit of that functioning and the finality by which art is companioned with the worship of God, we must leave to your voices the free and powerful song of which you are capable."[58] The overwhelming impression left by this address, and by the Society's program as a whole, is that the Roman Catholic artist has authority within the Church's decision-making structure, the authority to guide the Church in matters of appropriate liturgical art.[59]

THE ROLE OF THE VATICAN IN DECIDING MATTERS OF LITURGICAL ART

But throughout virtually all of the Liturgical Arts Society's history, the authority of the artist in matters of liturgical art was clearly derivative of the authority which the Vatican exercised over the life of the Church as a whole. It is true that those of the early founders who were intent upon establishing the Society as a monastic community[60] were more immediately concerned with obedience to the Rule of Saint Benedict than to Vatican pronouncements, and most of the documents authored by Everitt Harman and Ides van der Gracht say only that such a community should be "canonically established"[61] with "ecclesiastical approbation."[62] But as the Society moved away from consideration of a monastic form of organization, it became more emphatic about its reliance on the Vatican. The Liturgical Arts Society's bylaws are clear that its members were expected to act in "strict conformity to the liturgical laws of the Catholic Church,"[63] that their work should "conform to sound liturgical tradition and the decrees of the Sacred Congregation of Rites,"[64] and be "expressive of a truly Catholic spirit."[65] As the Society matured, it was concerned not only with the letter of ecclesiastical law but with the spirit as well:

128

"It has always been the policy of the Liturgical Arts Society to work in close harmony with the *mind* of the Church; and it is imperative that we do not deviate from the norms which have guided and inspired the work of the Society since the very beginning of its existence."[66]

At no time in its history, however, did the Society make any real distinction between the various kinds and degrees of ecclesiastical authority. The Vatican, the "mind of the Church," the liturgy, and canon law each had legitimate and equal claim on the Society and on its constituency:

"If theology is the human science that is built on the word of God spoken to men, canon law is a science concerned with the practical life of the Church founded on God's word. Its formulation is the work of human agents who are entrusted with the sanctification of God's Church. Consequently, the theological and juridical aspects of the Church cannot be entirely separated. It is by reflecting on the word of God that the Church concludes how she should act."[67]

In addition to having a legitimate claim on the life and work of artists, liturgical law, Vatican directives, and pronouncements of the Holy See were presented as the artists' most reliable source of creative energy and guidance:

"If ever there was a field granting maximum liberty for art, it is that offered by the Church. She welcomes the most varied aesthetics, admires art of all time, and even keeps in her museums the most beautiful treasures of pagan art."[68]

Church authority over the artist was likened to the banks of a river, or the sidewalks of a busy street, allowing movement without chaos, direction without impediment.[69]

Liturgical Arts and the Society itself very rarely discussed the theological underpinnings of Church authority in matters of liturgical art. Many contributors to *Liturgical Arts* declared that artists who work for the Church are really serving as theologians and that as such they must submit to the necessary discipline of the Church:

"The artist must bear in mind that he is engaged in making a sort of

129

theology, in graphic representation, and that therefore the Church claims the right to pass judgment on the suitability of the work."[70]

As the "qualified interpreter of the religious tradition of the community," the Church exercises legitimate control over the artist who serves that community.[71] The Church has the responsibility to insure that liturgical art is marked by integrity and conformity to doctrine,[72] that it is created "in very truth *ad majorem Dei gloriam*,"[73] and that it manifests "harmonious equilibrium between subjective and objective."[74] It is understood that art, per se, is not the Church's province:

"The Church's proper commission is to teach the truth taught by Christ and to save souls by the means which He instituted for salvation. Art, however, can come under the authority of the Church accidentally, namely, when the Church uses art for its own purposes. The Church is not concerned with art as art, but the Church *is* concerned with art as a service of the worship of God."[75]

Some contributors to *Liturgical Arts*, especially those influenced by medieval romanticism, voiced the opinion that the Church exercises legitimate authority in matters of art, not only for Roman Catholics but for the whole of society:

"Anyone who with an unbiased mind compares the products of any truly Christian century with those of our own can readily observe the wealth, spontaneity, and apparent ease of the former and artistic poverty of the latter. Two things are needed, therefore, to bring beauty into life through artistic expression: the one is religion, and the other is the application of right reason. The Catholic Church, under the guidance of the Holy Spirit, has retained both. She is, therefore, fundamentally best equipped to restore the right balance in the field of 'doing' and to furnish the guidance and leadership that the world needs. Conversely, the world has a right to expect from us the kind of direction that contributes so potently to the welfare of mankind."[76]

Still later, and especially as it became clear that Vatican II would make some changes in laws governing liturgical art, the Liturgical Arts Society began to discuss the marks of good legislation on ecclesiastical art and the ways in which ecclesiastical law could best

130

serve the art community. The Society also began to see how once appropriate laws had become disfunctional:

"The best law, the best decree, is based on common sense, which leads us to act intuitively and in a normal manner. Our troubles begin when the *spirit* of the law or decree is encrusted with the barnacles of unreasoned custom or when the clarity of the original law has been clouded by accretions which, while valid at one time, have become atrophied and useless."[77]

There is, then, a balance of responsibility between Church law and the artistic community. The Vatican must "encourage and promote the talents of artists" through its legislation and evince "willing acceptance of the highest degree of excellence" in the arts.[78] On the other hand, artists should acquaint themselves with current legislation and allow it to guide the creative process.

But there was always the suggestion that art, by its very nature, resists legislation by the Vatican, that "talent and genius should not be stifled by legislators who are not themselves conversant with the arts," because art is part of the "free and loving response of the whole man to the loving God."[79] In the end, art worthy of the Church is the result of dynamic cooperation between the authority of the Church and the freedom of the artist. If the Vatican and artists work together to "fortify the Christian community by faith and humanity, a complete, pure, and joyful house of God will appear."[80]

THE AUTHORITY OF BISHOPS AND PARISH CLERGY CONCERNING LITURGICAL ART

Because of the elasticity and generosity of Vatican pronouncements on matters of liturgical art, the Society was convinced that they were designed to "deal only in generalities and do not attempt to solve day-to-day problems."[81] The ordinary working life of the artist who wished to serve the Roman Catholic Church was, for better or worse, under the direction of local authorities, and especially the Ordinary of the diocese in which he or she was employed. Indeed the Society, as a Roman Catholic organization, believed that it could properly develop and grow only "under the watchful eye of our Ordinary and of the hierarchy."[82] Consequently, the Liturgical Arts Society had sought out the patronage of Cardinal Hayes (within whose archdiocese it had been incorporated)[83] and endeavored to make and maintain friendly contact with as many United States bishops as possible.[84]

In the eyes of the Society, episcopal authority was legitimately exercised on several levels. It was the bishop's primary function to act as mediator between the Holy See and the diocese. The bishop was to articulate to those under his care "what the Church has really said, what has been determined by the Holy Father, what the Sacred Congregations have laid down, and what is left to the discretion of the Ordinary"[85] in matters of sacred art. On a more practical level, the Society acknowledged the legitimate authority of bishops over the building and furnishing of churches in their dioceses, the selection of architects, and the allotment of funds, all of which were matters of grave concern to the Society.

Throughout its history, the Liturgical Arts Society endeavored to distinguish between the authority of the bishop on matters of legitimate Church teaching and the private opinion of the bishop on matters of artistic merit. Over and over again, the Society emphasized that although the bishop had the final say on the interpretation of canon law and theology, "in matters of taste , Church authorities may differ like anyone else."[86] It was at the level of episcopal decision-making that the two sets of law — ecclesiastical and artistic — were most likely to come into conflict:

"The Church indeed remains the ultimate judge of the fitness [of a work of art] for its task; a function which, in turn, is the office of the bishop as the representative of the Church. The bishop may, and frequently does, employ a commission to advise him in such matters and to help form his opinion, but his own judgment would be the ultimate local responsibility.

"But on the other hand, the Church recognizes the principle that art follows certain laws which are inherent in the art itself, even when, a 'noblest handmaid,' it is put at the service of the Church."[87]

Throughout its history, whenever the Society was asked about an artist's duty to obey the directives of a given bishop, the invariable answer was that any episcopal decision was entirely binding with

regard to the building and furnishing of churches within his jurisdiction:

"A subscriber writes that a bishop of his diocese is excited about a
statue recently placed in the vestibule of a rural church. His Excel-
lency wants the statue removed. What do do? Simple: The statue is
removed. Papal directives vest all *authority* in such matters in the
Ordinary of the diocese. All *we* can do is respectfully hold another
opinion, if we like, about the *quality* of the work of art involved and
hope for a more favorable artistic climate."[88]

Although the distinction between episcopal pronouncements on
doctrinal and theological matters and episcopal pronouncements
on matters of artistic taste appears over and over again in the pages
of *Liturgical Arts*, no thoroughgoing discussion of the foundations
of this distinction or its implications was ever attempted. In a 1969
Liturgical Arts editorial, Maurice Lavanoux admitted that his "philosopher and theologian friends could no doubt elaborate on this
distinction."[89]

The Society did, however, call for certain changes that would enable the artist or architect to balance more comfortably obligations
to Church and craft. Bishops were encouraged to identify clearly au-
thoritative pronouncements from opinion, to separate their role as
Church authority from their role as individual Christians interested
in art for the Church. They were encouraged to learn about art and
to accept the authority of those with special competence in such
matters:

"Unless [the authorities] are artistically competent they should
have the modesty to get out of the way and entrust the job to the
very best artists. What the architect and the artist needs is direction
on the liturgical and theological level."[90]

The Society also hoped that bishops would begin to work to create
a climate within which the arts could flourish, within which
"young artists can breathe freely and with zest to create the art we
need so much in our churches."[91] A major component in this
scheme would be a commitment by bishops to help artists understand the theological principles relating to liturgical art:

"Could not the bishops . . . speak more directly and positively to the artist and say to him: Here is what our holy faith expects you to embody in your work. Here are the deeper and ultimate norms that should guide it; here is the font from which you should especially draw your inspiration."[92]

That persons in authority who were untrained in matters of art should impose their own taste on the Church was something of a mystery to the leaders of the Society. Unlike the doctor, engineer, or physicist, the competent artist with the necessary academic distinctions found his or her work questioned at every turn:[93]

"It is one of the curious anomalies of the present time that we Catholics, who are so insistent upon what is objective in matters of rational conduct and ethical responsibility, should be so willing to yield to complete subjectivism in a field where the practice of the faith is so intimately concerned."[94]

As the years went on, the Society became increasingly realistic about this situation and suggested a variety of remedies to its constituency:

"Fortunately, in many places, good art has found a place in a new church because . . . few, if any, questions were asked of the diocesan commission . . . . In other words, don't ask too many questions of the chancery . . . . Use your common sense and liturgical intuition, and you can't be very far off. When faced with the intransigence of authority or the timidity of a conservative pastor, just be patient, and don't kick over the traces. Time often takes care of stubborn, unreasonable opposition to growth and living renewal."[95]

The Liturgical Arts Society longed for bishops who would study the arts in order to "personally . . . form a more intimate liaison . . . between the theoretical vision and its realization in space, form, and color,"[96] and for communication between artists and their episcopal clients that was marked by humility and mutual respect. The Society was convinced that where Vatican Council II affirmed the Church's right to pass judgment, it was not advocating that these judgments be based on the personal artistic prejudices of Church authorities. Rather, "it is talking about [the judgment of] competent, well-informed, and properly appointed individuals and groups."[97]

134

"We are all face to face with our personal responsibility in the matter of religious art. The artist, to whom God has granted the grace of talent . . . The Church, through the instrumentality of the bishops, exercises its authority to encourage and promote the talents of artists, all within the willing acceptance of the highest degree of excellence. It is a serious matter not to be ignored through ignorance or personal prejudice."[98]

PARISH CLERGY

Bishops garnered a certain amount of respect from the Liturgical Arts Society by virtue of their office, but the same cannot be said for parish clergy. Ides van der Gracht's contention that the low sociocultural status of immigrant priests had been a major contributor to the crisis in liturgical art was only the first hint of what would become the Society's overwhelming opinion. Over the years, some attempts were made to soften this negative and condescending attitude toward parish priests. But in spite of these attempts, the pages of *Liturgical Art:* (as well as private correspondence between Liturgical Arts Society leaders) were filled with anecdotal observations of the ways in which local clergymen had impeded the progress of liturgical and artistic renewal in the life of the Church. At best, these remarks are patronizing caricatures; often they are extremely derogatory. Some of these opinions were offered by other priests, who appear to have considered themselves more enlightened than their brethren in such matters.[99]

But at the same time, the Liturgical Arts Society realized that, more often than not, actual decisions about the building and furnishing of churches were made by parish priests, who thus became the usual point-of-contact between the individual artist or architect and the Church. Consequently, from the very beginning, the Society strove to create a program that would "explain [to clergy] the difference between good and bad [art], and why they should want the best, and what it is and where it is to be gotten."[100] In addition, the Society advocated certain courses of action designed to make parish priests better clients. "Educate the seminarians," an editorial in *Liturgical Arts* advised, "and all will be well."[101] Clergymen were encouraged to make a hobby of art and to visit museums and galleries in their leisure time.[102] At a somewhat deeper level, the Society recommended that parish clergy progressively hand over decision-making power in matters of art and architecture to competent parishoners:

"Much [of what is to be accomplished] depends on who runs the show, and I am more and more convinced of the necessity for having control in the hands of the laity, not because *some* clergy are not competent, but simply because they are not free. At any time — and it has happened — a priest who has been doing fine work at the "art level" may be removed from his post and sent elsewhere. What can he do in the face of legitimate authority?"[103]

The Society also emphasized that the employment of artists was not simply a matter of providing good art for churches, but presented a moral issue as well. The priest who refused to pay an artist a living wage denied him or her an "honest living."[104] Conversely, the Society was convinced of the necessity for the artist to understand the seriousness of the task of negotiating with clergy and to communicate clearly his or her own vision of how the work should be done with artistic integrity. "The Catholic artist," one Roman Catholic painter explained:

"is at one end of a tug-of-war, the Catholic worshipper at the other — or, to be realistic, the ecclesiastic that handles the parish money. If these were the only participants in the sport, the artist would have no choice but to bow abjectly to the aesthetic ideas of the non-artist; but it happens that this is a three-cornered proposition, with God as the referee. Before serving the Catholic flock or its pastor, the artist must give obeisance to God; he must not break the rules of sound aesthetics under penalty of ceasing to be a good man."[105]

As the years went by, the Society became more thoughtful about the decision-making power of parish clergy. In a rare explication of the nature of priestly authority in matters of liturgical art, Clement McNaspy claims that as *patron* of the arts, the priest extends his role as "father" (the word "patron" also being derivative from the Latin *pater*) in the creation of art for the Church. Although the artist acts as "mother," giving birth to art, "the genetic contribution of both 'parents' will result in true enrichment." Both patron and artist are called to work together in a humble and loving way, learning about one another and sharing their respective experiences of the Christian faith.[106] Although McNaspy's article was *Liturgical Arts'* only serious attempt at a theological explanation of the legitimate priestly authority over art, the Liturgical Arts Society began to see that the problem of ecclesiastical responsibility in such matters was more complicated than it had first believed.[107] Certainly, the presence in the Society of a number of scholarly and insightful clergymen contributed to a re-evaluation of the caricature of parish priests as the chief stumbling blocks to the liturgical movement and the sole perpetrators of bad taste in the United States.[108] It was increasingly recognized that much of the good work that appeared in the pages of *Liturgical Arts* was the direct result of the efforts of zealous and self-sacrificing parish priests, who were often misunderstood by fellow clergymen and ecclesiastical authorities. Many such priests suffered the disappointment of seeing years of painstaking effort to introduce fine art to local congregations completely dismantled by the next pastor.[109]

At no time in its history did the Liturgical Arts Society make a clear and consistent statement on its understanding of the nature of the authority of bishops and parish clergy in matters of liturgical art. The 40 years of *Liturgical Arts* do indeed leave the overwhelming impression that the Society recognized that it is entirely legitimate for bishops and parish clergy to make binding decisions in these matters as a part of their pastoral responsibility. But it is also clear that this situation does not provide the perfect context for the full flowering of ecclesiastical art and architecture. On one occasion, *Liturgical Arts* rather playfully suggested that the ideal solution to balancing a commitment to Church authority with a commitment to high artistic ideals lay in a system of "enlightened despotism":

"One of the justifications for the aristocratic principle is that it permits a few capable individuals, of taste and perception they must be, to act for the good of the many. Aristocracy's record of patronage in the arts is often argued in its favor. The aristocratic nature of the Catholic government certainly gives it powers of persuasion . . . which should make the establishment and maintenance of standards of taste a relatively easy task."[110]

Although these comments have a tongue-in-cheek quality about them, it is likely that they reflect very closely the actual sentiments of the Liturgical Arts Society and its leaders. In spite of its occasional protestations that art could not be legislated, the Society seems to have been committed to a system that combined the power of ecclesiastical authority to make actual changes in the life of the Church with sufficient artistic expertise to insure that those changes were made in the right direction.

THE CONTRIBUTION OF NON-ROMAN CATHOLIC CHRISTIANS AND NON-CHRISTIANS

The Roman Catholic identity of the Liturgical Arts Society established in its early years was reinforced in various ways throughout the organization's history. Aware that some opponents of the liturgical movement believed that interest in the liturgy and liturgical art was "Anglican,"[111] the Society did not make any effort during its first decade to rethink its decision to reject the contributions of Anglo-Catholic Christians such as Ralph Adams Cram.[112] Even so, the Society received criticism for the publication in *Liturgical Arts* of a series of articles by a Princeton historian of art,[113] for notice in the magazine's book review section of a book entitled *Anglicanism in Transition*,[114] and for presenting pictures of fonts that, although pre-Reformation, were then housed in Church of England parish churches.[115] Some members even objected to the awarding of a Liturgical Arts Society medal to Becket Gibbs, the devoted director of the Quilisma Club,[116] on the grounds that he was employed as choirmaster by an Episcopal Church and by Union Theological Seminary.[117] The subtitle of the magazine, "A Quarterly Devoted to the Arts of the Catholic Church," appeared on the front cover throughout its 40 years of publication, and as Lavanoux explained to one reader in 1947, "that is why all buildings illustrated in *Liturgical Arts* are either Catholic churches or other structures used by the Church."[118]

Toward the end of *Liturgical Arts'* years of publication, two non-Roman Catholic churches were described, one of which merited a cover photo.[119] More likely to receive attention in these final years were ecumenical facilities of various kinds, or community churches that accommodated both Roman Catholic congregations and those of other faiths.[120] Acknowledging that "ecumenism is really in the air,"[121] Lavanoux and Edward Sutfin compiled "A Selected, Annotated Bibliography on Ecumenical and Related Matters" that appeared in two installments in *Liturgical Arts*:[122]

"It may seem curious that this bibliography should appear in a publication devoted to religious art and architecture, yet a corollary of the ecumenical movement is surely a widening of our horizons. It is significant that in countries where the ecumenical movement has found marked impetus in recent decades, the evolution of religious art and architecture has undergone marked change — from ornate, overdecorated churches, cluttered with statuary and lacy Renaissance frippery, to bright and spacious interiors where the primacy of the liturgy is again made manifest and where the people take their rightful place."[123]

Throughout the late 1960s, the Society manifested the conviction that the best hopes for the renewal of religious art and architecture were to be found in an ecumenical approach. Gradually, religious labels (even the label "Roman Catholic") tended to disappear from the pages of *Liturgical Arts*.

Although the direction and identity of the Liturgical Arts Society itself was never a matter of any real debate, the more serious question of what authority non-Roman Catholic Christians and non-Christians had in deciding matters of Roman Catholic religious art was an important one for the Society. By the mid-1940s, the question "Can and should those outside the Roman Catholic faith provide adequate liturgical art for Roman Catholic use?" began to be a more frequent topic of discussion in *Liturgical Arts*. Despite its own clearly defined Roman Catholic identity, the Liturgical Arts Society generally displayed more concern with the product of creative genius than with the religious disposition of the artist. It did, however, at least in the beginning, make certain attempts to ascertain the denominational affiliation of those whose work was pictured or described in the pages of *Liturgical Arts*. To one critic, who admitted that he was canceling his subscription to *Liturgical Arts* because it had "a policy of encouraging well-known, present-day, non-Catholic artists to enter the Church field,"[124] Lavanoux replied:

"As for Catholic versus non-Catholic artists: it is true that the first thing I look for is professional competence, but I do ask an artist, first, if he is a Catholic."[125]

(Lavanoux added that a check of volumes 14-17 of *Liturgical Arts* had uncovered the work of 49 Roman Catholic artists and 32 non-Roman Catholics.[126]) Although some of the Society's leaders advised that the editors of *Liturgical Arts* "go very cautiously"[127] in presenting the work of non-Roman Catholic artists and architects in *Liturgical Arts*, as the years went by, Lavanoux and others were more and more inclined to say that "the only question should be: Is it a good piece or not?" In a 1960 editorial, Lavanoux wrote:[128]

"An ecumenical approach to our problems might . . . have the advantage of placing the choice of artists on a fair basis: first: competence, talent, and even a touch of genius; second: understanding of the subject matter; third: acceptance of the discipline of the commission, implicit when the work is to be done for a Catholic church. This sequence, we admit, is the proper one. On the other hand, the choice of an artist based primarily on religious affiliations is unrealistic and, in some cases, lacking in charity."[129]

The first in-depth discussion of these questions appeared in *Liturgical Arts* in 1946. In "Sacred Art and Sanctity,"[130] Herbert G. Kramer asked "What are the religious requirements for the creator of religious art?" and "Need artists be saints?" Kramer's thesis was that although many have believed religious art to be entirely dependent upon the artist's self-conscious acknowledgment of the Holy Spirit working within,[131] the demand for personal sanctity on the part of an artist who wishes to serve the Church is unrealistic in a world in which the divorce between sacred and secular, faith and work, is so explicit. In addition, the experience of wartime suffering had given many non-Roman Catholic artists a special claim to authenticity in conveying the sacrificial suffering of Christ. Since union with the sacrifice of Christ is at the heart of the Roman Catholic Church's self-understanding, those artists who have themselves lived sacrificially should be encouraged to contribute to the artistic expression of the Church.[132] After this article appeared, *Liturgical Arts* began increasingly to emphasize that one should not be too quick to judge the suitability of liturgical art by the religious affiliation (or lack of affiliation) of the artist. By about 1950, the evidence of humility and of an inspired genius seemed to have become the prime prerequisites in deciding who should provide liturgical art for Roman Catholic churches. Lavanoux remarked in a *Liturgical Arts* editorial in 1952:

"After all, 'the Holy Spirit bloweth where he will . . . ,' and can we not assume, until we have proof to the contrary, that many artists who may be condemned for no other reason than that damnable 'guilt by association theory' are on the high road to a Christian approach to religious art?"[133]

One event in particular seemed to focus and direct the Society's entire discussion of the degree to which faith is a determining factor in providing suitable liturgical art for the Roman Catholic Church. This event was the decoration of the Church of Notre Dame de Tout-Grâce at Assy, a small mountain town in the south of France. Serving primarily as a chapel for the numerous sanatoria in the area, Assy brought together the talents of artists who "until that moment had been strangers to the life of the Church"[134] under the direction of Marie-Alain Couturier, O.P. (1897-1954).[135] These artists, including Henri Matisse, Fernand Léger, Jean Lurcat, Pierre Bonnard, Georges Braque, Marc Chagall, and Jacques Lipchitz, provided the church at Assy with a wealth of interior and exterior decoration. Although the church was consecrated in 1950, the Assy project unleashed a storm of protest from conservative Roman Catholics who believed that neither the artists employed nor their mode of artistic expression was appropriate for a Roman Catholic church.[136] The Liturgical Arts Society entered the debate by making Assy the cover story of the February, 1951, issue of *Liturgical Arts*. In a brief introductory statement, Couturier said that although it had been a risk to commission art:

"born during a very first contact with Christian values, all we knew of those great spirits sufficed to assure us of the gravity and respect with which they would treat the sacred mysteries. And it is a joy to be able to say that even in this, they exceeded our expectations. The Spirit breathes where it will."[137]

Although the comments by Richard J. Douaire that accompanied the pictures of Assy in this 1951 issue were uniformly favorable toward both the concept and the result of the collaboration of the artists,[138] his earlier comments on the Assy project in *Liturgical Arts* had not been as laudatory. In August, 1950, he had been very firm

141

that because Georges Rouault was a "thorough and almost mystical Christian" the windows he had designed for Assy were decidedly the most successful parts of the design, "alive and [seeming to] vibrate with deep inspiration." "The rest is art," Douaire continued, "great art, indeed, but we require something more."[139] In the years following the consecration of the Assy church, other writers for *Liturgical Arts* echoed the theme that great art was not necessarily sacred art.[140] The answer to the problem of providing adequate religious art for the Roman Catholic Church was to induce more Roman Catholics to contribute to the task, not to involve non-Christians.

The Liturgical Arts Society itself admitted that self-professed Roman Catholic artists of deep faith and real genius were the ideal agents for the building and furnishing of Roman Catholic places of worship. But lacking them, the Church has every right to turn to "'men of good will' who possess the secret of dynamic technique."[141] In the end, the Society and *Liturgical Arts* pursued the idea that all great art is, by its very nature, inspired, and therefore sacred on a deep and elemental level. The Society advocated that the Church look for religious truth in a work of art and, when found, attribute it rightly to the work of the Holy Spirit, whether or not the artist openly acknowledges it:

"Instead of advocating an ostrich-like policy of pretending to ignore a great human medium, it would seem right to do now what the Church has done from the beginning — invite all the best artists to show what they, in their own fashion, can do toward embellishing the House of God, inform them plainly of the needs of the Christian community, and then judge the result."[142]

THE ROLE OF NON-WESTERN CHRISTIANS

A final word needs to be said about the Liturgical Arts Society's attitude toward the contribution of non-Western Christians to the evolution of Roman Catholic religious art and architecture. Although the right of native peoples to self-determination with regard to their own religious and artistic expression was rarely raised by the Society before 1950,[143] both Lavanoux and Binsse showed early evidence of openness to the problems involved in transplanting Western art to missionary lands. "One should always try to express

142

Catholicism in an art that bears a definite relation to the place for which it is intended as well as the time in which it exists," Binsse wrote to a colleague in 1934.[144] In the early 1940s, Lavanoux came under the influence of Marie-Alain Couturier, O.P.,[145] who taught him valuable lessons about the boundaries between sacred and secular art:

"I went to Altman's one sunny day to watch [Couturier] at work purchasing material for his own vestments. He roamed the ladies' dress department. When he asked the saleslady for a sample of a particularly fine white material draped on a mannequin, she immediately excused herself and ran to the floor manager, who hurried back to assure Fr. Couturier that Altman's had a very good and well-stocked religious goods department."[146]

This sense that the goods of the whole world were available for the Church's use, regardless of how they had been categorized, was to be an important foundation for the Society's later commitment to the indigenization of religious art and architecture.

But during the Society's early years, there was more than enough work closer to home to keep it occupied, and in any case, it had no real access to sources of information on work being done in the mission field.[147] Consequently, for nearly 20 years of publication, *Liturgical Arts* devoted itself to art and architecture in the United States, with some attention to those Western countries to which it had ready editorial access.[148] But in the fall of 1950, there was a dramatic widening of the Society's sphere of interest. This was due in part to the more general awareness of questions of indigenization but more specifically, to Lavanoux's participation in the First International Congress of Catholic Artists.[149] In Rome, a visit to an exhibition of missionary arts aroused in Lavanoux an intense interest in "investigating the possibilities of a sane evolution of religious art and architecture in a largely unknown situation."[150]

Between 1950 and 1960, grants from the Grace Fund[151] allowed Lavanoux to travel the world and to make extensive editorial contacts with those who were on the front lines of the quest for an indigenous religious art for non-Western Christians. This "editorial network" would provide *Liturgical Arts* with a constant source of material on indigenous Christian art, resulting in issues of the magazine devoted to the art and architecture of Mexico (23:3), India (22:1), the Philippines (21:4), Japan (21:3), and Africa (26:3 and 26:4). Each of these issues contained photographs and articles on the pre-Christian native art of the area, the theoretical and practical problems encountered in adapting native art forms to a Christian point of view (and vice versa), and examples of modern attempts at an indigenous Roman Catholic art and architecture. (The logical outcome of this interest in indigenization was perhaps the 1967 issue of *Liturgical Arts* devoted to a theoretical "Chapel on the Moon."[152])

During this period, *Liturgical Arts* explored many aspects of the process of the indigenization of Roman Catholic art and architecture. Although the Society was clearly committed to the full assimilation of native art with Western,[153] the difficulties seemed, at times, insurmountable. There was, in the first instance, strong opposition from those who believed that Latin art forms were so closely wedded to the essence of Christianity, that they were the only acceptable artistic language for the entire world:

"In Professor Raoul Villedieu of France we have an exponent of the theory that the Latin soul encompasses all that is good and holy and little is left for the non-Latin world to boast about. In his paper 'The Latin Soul in the Figurative Arts,' our friend from France calls the Latin soul a flag of three colors: clarity, beauty, sanctity. The Latin soul is the fruit of Christian virtues and the flower of Mediterranean greatness. The Latin soul has, as artisans, after Jesus and the Evangelists, Cicero and Virgil, the martyrs and troubadours, Dante and St. Francis, St. Louis and St. Joan of Arc, and the architects of all of the great cathedrals."[154]

Although many Western missionaries had adopted the idea that their task was to "rid converts of all pagan evidences,"[155] this same attitude had come to prevail among native converts, "who wanted to celebrate their new found faith by forgetting, as soon as possible, all physical elements of their religious past."[156] As Lavanoux reported after an extensive African tour:

"The trouble is that the literate minority, through an inferiority complex on a national scale, repudiated its own culture in favor of that of the 'whites.' They unconsciously equate all efforts to introduce native forms in Church art with the oft-expressed wish of Europeans that they 'keep in their place' and 'develop along their own lines,' which is the official policy of the Union of South Africa."[157]

But the Liturgical Arts Society was firm in its conviction that these sentiments should not be allowed to prevail and that every effort should be made to ensure that the art of native peoples make "a contribution to the outworking of the missionary command of Christ."[158] Underlying this discussion was the belief that "if Christianity penetrates into the sources from which an artistic expression arises, that which arises will be naturally impressed with Christian character."[159] Nevertheless, according to one *Liturgical Arts* article, responsible and successful adaptation of native art could only take place when a number of conditions were met. Adaptation of indigenous art and architecture to Christian purposes, claimed the author of this article, takes place on three levels: the material (including adaptation to climate, landscape, labor conditions, and available materials), the "ideational" (respect for the nature of the building materials, the environment, and simplicity and clarity of design), and the pastoral (respect for native spirituality).[160] A Christian art which took these principles seriously would be able to speak to the "deepest symbolic meanings of a civilization"[161] and thereby reach into the heart of its spiritual expression.

But indigenous art was not simply seen as a matter of giving Christian themes native treatments. Writing about the state of religious art in India, Indian Jesuit S. Nohonra explained that:

". . . the task facing the Indian Christian artists today is virtually that of creating a new genre: the mere adoption of Indian forms will not do — there must be an adaptation not only to the new Christian content they must embody but also the changing setting of modern India. And this calls for creative Christian vision rooted in Indian tradition."[162]

The Society, then, sought a new genre, a native rendering of Christian truth "which would evolve normally and in a healthy fashion without too much of an overlay of Western notions."[163] Native Christian artists, trained in their own country and tradition and deeply inspired and guided by the Christian message, were the key to the revitalization of art for non-Western Roman Catholicism.

It is clear that the Liturgical Arts Society believed that indigenous art and architecture had much to contribute to the development of missionary Christianity, and that non-Western Christians should have the right to self-determination in these matters without the interference of Western notions of appropriate Christian art. But while it actively promoted the idea that the indigenization of liturgical art and architecture was a powerful, and too often neglected, tool in the conversion of native peoples to Christianity, the Society also believed that the principles of indigenization had much to teach Western Christianity about the relationship between art and religion. First, Western Christians could profit from native peoples' clear sense of the deep connections between art and spirituality. In addition, indigenous art had the power to uncover the meaning of spiritual poverty and simplicity, and of basic and direct approaches to artistic expression. And finally, the adaptation of native art and the employment of native craftsmen were seen to be matters of social justice in countries where the import of foreign elements compromised the native economy. All of these issues, taken together, convinced the Liturgical Arts Society that intensive exploration of the role of indigenous Christian art was vitally important, and the interest of Vatican Council II was seen as clear confirmation of the rightness of this work.

Constant re-evaluation of the problem of who is to decide what liturgical art is appropriate for the Roman Catholic Church occupied the Liturgical Arts Society from its very first meeting to the final issue of *Liturgical Arts* magazine. Clearly, each of the participants in the discussion — clergy and laity, artists and bishops, non-Roman Catholics and non-Christians — had something to contribute, to one extent or another. Overall, the Society seemed to place high value on expertise, artistic and cultural, and on the decision-making power of ecclesiastical authorities.

The striving for artistic quality seems to have driven the Liturgical Arts Society to increasingly wider definitions of Church and ministry. But it was soon recognized that the hierarchy did not always guide the Church in the direction the Society would have it go in matters of religious art and that one might find legitimate authority in other places in and outside of the Church. In the end, the Society became convinced that legitimate authority was identified not by

146

rank in the institutional structure but by evidence of the working of the Holy Spirit. If that evidence was found in the less developed countries or among non-Roman Catholic artists, then it was to be accepted as readily as if it had been found in Rome.

CHAPTER NINE

The Issue of Appropriate Liturgical Art

LITURGICAL ART: A "GOLDEN AGE"?

During the decade in which the Liturgical Arts Society was founded, various manifestations of a romanticism of the past were continuing to have wide influence on the forms of literature, art, and architecture by which Roman Catholicism sought to express itself. For many Roman Catholics, this nostalgia manifested itself as neo-medievalism, and was reinforced by Vatican II's emphasis on medieval philosophy, theology, and forms of monasticism and the chant. In part a reaction to the rise of industrialism and mechanization, this romantic interest often took the form of revivalism, a desire to recapture and reproduce a more humane and cohesive era.

In the United States, there were many examples of the flowering of medieval nostalgia. James J. Walsh's *The Thirteenth: Greatest of Centuries*,[1] originally published in 1907, was immensely popular among clergy and laity alike in the 1920s, giving neo-medievalism the status of doctrine in the minds of many Roman Catholics. For Walsh, Gothic architecture was a principal piece of evidence for the superiority of the 13th century:

"No more perfect effort at worthy worship of the Most High has ever been accomplished than is to be seen in the Gothic cathedrals. . . . [The 13th-century cathedrals] are the compendious expression of the art impulses of a glorious century. Every single detail of the Gothic Cathedral is not only worthy of study, but of admiration."[2]

Although the medieval romanticism of this period had important intellectual and literary manifestations, one particularly identifiable feature was the attempt to reproduce this Gothic architecture. (Indeed, Kenneth Clark has called neo-Gothic architecture "the clearest symptom of Romanticism."[3]) Popularized throughout the Anglican communion through the efforts of the Cambridge Camden Society,[4] neo-Gothic architecture had been transplanted to the 20th century Roman Catholic Church in America through the work of James Renwick,[5] Ralph Adams Cram,[6] and Bertram Grosvenor Goodhue. But although the Gothic Revival has been described as "an episode in the history of taste,"[7] for Roman Catholics in the 1920s, it was much more than that. It was a path to authentic religious life. By restoring to the Church the architecture of the Great Age of Faith, Christianity would itself be restored to its former vitality.

THE LITURGICAL ARTS SOCIETY AND THE NEO-GOTHIC REVIVAL

Given the pervasiveness of neo-Gothic revivalism, it would be surprising if a number of the founding members of the Liturgical Arts Society had not been deeply affected by it. But the records of the 1927 and 1928 Portsmouth Priory meetings show that stylistic revivalism was rarely, if ever, a topic of discussion, and the betterment of ecclesiastical art was not explicitly tied to medieval styles or methods of construction. Most of the young founders were, however, then employed by architectural firms that catered to the neo-Gothic tastes of the American Roman Catholic Church of the period, and this cannot help but have colored their attitudes. Charles D. Maginnis, the president of the Liturgical Arts Society for its first four years, headed the architectural firm of Maginnis & Walsh, which built many neo-Gothic parish churches, collegiate chapels, and public and educational facilities,[8] and he wrote and lectured extensively on the natural superiority of the Gothic style for the Roman Catholic Church.[9] In addition, the brother of Society chaplain John LaFarge was selected as architect for the Cathedral of Saint John the Divine on the strength of his neo-Gothic competition designs.[10] Founding members Oliver Reagan, J. Sanford Shanley, and Jacques André Fouilhoux were all engaged in the design and construction of Gothic churches for Roman Catholics. It was likely, then, that when many members of the Portsmouth Priory group thought of the improvement of Roman Catholic art and architecture, they naturally assumed that this improvement would consist of a return to medieval design.

This belief was certainly represented in the early numbers of *Liturgical Arts*. Although there was a general editorial policy stating that work of the Society's officers and directors would not be highlighted in *Liturgical Arts*, the impact of the Gothic ideal on Roman Catholic church building is clearly evident in early issues of the magazine.[11] Volume 1 featured the newly erected neo-Gothic Church of St. Vincent Ferrar, New York City (Bertram Grosvenor Goodhue, architect)[12] and contained a substantial article on the Church of the Sacred Heart (Pittsburgh, Pennsylvania).[13] The A.W.N. *Pugin* retrospective[14] and a description of the Church of St. Catherine of Siena (New York, New York)[15] gave neo-medieval concerns a prominent place in subsequent issues of *Liturgical Arts*. In addition, articles on art history emphasized the importance of research into the sources of the Gothic revival.[16]

It would be a mistake, however, to assume hastily from this attention to neo-Gothic churches in *Liturgical Arts* that the Liturgical Arts Society had absorbed medieval romanticism in its entirety and that the Middle Ages was the Church's architectural "Golden Age." In the first place, neo-Gothic churches by no means have a monopoly of editorial attention in *Liturgical Arts*. Neo-Romanesque churches, such as the Church of the Holy Child (New York, New York),[17] and churches in neo-Byzantine style, such as the Church of the Most Precious Blood (Astoria, New York),[18] appear with some regularity in the early issues of *Liturgical Arts*.[19]

The articles that make up the 1933 retrospective issue on the architecture and writings of A. W. N. Pugin provide additional evidence of some disillusionment with the idea of neo-medievalism:

"The trouble was that Pugin made two fundamental mistakes. The first was in failing to see that art and religion were two different things; the second, in believing that only one form of art — the Gothic — was suitable for Christians. The origin of these errors is plain enough. . . . It was but a step from finding Catholicism through the Gothic to the belief that Gothic was the only true Catholic — or, as he preferred to say, 'Christian' — architecture."[20]

150

In spite of the presence of neo-Gothic church buildings in *Liturgical Arts*, the Society was quite emphatic that the architectural return to a medieval *âge d'or* would not serve the Church of the future:

"In the recent past, Catholic architecture has been a mere reproduction and adaptation of the inspired works of the Middle Ages, because of the current notion that only by building in these styles would Catholic tradition be maintained. This is a misinterpretation of the Church's conservatism."[21]

The Society's reaction against neo-medievalism coalesced in the case made against giving Ralph Adams Cram, the chief protagonist of neo-Gothic church architecture, a leadership role in the work of the organization.[22] Certainly, some (although by no means all[23]) of the criticism against Cram was the result of the desire of a few of the Society's leaders to move away from neo-Gothic as the Church's only stylistic alternative. Maurice Lavanoux would later remark that much of the Society's work was directed toward reversing the trend that Cram had so clearly advocated. "Cram's insistence on the virtue of one style to the practical exclusion of any other manifestation," Lavanoux reflected, "set back religious art in the United States about fifty years."[24]

ANTI-REVIVALISM AND THE LITURGICAL ARTS SOCIETY

There were many reasons for the Liturgical Arts Society's refusal to embrace the contemporary Roman Catholic enthusiasm for the Middle Ages as a golden age of religious art and architecture. One of these was the belief of many of the Society's founding members that all forms of stylistic revivalism were perversions of the creative enterprise.

Perhaps the most vocal critic of the revivalist approach to religious architecture was Maurice Lavanoux. Although Lavanoux was employed as a draftsman for Maginnis & Walsh from 1925 to 1930, he was not enthusiastic about the work the firm was doing and was uncertain about the extent to which he wished to commit his future to it:

"I was faced with the prospect of becoming another cog in the pseudo-Gothic machine in which steel beams and girders were used to *buttress* brick and stone buttresses — the whole miserable

151

fake capped off by plaster vaults on which were painted stone 'joints'."[26]

Lavanoux traced his dissatisfaction with architecture as an "archaeological pastime"[27] to his years in Europe during the war, when he had the opportunity to see and study the great medieval cathedrals. Especially important to the formation of his architectural convictions was a visit to Rheims:

"The Germans were still shelling the city and had bombed the Cathedral. This, in a way, gave me an extraordinary opportunity to study the 'structure' of a gothic cathedral as there was a great hole in the transept walls, and I could *see* how the vault was buttressed by the buttresses and the whole structure was a logical one."[28]

Returning to the United States, Lavanoux's wartime experience convinced him of the futility of building "churches which were Gothic in style but really monumental lies."[29]

Others of the founding members shared Lavanoux's skepticism about the validity of stylistic revivalism as the most appropriate mode of architectural expression for the Church. John Walter Wood, for example, lamented that "America and Europe are strewn with the failures resulting from the unhappy attempts to reproduce or adapt church architecture of the past, in an age economically and artistically unfitted to do so."[30] The addition of Henry Lorin Binsse to the Liturgical Arts Society staff in 1930 further bolstered the Society's move away from the domination of stylistic revivalism. Beginning in November, 1931, Binsse delivered a series of radio lectures on the Society's behalf, in which he argued that the Church could not be truly served by "the imitation of the architecture of the past."[31] The Liturgical Arts Society was convinced that for the first 19th centuries the art of the Church had reflected "a splendid contemporaneousness,"[32] mirroring successive ages of faith. But in the 19th century:

"Church art . . . ended its splendid cycle of fresh and original styles and became as an animal devouring itself. From then on, it has survived on pre-digested styles and stylistics foreign and abhorrent to the true spirit of contemporaneity."[33]

Two important articles, one by Binsse, in July, 1939,[34] and another

152

by Henry Clifford, in August, 1942,[35] outlined the reasons for the death of church art as a vital, living reality. According to Clifford, it was the "depressing wave of industrial literalism, with its atmosphere of coal mines and factory smoke" that had effectively killed the drive for contemporary church art and architecture:

"As the original minds disappeared, there emerged a group of skillful restorers, quacks, one might say, whose nostrums kept the patient functioning through the obscuring use of mirrors."[36]

Binsse attributed the wave of architectural nostalgia to the rise of a fashionable interest in archaeology:

"The 18th century, for some mysterious reason, saw the beginning of a very serious study of archaeology among the "better people" in England. It became fashionable to know about ruins and even to have a ruin on your front lawn. . . . After a little, someone conceived of a thoroughly insane idea, which was to live in your ruin, and the Gothic Revival was born. . . . It is always hard to know whether it was clients who gave architects the idea of building ruins for everyday use, or, *per contra*, it was the architects who sold their clients on the notion. . . . But anyhow, the idea of building in imitation of things spread until everyone forgot how to build in any other way."[37]

Because the United States in the 19th century had not yet found a native form of architectural expression, Binsse continued, and because it looked to Europe for guidance, this archaeological way of thinking about architecture was transplanted to this country and took root. By the time the Liturgical Arts Society was founded, the philosophical and theological underpinnings of this trend were so strong that it was widely believed that the Church had a special responsibility to build according to the styles of the past.[38]

For the Liturgical Arts Society, true art in any age was creative and not imitative.[39] Thus, the second major objection to the neo-Gothic and other revivalist architectural styles was that they were dishonest and therefore contrary to the nature of true art. At the heart of the artistic endeavor was the creative use of the new spiritual and material resources that each age offered, and to return to the agenda of a past age was to violate the divine gift of artistic talent.

Because of these convictions, the Liturgical Arts Society gradually strengthened its stand against the trend toward medieval romanticism and revivalism that was so prevalent in Roman Catholicism during the period between I and II World War.[40]

In its choice of articles and photographs for *Liturgical Arts*, the Society stated over and over again that there were viable alternatives to neo-Gothic, neo-Byzantine, and neo-Romanesque architecture for the Roman Catholic Church. After about 1935, revivalist architecture was only rarely pictured in *Liturgical Arts* and articles on archaeology and art history virtually disappeared, "left to other publications better equipped to handle these matters."[41]

A CONTEMPORARY APPROACH TO TRADITION IN ART

Clearly, the Liturgical Arts Society did not see the recreation of the medieval world as the solution to the Church's architectural poverty. But the use of evidence from the Middle Ages did support the argument for the contemporary approach the Society was seeking. Again and again in the early years, *Liturgical Arts* stressed that the builders of the great medieval churches were themselves concerned with being contemporary: "Why should we not do *as* the medieval builders did, rather than copy *what* they did?"[42] But in order for the Roman Catholic Church to appreciate the value of a contemporary approach to church art and architecture, it would first have to come to a renewed understanding of the term "tradition":

'Christian tradition is that body of doctrine and discipline preached by Christ and the apostles and not committed to them in writing. But the Church, as a living organism, has maintained a living tradition. The term is too often taken to mean a long-established convention, a set of fixed formulae regulating external appearance and performance; a repository of material, precious but inert. Actually, the Christian tradition is an animating spirit, and this spirit should infuse religious art as well as theology."[43]

Tradition, including artistic and architectural tradition, was viewed as a "great stream," a "golden chain to which the present day adds its own link by accepting and loving the world as it is."[44] Again, the Society turned to Jacques Maritain for inspiration in this matter, on several occasions quoting his statement that failing to see tradition

154

as an ongoing reality is "blasphemy against God's government of history." For the Liturgical Arts Society, "nothing is more traditional than handing down the newness of life in God in a contemporary way."[45]

Very often, biological imagery was employed to describe the Christian tradition, and in particular the tradition of Christian art. Growth and decay, motion and inertia, health and disease are recurring metaphors for the state of the Church's architectural expression. Above all, the Liturgical Arts Society stressed that art was to be a vigorous, living thing. "The quality of life is the essential soul of an artwork," wrote architect Barry Byrne in 1933. "Without it, art cannot exist as a reality."[46] Indeed, the Society saw itself as something of a physician to diseased art forms:

"While it is possible to cure a skin disease (and that is what we are suffering from nowadays in the architectural field), the cure must be worked on a living tissue and not on the corpse of fantasy and past dreams."[47]

In using such physiological language, Lavanoux was undoubtedly influenced by his friend Marie-Alain Couturier, who said that just as the Church does not baptize still-born babies, neither should it "baptize" still-born forms of art and architecture.[48]

MODERN ART AND THE LITURGICAL ARTS SOCIETY

Although the Liturgical Arts Society could state with confidence that art for the Church should be "living" and "contemporary," it found it difficult to describe or define what a living Christian art in the 20th century would be. Article I of the Society's (Objects and Standards) stated that the Society "aims at encouraging the evolution of ecclesiastical art along new lines, provided that such work seems expressive of a truly Catholic spirit,"[49] but no further elaboration of this idea is offered in the founding documents.

During the years that followed incorporation, the Society was greatly influenced in the development of this theme by the work of Barry Byrne. Byrne had been a student of Frank Lloyd Wright and was an advocate of modern building principles, methods, and materials. In May, 1933, the Society sponsored a lecture by Byrne, in which he outlined his understanding of modern design for the

Christian Church. His fundamental argument was that the first task of contemporary church architecture was to analyze the function of a structure; then and only then should design begin. The primary function of a church building is the celebration of the Mass, and the church architect must be primarily concerned with housing the altar, the celebrants at it, and the people who come before it:

"The liturgy of the Mass is not for the few, it is for all to follow as intimately as they can. The altar and the worshipers, then, must be as one, or as much so as space and a large number of worshipers permit. The modern church is for the people who build it and of the day which produces it. If it fulfills that function of its use, it is a modern church in the truest sense of the word."[50]

Byrne's insistence on a functionalist approach to ecclesiastical architecture would color the Society's work throughout its history, serving as something of a litmus test of adequate church design.

Beginning in 1938, a series of articles appeared in *Liturgical Arts* that explored the relationship between religion and modern art.[51] Taken together, these articles serve as the Liturgical Arts Society's apology for modern religious art and architecture. The argument can be summarized as follows:

1) Modern art is suitable for the Christian Church because it has the quality of simplicity, offering "a direct oneness of purpose of great driving force with a consequent heightening of desired intensity of emotion."[52] Confining itself to one element at a time, modern treatment of religious themes has a great "teaching power" for modern human beings.

2) The abstract quality of modern art forms corresponds to the abstract quality of mystical experience.[53]

3) Because modern art operates under the principle of economy of expression, it gives religious themes a special dignity, which is "the most adequate to the tradition of ecclesiastical institutions."[54]

4) Modern art tends toward honesty and sincerity. It is therefore most suitable as a setting for the liturgy, which is itself "based on reality and not illusion."[55]

5) Modern art claims only to be the genuine expression of a particu-

lar time and place and asks only that that historical situation be treated with respect. Since liturgical art is always "a function of the life of a community," which is addressed by God in a particular historical moment, modern expression is most appropriate to it.[56]

6) Modern art fully expresses the goals and principles of the liturgical movement.

This last proposition was the one upon which all future arguments for the adequacy of modern art for the Church would ultimately depend. For the Liturgical Arts Society, it is through modern art that the spirit of the liturgy will most surely be conveyed in the 20th century:

"Modern art owes to the liturgy the most perfect and lasting example of application of its principles. . . . In its boundless sincerity, modern art confines itself no longer to a merely historical or aesthetic appreciation of the liturgy but has become susceptible to its metaphysical influence. Cheap sneering at the dark ages has long given room to genuine preparedness, however romantic and irresponsible its foundations may be, for harmonious coordination between nature and supernature in artistic activities."[57]

The Society recognized that the modern approach to church architecture had not yet developed into an architectural "style." Rather, in the early years, the modern was seen as an approach, an attitude toward the problems of church building. But the Society expected that just as a "rational approach"[58] to church architecture in the Middle Ages had led to the style called the Gothic, so, too, would a rational approach to church building in the modern period lead to a modern style. One of the components of this modern style would surely be the acceptance of modern materials and construction methods (such as, for example, the use of reinforced concrete[59]). More important would be a willingness on the part of the artist or architect to follow the form and spirit of the liturgy in the design of churches. Maurice Lavanoux expressed the Society's views on the matter in 1939:

"The *idea* of a Church should come first, its use and requirements; then, and only then, should anyone think of style. As a matter of fact, we feel that style flows from a sensible and logical understanding of the purposes for which a church is built."[60]

For the Liturgical Arts Society, then, a modern *style* of art and architecture would be the natural result of the application of contemporary liturgical and theological principles to the design of church buildings. It would always be a by-product, and never simply an end in itself.

MODERN SACRED ART AND THE CHURCH AT *ASSY*

Just as the decoration of the church at Assy had brought special urgency to the question of non-Christian participation in creating liturgical art,[61] it also provided the occasion for addressing more directly the question of modern art for the Church. Although modern church art and architecture had been given several trials in Europe (and especially in Germany) between World War I and II, the variety and quality of modern expression in the Church of Notre Dame de Tout-Grâce put it at the center of the Church's attention. In the decoration of Assy, Marie-Alain Couturier sought what the Liturgical Arts Society had been seeking (albeit hesitantly) since its inception: "to bring to an end, by means of a direct achievement, the absurd divorce which for the past century has separated the Church from living art."[62] The energy of the bold and innovative designs at Assy gave the Liturgical Arts Society renewed confidence in the stance it had taken on the issue of modern art for the Church and provided a vision of what could be accomplished:

"When Canon Devamy and Fr. Couturier teamed up to produce the Church of Our Lady of Grace at Assy in the heart of the French Alps, a great change came over many of us in our attitude toward religious art. The work of great artists in that little church opened up vistas for the future. [After that] daring adventure, nothing can stop the march of events."[63]

Beginning in 1950, the year that Assy was consecrated, *Liturgical Arts* and the Liturgical Arts Society became increasingly direct and unequivocal in advocating modern art for the Church. Lavanoux seemed to seek out daring ecclesiastical design projects to highlight in *Liturgical Arts*. The work of such notable artists and architects as Marc Chagall, Rudolf Schwartz, André Girard, Jean Charlot, Barry

Byrne, Marcel Breuer, and Georges Rouault was regularly featured. Although the Society's argument for modern art was strengthened after 1950, it shows little real development. In the pages of *Liturgical Arts*, the Society repeated the call for a "living" art, for a contemporary, rather than a nostalgic, architecture, for freedom for those who wished to offer their talents to the Church, and for churches designed "to accommodate the total needs of the community."[64]

THE DEBATE OVER MODERN ART FOR THE CHURCH

There was by no means universal acceptance of the idea that modern art was a suitable form of expression for the Roman Catholic Church. Many believed that any relationship between Roman Catholicism and modern art would do violence to the essence of the Christian faith. The long shadow of the modernist controversy put even the word "modern" under a cloud of suspicion during the Society's early years, giving particular urgency to the matter of appropriate terminology for the kind of work the Society was advocating.[65] "The word *modern* suffers from unfortunate connotations," Lavanoux admitted in 1955, "and the word *contemporary* is equally misleading, [since] anything done today would be contemporary and yet violate all the norms of a living art."[66] (During the McCarthy era, modern art would also be linked with communism, providing political as well as religious difficulties for the use of the term.[67]) But even after the fear of the modernist label had begun to fade, the more generalized fear of the Church's engagement with the world of modern subjectivity through modern art persisted.[68] Many of the most conservative Roman Catholics believed that the forms by which the Church expressed itself could change only when underlying beliefs changed. Since the Church was a permanent and immutable reality, no such change in its visible forms was acceptable.[69]

Other critics of modern art for the Church were disturbed by the strangeness of modern art forms and the lack of objectivity with which the subject matter was treated.[70] During the previous century, religious truth had come to be equated with realism in artistic style. If a person or event in Christian history was not presented realistically in a work of art, it was considered defective or unorthodox and presumed to be tainted with atheism and liberal Christian theology.

And finally, even those who accepted the possibility of *evolution* in religious art, viewed the introduction of modern art as a disruptive *revolution*, an utter breach with the Church's artistic and architectural tradition. Dissonance in music, the lack of ornamentation in architecture, the immaterialization of the human figure in painting, the use of radically new materials in every medium all seemed clear evidence that modern art was outside the boundaries of the Christian art heritage.

The Society had heard these criticisms in various forms since the earliest years of *Liturgical Arts'* publication. Some were of a general nature, offered by Church leaders, architects, and lay people who were "considerably concerned that some Catholic Church leaders [were] encouraging what seemed to be very new and rather startling things in architectural design."[71] Other objections were aimed directly at the Liturgical Arts Society's contribution to the encouragement of modern art for the Church. Frontispieces in *Liturgical Arts* by Georges Rouault and Jean Charlot unleashed a storm of protest from readers.[72] During the first 20 years of *Liturgical Arts'* publication, the Society attempted to give balanced and reasonable answers to each of these objections. The Society's motto in these matters was taken from Ben Jonson: "Art hath an enemy called ignorance,"[73] and in articles, editorials, and the careful selection of letters to the editor it sought to dispel that ignorance. But the Society discovered that it was often arguing against something more than simple personal prejudice; many critics of modern art for the Church were also convinced that the Vatican stood firmly in support of their position.

THE VATICAN, MODERN ART, AND THE LITURGICAL ARTS SOCIETY

On October 27, 1932, on the occasion of the dedication of the new Vatican Picture Gallery, Pius XI made remarks that, in the minds of many Roman Catholics, specifically addressed the question of modern art for the Church.[74] In this address, the Pope said that since "much of the art of the day reverts to the crude forms of the darkest ages," it is therefore unfitting for the service of the Church. Citing canons 1164 (paragraph 1), 1279 (full paragraph 2), and 1296 (paragraph 3) of the Code of Canon Law,[75] Pius XI made it clear that what he referred to as "this unworthy school of art" should be excluded from the building, remodeling, and decoration of churches. Many Roman Catholics viewed this 1932 document as utter condemnation of the ecclesiastical use of modern art.

The Liturgical Arts Society, however, found in the papal address certain phrases that seemed to support its own convictions on the place of modern art in the Church. The Pope had called upon the Church to:

"Open wide the portals and give cordial welcome to every good and progressive development of the approved and venerable Christian traditions, which, in so many centuries of Christian life, in such diversity of circumstances, have given such proof of their inexhaustible capacity to inspire new and beautiful forms, whenever they have been called upon or studied and cultivated by the twofold light of genius and of faith."[76]

Since the Liturgical Arts Society understood the word "tradition" as the ever-new articulation of Christian faith,[77] it could say with conviction that the tradition could include modern art as a "good and progressive development." But Pius XI's address received little public attention, and the Liturgical Arts Society was rarely called upon to defend its actions and attitudes in light of the document.[78] More influential was the pronouncement on sacred art found in *Mediator Dei et Hominum*, promulgated by Pius XII on November 20, 1947.[79]

THE ENCYCLICAL *MEDIATOR DEI*

The Liturgical Arts Society discovered that the 1947 statements on sacred art in *Mediator Dei*, like those in the 1932 address, were open to a variety of interpretations. Certainly, the Society viewed the document as encouragement for its own artistic agenda, but it recognized that others might disagree:

"Those who always look for rules and regulations in neat packages (in areas which can only function properly in an atmosphere of elastic common sense) will find in this papal document arguments to bolster whatever prejudices are entertained at the moment."[80]

Maurice Lavanoux later admitted that he had "never worried unduly about the passage on art in the encyclical *Mediator Dei*" because of its balanced and elastic treatment of the subject. But those who argued against modern art for the Church saw *Mediator Dei* as proof that the Vatican had at last ruled authoritatively in the matter. The encyclical denounced "distortions" and forms of art that shock Christian "taste, modesty, devotion, and shamefully offend the true religious sense." Works of art such as this, the document continued, "must be entirely excluded and banished from our churches like anything else that is not in keeping with the sanctity of the place." For many conservative Roman Catholics, these passages were clear evidence that the use of modern art was absolutely forbidden.

In the years following *Mediator Dei*, the Liturgical Arts Society strove to articulate its own interpretation of the document:

"The much quoted *Mediator Dei* is far more tolerant than some of us. . . . It bans 'distortion and perversion of true art' and open shock to Christian 'taste, modesty, and true religious sense.' All these words allow for various interpretations."[81]

The Society claimed that while modern art may at times display a distortion of *form*, it does not in any way represent a distortion of "true art," and that, conversely, anatomical correctness does not in any way insure that art will not cause "open shock." Over and over again, in response to criticism of its promotion of modern art, the Society quoted *Mediator Dei*'s statement that "modern art should be given true scope in due and reverent service of the Church and the sacred rites."[82] For the Liturgical Arts Society, the beauty of *Mediator Dei* was that it "swept out the rubbish of one very common misunderstanding fostered by salesmen, half-hearted teachers, and superficial magazines that there is a 'liturgical style' of art and architecture."[83]

THE INSTRUCTION OF THE HOLY OFFICE, 1952

The 1952 Instruction of the Holy Office (*De arte sacra*),[84] issued in part as a response to the controversy over the decoration of the church at Assy by nonbelieving artists such as Fernand Léger, was clearly a more conservative (and less ambiguous) document than its predecessors. In its opening paragraphs, the document quotes

Pius X's warning against any form of art that "disturbs or even merely diminishes the piety of the faithful [and] which is unworthy of the House of God."[85] Citing the same canons as did the 1932 address,[86] as well as the more restrictive portions of *Mediator Dei*,[87] *De arte sacra* declared that:

"The objection raised by some that sacred art must be adapted to the needs and circumstances of changing times, is of no weight. For sacred art, which originated with Christian society, has its own ends from which it can never diverge and its proper function which it can never abandon."[88]

If the restrictive tone of this document disturbed the Society's convictions about the suitability of modern art for the Church, there was no evidence of it. The document was simply not mentioned, either in the pages of *Liturgical Arts* or in correspondence. (In 1964, the Society did finally refer to the Instruction as having been a "disturbing document."[89])

In August, 1959, only seven years after the publication of *De arte sacra*, the Liturgical Arts Society took great pleasure in announcing the addition of several contemporary works of art to the Vatican museum.[90] Accompanying the report in *Liturgical Arts* was a long quotation from an address delivered on the occasion by the director of the Vatican museum:

"This is only a continuation of the close relations the Church has always had with the finest artists of every age. . . . The Church has always collected the best art of each age and in centuries past has called the greatest artists to her own service. Today, with this small and modest collection, the Church wishes to give a demonstration of her encouragement and good relations with the artists of this age."[91]

This positive action on the part of the Vatican gave the Society renewed confidence in its struggle to promote a contemporary style of religious art and architecture. "With Rouault, Utrillo, Jacques Villon, Zadkin, and others admitted to the Vatican Museum," the editor continued, "I wonder what the modernistically-mad worriers will now use for ammunition?!"[92]

The 1950s had been something of a watershed in the matter of modern art for the Church, although by the middle of the decade the prophetic work of M.-A. Couturier at Assy and the positive tone of *Mediator Dei* had provoked an intense conservative reaction. During this period, criticism of the Society and of *Liturgical Arts* for its support of modern liturgical art increased dramatically. Many subscriptions and memberships were lost. But the design and construction of modern churches in Germany and France continued,[93] and with the addition of modern art works to the Vatican museum, it seemed to the Society that it had weathered the storm and that brighter days for modern art were ahead.

MODERN SACRED ART COMES OF AGE

The *Constitution on the Sacred Liturgy* [94] (as well as the conciliar allocution by Pope John XXIII which preceded it,[95]) was further confirmation that the Church had at last found room for modern art. In the chapter "Sacred Art and Sacred Furnishings," the *Constitution* affirmed the relationship between the Church and "the art of our own days," and encouraged bishops and others in authority to seek out the best in religious art. Although the *Constitution* used the same language as *Mediator Dei* in banning art that is "repugnant to faith, morals, and Christian piety,"[96] it was the "lack of artistic worth, mediocrity, and pretense" that identified such works. Five months after the *Constitution* was promulgated, after the death of John XXIII, the new Pope Paul VI offered additional reflections on sacred art in the allocution *Le nobili espressioni*.[97] This document was particularly encouraging to the Society in that it was specifically aimed at "reestablishing the friendship between the Church and artists":

"But to be sincere and daring . . . we admit that we, too, have caused trouble. We have caused you trouble because we have imposed on you as a first canon that of imitation, on you who are creators, vivacious people, spurting a thousand new ideas and a thousand innovations. We have this style, and we must adapt ourselves to it; we have this tradition, and we must be faithful to it; we have these masters, and we must follow them; we have these canons, and there is no way out. We have placed a lead hood over you. We may as well say it, pardon us!"[98]

Undoubtedly, the Liturgical Arts Society felt that its aspirations for a positive relationship between modern art and the Roman Catholic Church had been realized in these documents. There seemed little more left for the Liturgical Arts Society to do but to affirm and promote them.

While a few influential Roman Catholics continued to speak out against artistic innovation,[99] modern art and architecture were no longer contested issues in the Church. The atmosphere of the 1960s allowed the Society to give more nuanced evaluations of the various manifestations of ecclesiastical modern art, which it had been unable to do when the genre itself was under attack.

THE ISSUE OF ABSTRACT ART

One of the most difficult questions addressed by the Liturgical Arts Society was the value of abstract art as a form of Christian artistic expression. It was suggested as early as 1954[100] that abstract paintings, glass, mosaics, and textiles might find their place in liturgical art, and the decoration of the Church of the Sacred Heart at Audincourt was cited as an example. In the article that accompanied the photographs of Audincourt, the author claimed that abstract art was a valid form of Christian expression because:

"Certain tendencies in modern art are essentially born out of the need to free itself from dependence on the external visual reality. This in no way implies that this external reality is being rejected. Rather, it is possible that it is being more fully realized. The artist seeks to respond to deeper forces, which live in us individually and collectively. He seeks to respond to them, to identify them, and finally to recreate them into a new visual reality."[101]

But the Society felt it necessary to make an editorial disclaimer to this argument, saying that the article had been published "as a counterweight to the vastly over-prevalent, pseudo-traditional religious art in the other direction."[102]

Beginning about 1960, however, the Liturgical Arts Society had begun to suggest more forcefully that the absence of recognizable subject matter could be a barrier to the liturgical use of abstract art. Although the Society constantly affirmed the freedom of artists to follow their creative instincts, "any art which contains no recall, no evocation of observed reality" was seen to have limited value to the

165

Christian community.[103] It was argued that artistic liberty was useless to the Church if the result was art that required the "continuous presence of the artist to express his work to the faithful."[104] Without appeal to the collective religious memory of the Church, abstract art ran the risk of becoming "mere decoration:"[105]

"It is possible to consider works of 'abstract art' as valid in themselves, but it cannot be objected that the painting, for example, which does not convey at least a glimmer of reality to the members of the congregation is not *appropriate for use* in a church."[106]

It was granted that "there might be more spiritual value in abstract art than in sentimental representations"[107] and that a fine piece of abstract art would be preferable to "the pap which is fed to so many of us." But the Society continually hoped that it could find a creative middle ground between these two extremes.[108]

Abstract art raised forcefully the question of the starkness and sterility that marked many church buildings designed after Vatican Council II.

"[There is the] notion, so prevalent at the moment, that the simplicity of new, multipurpose church interiors needs no visual embellishments — no paintings, murals, mosaics, sculpture, perhaps only an occasional banner."[109]

Although this sterility was decidedly preferable to the "old-fashioned, dull, stencil-decoration which seemed to be the sacred cow of church embellishment,"[110] the Society believed that a church interior should possess the quality of hospitality and that tapestries, statuary, and other art forms could "clothe it with warmth."[111] *Liturgical Arts* editorialized:

"It took a long time . . . to get rid of the stencil decoration, and we have at last reached the bottom of that barrel. It seems that now is the time to pour in the work of first rate . . . painters and sculptors — otherwise we will have been rid of one cliche to fall into another."[112]

The clinical approach to church architecture had some ardent proponents, who took their inspiration from the central principles of the liturgical movement. They claimed that the interior of a church should be empty, since it was the community itself that was the primary religious symbol and the only visual element whose presence required a sacred space. "Sacred art in a church," these architects said, "is a distraction to the positive current liturgical atmosphere."[113] The Liturgical Arts Society argued that those who held this opinion refused to take seriously the power of art in Christian life and that, like the neo-Gothicists, they wished to put a "stop to the normal and healthy swing of the pendulum of life."[114] As a further response, the Society continued to encourage the work of artists in all media, so that their work might become better known and thus find a place in newly designed church buildings.

Although these issues touching upon abstract art had not been fully resolved by the time the Liturgical Arts Society disbanded in 1972, the group could look back on its work with considerable satisfaction. Its efforts to make peace between modern art and the Church in the United States had brought together artists, architects, theologians, and liturgists to forge new and creative options for contemporary religious expression. Over the years, the Society had come under severe criticism for its stance on the place of modern art in the Church. Bishops,[115] clergy,[116] lay people,[117] and even some of the leaders of the American liturgical movement[118] had spoken out in opposition to the Society's position in the matter.[119] Because the Liturgical Arts Society took art seriously, not as mere decoration but as an integral part of Christian life, such criticisms had left its leaders disappointed, though not discouraged. Because the Society took history seriously, as a manifestation of God's will for the Church, it could be bold and emphatic in its approach to contemporary religious art. Indeed, for the Liturgical Arts Society, the modern period of religious art and architecture had all the earmarks of true greatness:

"Freed from the obsession of copying monuments of a day that is past, and likewise freed from the fetish for naked structural simplicity, modern American architecture may well be on its way to its own golden age."[120]

But, at the same time, the Society's view of history forced it to admit that its call for a modern art for the Church was conditioned by the needs and demands of the Church in the 20th century, and such art was not necessarily of perpetual value. The Society's work had been founded on the principle that each age added its own link to the golden chain of tradition, its own contribution to the life of the Church. Even when the Society's own agenda was established as the norm, it was understood that the Christian faith would always call forth fresh forms of self-expression.

CONCLUSION

The Contribution of The Liturgical Arts Society

THE LITURGICAL ARTS SOCIETY IN HISTORICAL AND THEO-
LOGICAL CONTEXT

The period between the First and Second World Wars was a time of
transition for American Roman Catholicism.[1] The world around it
was beginning to come to terms with the forces of modernity, unleashed during the previous century, which were compelling a
transformation in the ways of thinking about the human person
and society. As the Church at large sought to insulate itself from a
world which believed it could create its own future,[2] Roman Catholics in the United States were searching for a self-definition which
took seriously both their religious heritage and their experience as
Americans.

At the same time, a new generation of American Roman Catholics
was coming into its own. Many had become affluent during the
war years, and in the 1920s the first substantial numbers of Roman
Catholics were graduating from prestigious Ivy League universities, anxious to make a contribution to their Church and to society.
Taking their inspiration from the resurgence of Roman Catholic intellectual life in Europe, these individuals participated in the quest
for religious identity by forging the foundations of an American intellectual revival.[3]

By the last half of the 1920s, this intensified intellectual activity had
made an impact on nearly all aspects of Roman Catholic life: education and politics, theology and literature, social welfare and liturgy.
But there was one area of life that had been left relatively un-
touched by the flowering of Roman Catholic intellectual life: ecclesiastical art and architecture. Most of the existing churches had

169

been built before the war, during the period of transplanted ethnic values and tastes, but even those which were being erected in the 1920s were inspired by a nostalgic and sentimental religious ideal. To compound the problem, catalog sales houses made a good living from catering to the sentimental tastes of most American Roman Catholics, and flooded churches with poorly-designed and tasteless mass-produced furnishings, statues, vestments, and altarware.

The fourteen young men who gathered at Portsmouth Priory in the fall of 1927 were very much children of the American Roman Catholic intellectual revival. With few exceptions,[4] they were financially secure, Ivy-League educated, convinced of the rightness of a revitalized Scholasticism, and talented enough to put it to work toward changing the face of American Roman Catholic art and architecture. As a group, they mirrored the conflicting strains in the Roman Catholicism of the period between the wars, the longing for a positive identity and status in a society dominated by Anglo-Saxon Protestantism and, at the same time, the fear of succumbing entirely to the forces at work in the present age. They combined romantic medieval nostalgia, intellectual energy, optimism, social conscience, and ambivalence about the value of technology.

In a very real sense, the dialogue between the Church and modernity was played out, in microcosm, among the early members of the Liturgical Arts Society. As we have seen, those individuals who felt that the Church could not come to terms with the modern world without losing its essential identity soon discontinued their association with the Liturgical Arts Society,[5] while those more optimistic about the relationship came to dominate it.[6] As a result, during most of the Society's history its agenda was shaped by the desire to make peace between modernity and the Roman Catholic Church through the medium of ecclesiastical art and architecture.

THE GOALS OF THE LITURGICAL ARTS SOCIETY

There were several elements in the Society's agenda, some made explicit, some left unarticulated. The first of the Society's goals was to embody the principles of the liturgical movement in the design of church buildings and furnishings.

"The theologian and the artist have the power to infuse our ever-

170

growing life into the religious arts, and it is within such collaboration that we, as Christians, can find solutions in humble and willing acceptance of the primacy of the liturgy. For within this primacy is contained the seeds of a dynamic and creative tradition and our freedom from inveterate prejudices."[7]

As the reform agenda of the liturgical movement changed, every step of that change was mirrored by changes in the Liturgical Arts Society's agenda for the reform of ecclesiastical design. Attention to rubrics led to the call for rubrical correctness in the design of altars, tabernacles, and altarware; focus on the spirit of the liturgy led to the demand for churches which proclaimed the public nature of Christian worship; emphasis on full participation of the faithful resulted in the call for a free-standing altar and a more hospitable sacred space; and the importance and dignity of the liturgy freed from accretions was mirrored in the Society's plea for honesty of materials and simplicity of design.

The second item on the Society's agenda was to make actual changes in Roman Catholic church architecture based upon these liturgical principles. The sentimental fakery of neo-stylistic church buildings, with decoration "stuck on like band-aids on a cancer,"[8] which were so prevalent at the time of the Society's founding, were to be replaced by those which were honest, simple, and functional. Undoubtedly, in the forty-four years of the Society's existence, the face of Roman Catholic ecclesiastical art and architecture did change dramatically, and it did change in the direction of closer adherence to liturgical principles. But the extent to which the Liturgical Arts Society was directly responsible for that change is more difficult to determine. At its height, *Liturgical Arts* had only slightly more than 2500 subscribers. Even assuming that some of these were library subscriptions (giving several people access to each issue) only a very small number of American Roman Catholics saw *Liturgical Arts* or knew directly of the Society's work at any given time.

The leaders of the Society recognized this problem, and admitted that it could be argued that "the magazine appeals only to those who were already in agreement, and does not reach nor does it influence the greater number of those in need of basic instruction."[9]

However, some of the Society's members did have significant impact on American ecclesiastical architecture, and their work was undoubtedly encouraged and informed by the Society. Over the course of the organization's history, at least fifty American bishops and a number of architects who did considerable church work were members.

In one particular case, we can document the direct influence of the Liturgical Arts Society on an important piece of church architecture. In 1958, the pastor of St. Francis de Sales Church, Muskegon, Michigan, a member of the Society, was given permission to build a new church. During the process of deciding on an architect, the name Marcel Breuer was suggested. Breuer was contacted, but when the question of his fee was raised, the pastor became discouraged, feeling that the design costs were too great a percentage of the small amount budgeted for the project. A short while later, the pastor and the chairman of the diocesan building committee attended a lecture by Maurice Lavanoux at the University of Notre Dame:

"I shall never forget [his] advice to the pastors in the audience that afternoon. 'If you have a lot of money to spend, you can hire the usual type of "church" architect, but if you have limited funds then you must look for the highest type of professional competence.' At a meeting of the [building] committee the next week, Marcel Breuer was unanimously selected as architect and the result is St. Francis de Sales, Muskegon."[10]

The church of St. Francis de Sales is, by most assessments, one of the great pieces of American church architecture. It is the only parish church which Breuer was ever commissioned to build, and without the timely intervention of the Liturgical Arts Society, it would probably remain today a sketch on Breuer's pad. St. Francis and other churches like it which were built in direct response to and conformity with the Liturgical Arts Society's liturgical and architectural principles, stand today as monuments to the life of the Society.

Unfortunately, for every St. Francis de Sales that was built, there were also erected four or five prominent and influential buildings which directly contradicted the Society's liturgical and architectural principles. The publicity surrounding the construction of the National Shrine of the Immaculate Conception in Washington put it at the center of Roman Catholic attention during the mid-1950s, sending a clear message that stylistic revivalism was still the most adequate architectural expression for the American Church. Many began to wonder why the Society did not wield more influence in the situation:

"We have received a number of telephone calls in which the speaker wanted to know, in no uncertain terms, what we were going to do to stop certain building operations in Washington. Our demurrers dropped sarcastic hints that twenty-five years of any Society's existence should yield a greater measure of influence or authority than we, at the moment, can exercise in any one case."[11]

But the Society was not intimidated by the ecclesiastical machinery and high finance which produced the National Shrine, believing that humility and simplicity would eventually be victorious.

"In a way it is ironic, but work for the Church when operating on a subsistence level because of indifference in certain quarters, is more deeply productive in the long run then [sic] the more glamorous undertakings bolstered by papal titles and elaborate banquets in fancy hotels."[12]

(As financial constraints became more and more a factor in church building, churches designed in accordance with the Society's principles were indeed more economical than were pseudo-Gothic and Romanesque designs which were always very expensive to build.)

In addition to the distress caused by well-publicized examples which displayed all the errors which the Society strove to correct, further discouragement came when good churches were "vandalized," due to changes in ecclesiastical personnel. A close friend of the Liturgical Arts Society, Fr. Edward Sutfin, working on a limited budget in the 1950s, had produced a wonderfully gracious and engaging sacred space in a tiny church in Montgomery Center, Vermont. Over the course of five years, Sutfin had introduced a free-standing altar, a large baptismal font surrounded by murals by Robert Bonnette, vestments by Marywood Studios, and a fine set of stations by Lambert-Rucki. Sutfin reported what happened after he left the parish:

"More news from Montgomery and, of course, worse. Am really

just about holding together with the prospect of seeing five years of patient labor going to pieces in just a few days of progressive demolition. They now have a galaxy of plaster statues and no participation whatsoever. Stations go out as soon as possible."[13]

In the end, despite these disappointments, the Liturgical Arts Society felt that it had made some important contributions to the American Roman Catholic Church by giving the principles of the liturgical movement artistic and architectural expression. At the time of the Society's demise, much of its liturgical design agenda was widely accepted, and many churches built as a result of their direct intervention were being (and would continue to be) appreciated and used by Christian communities.

CREATING A HEALTHY ATMOSPHERE FOR THE ARTS OF THE CHURCH

The final goal which the Liturgical Arts Society had set for itself was "to help in creating an atmosphere, a climate, in which good work will be produced in a normal, healthy manner."[14] The Society was "not trying to offer solutions for all problems in religious art and architecture, but only to point the way . . . to offer the impulse of a fresh start."[15]

Part of this task of establishing a climate involved convincing artists and architects that the Church would rejoice in their work, rather than impede it. Many of the most talented artists had sincerely believed that a Church commission necessarily required a compromise and restriction of their creativity, and the Liturgical Arts Society worked diligently to convey the message that "to work for the Church is not to subject oneself to the inhibiting of their talents, but rather will be a context within which talent will be freed for its full flowering of genius."[16] Undoubtedly, *Liturgical Arts'* editorial policy of publishing the work of the very best artists and architects of the time — Rouault, Chagall, and Breuer, for example — was a great encouragement to young artists searching for commissions. Much of the success of this work can be attributed to the special gifts of Maurice Lavanoux, whose "gentle openmindedness was able to coax and encourage creative genius from many artists who were timid or unsure of their work."[17]

174

On the other hand, the Liturgical Arts Society also sought to make changes in the Church which would make it more accepting of the work of the most talented artists and architects. One-third of the Society's membership was clergy and much of the material in *Liturgical Arts* was directed toward making them more familiar with the principles and process of ecclesiastical design, and with the work of the most competent and sympathetic artists and architects. Lectures at seminaries, convents, and parish churches were aimed at dispelling the fear of genuine creative energy.

In 1960, after thirty years of slow and painstaking work on the national level, the Society was given the opportunity to make a wider contribution to creating a climate within which the arts could flourish and develop. Through the good offices of long-time friend of the Society Joachim Nabuco (who was one of the members of the Pontifical Commission Preparatory to the Second Vatican Council) Lavanoux was asked to serve as a consultant to the Subcommission on Sacred Art of the Pontificial Commission on the Sacred Liturgy.[18] In his notes submitted to the subcommission,[19] Lavanoux argued for an official Vatican statement on art which would be "positive" and "generous."

Although it is difficult to determine the actual impact Lavanoux's notes had on the final draft of the *Constitution,* we do know that the members of the subcommission accepted them with approval,[20] and that the final statement in the *Constitution on the Sacred Liturgy* was indeed a "positive and generous" one. It emphasized that sacred furnishings were to be worthy to "serve the dignity of worship," (chapter 7, paragraph 122), that the number of sacred images is to be "moderate" and their placement reflect "right order," (paragraph 125), and that clergy are to be instructed in the principles and history of sacred art as a part of their seminary training (paragraph 129). Most important, the *Constitution* affirms that the Church "has admitted changes in materials, style, or ornamentation prompted by the progress of the technical arts with the passage of time" (paragraph 122) and accepts "styles from every period according to the natural talents and circumstances of peoples and the needs of the various rites" (paragraph 123).

Chapter Five of the "Instruction on the Sacred Liturgy" (September

26, 1964) went even further in establishing liturgical principles as the norm for the design and furnishing of church buildings, making the liturgy the first consideration in the building and furnishing of churches.

"In the new construction, repair, and adaptation of church buildings great care shall be taken that they are suitable for the celebration of divine services according to the true nature of the services and for the active participation of the faithful."[21]

Over the years, each of these recommendations had been an important part of the Liturgical Arts Society's agenda, and so the *Constitution* and "Instruction on the Sacred Liturgy" served as final confirmation that the Society's goals were, in some measure, to be realized in the Church's future. A simple, honest, and dignified ecclesiastical architecture, freed from the accretions of pious sentimentalism and rooted in the spirit of the liturgy, was not only *allowed* by the document but actively encouraged. More important, the Council documents had strengthened the foundations on which the Society's work had always been based — simplicity, sincerity, and integrity of design:

"The *Constitution on the Sacred Liturgy* and the generous directives of Vatican Council II herald a new era of life, an era in which the emphasis has shifted from a misguided triumphalism to a consideration of the dignity of the human person and of that poverty (not destitution) which insists on the importance of *first things first*."[22]

THE LITURGICAL ARTS SOCIETY AND THE DIALOGUE WITH MODERNITY

During the period in which the Liturgical Arts Society operated, the American Roman Catholic Church was constantly asking and answering the essential question of modernity: "Can the insights and information about the world and its contents which arise from sources *outside* the formal boundaries of the Church be reconciled with the Christian faith without doing violence to it?". Over and over again, in words and in actions, the Liturgical Arts Society answered a resounding "yes" in the specific case of ecclesiastical art and architecture. In so doing, it challenged nearly all of the assumptions about religious art which were operative in the Church at the time of the Society's founding. The Society declared that beauty was a logical and not an emotional matter, and that churches should be designed as settings for the liturgy, and not as manipulators of pious sentiment. It stated that every Christian community has the right to determine the art forms which serve it best, and that artistic truth does not rest on photographic realism, but on its ability to uncover the hiddenness of divine presence. And perhaps most important, the Society proclaimed that wherever evidence of creative genius is found, inside or outside the Christian faith, it is to be regarded as a God-given gift, and invited to serve the Church.

The American Roman Catholic Church continued to ask and answer the question of modernity throughout the period of the Society's existence (and continues to do so today, more than fifteen years after the Society's demise). But in the case of religious art and architecture, there seems to have developed something of a truce between the Church and modernity, and the Liturgical Arts Society played an important part in negotiating that truce. Imitative and liturgically insensitive churches are still being built, to be sure. But they are fewer and less influential than in the past, and evidence is mounting that, as Maurice Lavanoux predicted, the modern period of ecclesiastical art and architecture may well be looked upon as a golden age by future generations.[23]

Winston Churchill said, "We shape our buildings and ever after they shape us." For forty-four years, the Liturgical Arts Society worked to shape a thoroughly modern ecclesiastical art and architecture that was grounded in the theology and practice of the Church's public worship. To the extent Churchill's dictum is true, churches built as a result of the work of the Liturgical Arts Society have shaped and continue to shape the corporate life and faith of the American Roman Catholic Church in the twentieth century.

Notes

CHAPTER ONE

1. Everitt Harman to the Editor, *American Institute of Architects Journal*, May, 1927.
2. Maurice Lavanoux (hereafter Lavanoux), "The Past is Prologue," *LA*, 31:2 (February, 1963), 40. Although Lavanoux here described Harman as "in the novitiate at St. Benedict's Abbey at Fort Augustus, Scotland" and as "a member of the community of the recently founded Priory of St. Gregory the Great," Harman's actual relationship with the Order of St. Benedict is unclear. In the first instance, a survey of Harman's correspondence shows that he never seems to have settled in any one place long enough to have established himself in a religious vocation. He was ordained priest in 1949 in the Diocese of Salt Lake City, and biographical information in diocesan records there gives no indication of any previous alliance with the Benedictines. He occasionally signs himself "Brother Wilfrid," but that name is by no means universally accepted by his colleagues. Given Harman's rather romantic feelings about monasticism, "Brother Wilfrid" may have simply been a pious affectation rather than an officially given religious name.
3. See Dom Wilfrid Bayne, O.S.B., "Thirty-three Years of Portsmouth History," *American Benedictine Review* 3:4 (Winter, 1952), 315-339.
4. Everitt Harman to Lavanoux, May 17, 1927. LAS, 5.
5. The members of the group from New York were Louis Boislinere, Adlai Hardin, L. Bancel LaFarge, Ides van der Gracht, Oliver Reagan, J. Sanford Shanley, and John J. Stanton, and from Boston, John Howard Benson, A. Graham Carey, Wright Goodhue, Lavanoux, John Walter Wood, Donald Wood, and Francis White.
6. See William Halsey, *The Survival of American Innocence* (Notre Dame: University of Notre Dame Press, 1980) and Walter J. Ong, S.J., *Frontiers in American Catholicism* (New York: Macmillan Company, 1957).
7. Everitt Harman, "A Benedictine Oblates Guild of Architects, Artists and Craftsmen," unpublished paper, ca. January 15, 1928. LAS, 188.
8. Everitt Harman never clearly spelled out his understanding of the relationship between these groups and already established Benedictine houses. He did speak of his select oblate group as being located "in the vicinity of one of the great Benedictine houses" but never explicated the direct connections. Harman acknowledged that what was required for the revival of art was not a "collection of pious souls," such as one would find in a regular monastery, but rather a "community of scholars." Everitt Harman to Ides van der Gracht, January 14, 1928. LAS, 5.
9. Ides van der Gracht to Dom Suibert Kramer, March 23, 1928. LAS, 188.
10. Benjamin Musser, "Letter to the Editor," *LA* 1:2 (Winter, 1932), 78.
11. September 10, 1927.
12. January 1-2, 1928.
13. Ides van der Gracht to Max Jordan, May 15, 1928. LAS, 188. (The large volume in the Archives of similarly "rambling and pointless letters" from Harman to various members of the Society attests to the truth of van der Gracht's observations.)
14. Although this is a second-hand report from one who was obviously uncertain about Harman's leadership capabilities, it is very likely that Harman's rather overzealous approach to this project had indeed alienated him from the ecclesiastical au-

thorities, and that enthusiasm for establishing the planned organization under the jurisdiction of Portsmouth was not shared by the Priory's leadership.

15. Among those of this opinion were Harman's old friends Oliver Reagan and John Stanton. Ides van der Gracht to Dom Suibert Kramer, O.S.B., March 23, 1928. LAS, 6.

16. Ides van der Gracht to Max Jordan, May 19, 1928. LAS, 6.

17. See *Who's Who in America* 31 (Chicago: Marquis, 1962), p. 953.

18. Ides van der Gracht, "Brother Harmon [*sic*] on the Priory" (excerpts from letters from Everitt Harman with van der Gracht's commentary), ca. February 15, 1928. LAS, 188.

19. Ides van der Gracht, "Some Notes on a Movement to Make Catholic Spirit, Culture, and Liturgy More Effective and Fertile in Our Modern Intellectual and Artistic Life," unpublished paper, May 13, 1928. LAS, 188.

20. *Ibid.*, 2.

21. *Ibid.*, 2.

22. *Ibid.*, 3.

23. *Ibid.*, 3.

24. *Ibid.*, 3.

25. Max Jordan to Ides van der Gracht, June 13, 1928. LAS, 16. Others seem to have generally accepted the European elitism in van der Gracht's approach without question, and it appears, in various guises, for at least the first years of the Society's history. See page 121.

26. Ides van der Gracht to "Mrs. Tiers," August 9, 1928. LAS, 188.

27. Ides van der Gracht, "Brother Harmon [*sic*] on the Priory," 2. LAS, 188. It is indeed difficult to comprehend completely Harman's understanding of oblation. He seems to think that the "select group of oblates," who were to make up the first component of his scheme, should live exactly as if they were a monastic community. The second, "wider oblate movement" seems closer to the common understanding of an Oblate, namely, a person trying to live under monastic discipline in the world.

28. *Ibid.* and Ides van der Gracht to Everitt Harman, March 15, 1928. LAS, 188.

29. Abbot Andrew Joseph McDonald, later Archbishop of Edinburgh and Primate of Scotland, had remained in close contact with Harman throughout the process of organizing the Guild. While in America to visit Fort Augustus' foundations at Portsmouth and Washington, D.C., he met with Harman on several occasions and addressed the Portsmouth Priory group at their June 16-18, 1928, retreat. Portsmouth was not under consideration as a potential sponsor because it was itself still struggling as a foundation of Fort Augustus.

30. See *Beuron, 1863-1963: Festschrift zum hundertjahrigen Bestehen der Erzabtei St. Martin* (Beuron: Hohenzollern, 1963), 531.

31. Ides van der Gracht to "Mrs. Tiers," August 9, 1928. LAS, 188.

32. Ides van der Gracht to Dom Suibert Kramer, March 23, 1928, and response, July 7, 1928; Ides van der Gracht to "Mrs. Tiers," August 9, 1928. LAS, 188.

33. Ides van der Gracht, "Some Notes on a Movement . . .," 8. LAS, 188.

34. This group included Michael Williams, editor of *The Commonweal*, and architects L. Bancel LaFarge and Joseph Shanley.

35. Ides van der Gracht to Everitt Harman, March 15, 1928. LAS, 188.

36. Ides van der Gracht to Max Jordan, May 15, 1928. LAS, 6.

37. Ides van der Gracht, "Brother W. has very ably . . ." unpublished paper, June, 1928; Ides van der Gracht to Max Jordan, May 15, 1928. LAS, 188.

38. Oliver Reagan to Lavanoux, December 9, 1930. LAS, 7.

39. Lavanoux describes the group's rather romantic vision of its own future in his (unpublished) autobiography, *Never a Dull Moment*, 221. ML, 3.

40. Ides van der Gracht to "Mrs. Tiers," August 9, 1928. LAS, 188.

41. Indeed, at meetings in New York on September 4 and 24, 1928, a draft constitution and bylaws was discussed, and it contained no mention of any religious community whatsoever.

42. "Constitution of the Liturgical Arts Society," Article II: Object. See Appendix A.

43. The others were L. Bancel LaFarge, Oliver Reagan, J. Sanford Shanley, John J. Stanton, and Louis Boisliniere from New York, and Wright Goodhue and Maurice Lavanoux from Boston.

44. Everitt Harman to Lavanoux, September 29, 1928; Everitt Harman to Ides van der Gracht, August 30, 1928; Charles Maginnis to Everitt Harman, August 28, 1928. LAS, 188.

45. Presumably through his nephew L. Bancel LaFarge, one of the founding members.

46. George N. Schuster, colleague of Williams at *The Commonweal*; Robert Walsh, partner of Charles Maginnis; Bancel LaFarge, mosaicist and muralist and brother of John LaFarge; and the Rev. T. Lawrason Riggs, Catholic chaplain at Yale University, were also a part of this second group, and their expertise would be invaluable to the Society in the years to come.

47. The meeting was held on the evening of December 28, 1930.

48. See page 1.

49. The first directors were the Rt. Rev. James H. Ryan, rector, Catholic University of America; the Rev. T. Lawrason Riggs; Michael Williams; Bancel LaFarge; Hildreth Meiere, muralist (the only woman in the group); Eugene Savage, muralist; Augustus Vincent Tack, muralist; John LaFarge, S.J.; and Charles Maginnis. Within four years, the duties of the directors as outlined by the bylaws had been reduced to occasional votes on important matters. This change was not the result of any amendment to the bylaws.

50. President, Oliver Reagan; Vice President, Wright Goodhue; Secretary, Ides van der Gracht; Treasurer, Joseph Shanley; Chairs: Membership, L. Bancel LaFarge; Finance, John Stanton; Professional Activities, Maurice Lavanoux.

51. Architect Oliver Reagan.

52. Oliver Reagan to Lavanoux, February 23, 1929; Lavanoux agreed that, at least for the present, a limited membership was most desirable. Lavanoux to Oliver Reagan, February 26, 1929. LAS, 188.

53. Ides van der Gracht to Lavanoux, November 4, 1930. LAS, 188.

54. John LaFarge, S.J., "The Liturgical Arts Society," *America*, XLIV:9 (December 6, 1930), 519.

55. XIII:3 (November 19, 1930), 61, and XIII:6 (December 10, 1930), 146.

56. Ides van der Gracht to Charles Maginnis, December 15, 1930. LAS, 8. Van der Gracht suggested making it clear to such individuals that the group had announced itself "in order to get a more widespread reaction from which we would select our membership." Ides van der Gracht to Lavanoux, November 4, 1930. LAS, 188.

57. Ides van der Gracht to Lavanoux, February 28, 1931. LAS, 7.

58. See Appendix A for complete Constitution and bylaws.

59. Binsse to Lavanoux, June 18, 1931. LAS, 7.

60. Lavanoux and J. Sanford Shanley, "Annual Report to the Society," January 28, 1932. LAS, 8.

61. Binsse to Lavanoux, June 18, 1931. LAS, 7.

62. Lavanoux to Everitt Harman, March 9, 1930. LAS, 7.

63. Such a church, the Church of St. Vincent Ferrer in New York City, was the centerpiece of several early issues of *Liturgical Arts*.

64. The bylaws actually make no such stipulation for Sustaining Membership.

65. Lavanoux to Binsse, March 25, 1931. LAS, 7. Of course, it is possible that Lavanoux's sentiments are colored by the fact that Charles Connick had had a long and fruitful working relationship with Ralph Adams Cram, the chief competitor of Lavanoux's employer, the architectural firm of Maginnis & Walsh. At the time of his comments directed against Connick, however, Lavanoux was not aware that it had been Connick's special intercession with Charles Maginnis that had secured him his first drafting job with Maginnis & Walsh. See Lavanoux, *Never a Dull Moment*, p. 213. ML, 3.

66. Virgil Michel and Martin Hellriegel.

67. Michael Williams and Michael Chapman.

68. Peter Guilday and Thomas J. McCormick.

69. Carleton Strong and Edward J. Weber.

70. Pierre LaRose and James A. Ryan.

71. Lavanoux to Alcuin Deutsch October 28, 1930. LAS, 7.

72. *Ibid.*

73. The members of the advisory board, in addition to those listed in footnotes 66-69, were: Rev. Thomas F. Coakely, Rev. J.T. Creagh, Rev. Alcuin Deutsch, O.S.B., Rev. Hugh Diman, O.S.B., Frederick V. Murphy, Dom P. Raphael, O.S.B., Rev. T. Lawrason Riggs, Rev. James A. Walsh, Rev. L. Zirbes.

74. Lavanoux to Everitt Harman, November 6, 1930. LAS, 7.

75. Lavanoux to Oliver Reagan, February 26, 1929. LAS, 7.

76. See Ralph Adams Cram, *The Substance of Gothic* (Boston: Marshall Jones, 1917); *Church Building* (Boston: Marshall Jones, 1924); and *My Life in Architecture* (Boston: Little, Brown & Co., 1936) for an explication of Cram's thinking on these matters.

77. See Robert Brooke Clements, *The Commonweal, 1924-1938 The Williams-Schuster Years* (Ph.D. dissertation University of Notre Dame, 1972), 39ff; and Rodger van Allen, *The Commonweal and American Catholicism*, (Philadelphia: Fortress, 1974), 5ff.

78. Ralph Adams Cram, *The Catholic Church and Art* (New York: Macmillan, 1930).

79. Everitt Harman to Lavanoux, August 11, 1927. LAS, 188.

80. Charles Maginnis to Everitt Harman, August 28, 1928. LAS, 10.

81. Ralph Adams Cram to Everitt Harman, August 27, 1928. LAS, 188.

82. Everitt Harman to Lavanoux, November 6, 1930. LAS, 10.

83. See above footnote 65.

84. John LaFarge, S.J., the Society's chaplain, was equally strong in his feelings against Cram. His prejudice against Cram may have been exacerbated by the fact that an important architectural commission, the (Episcopal) Cathedral of St. John the Divine, had been taken away from LaFarge's brother Grant and given to the Cram firm. John LaFarge to Lavanoux, April 11, 1930 (LAS, 7) and John LaFarge, *The Manner is Ordinary* (New York: Harcourt Brace, 1954), 389-391.

85. Ralph Adams Cram, *The Catholic Church and Art*. (New York: Macmillan, 1930).

86. Lavanoux to Everitt Harman, March 16, 1930. LAS, 188.

87. *Ibid.*

88. *Ibid.*

89. *Ibid.*

90. Everitt Harman to Lavanoux, March 17, 1930. LAS, 188.

91. *Ibid.*

92. Everitt Harman to Lavanoux, November 6, 1930. LAS, 188.

93. Lavanoux to Everitt Harman, November 11, 1930. LAS, 188.

94. Dan Anderson, Press Release for the Liturgical Arts Society, November 20, 1931. LAS, 188.

95. Ralph Adams Cram to Binsse, July 10, 1933. LAS, 3.

96. Lavanoux to Bishop James Cassidy, July 15, 1933. LAS, 7.

97. *Brooklyn Tablet* 25:7 (July 8, 1933), 2.

98. James Cassidy to Lavanoux, July 29, 1933. LAS, 7.

99. George Lovatt to Binsse, August 3, 1933. LAS, 10.

100. Charles Maginnis to Lavanoux, July 22, 1933. LAS, 10.

101. Ralph Adams Cram to Lavanoux, August 8, 1933. LAS, 3. Maginnis, having been sent a copy of Cram's response, wrote to Lavanoux: "I was interested to notice the phraseology of the last line of the first paragraph. One wonders how much that is disingenuous lies behind the words 'at present.' " Charles Maginnis to Lavanoux, August 12, 1933. LAS, 10.

102. "Editorial," *LA* 11:1 (November, 1942), 1.

103. Oliver Reagan to Lavanoux, February 23, 1929. LAS, 188.

104. T. Lawrason Riggs to Bancel LaFarge, February 13, 1930. LAS, 13.

105. See pages 28-30.

106. Ides van der Gracht to Charles Maginnis, December 8, 1931. LAS, 10.

107. Lavanoux to Ides van der Gracht, March 24, 1930. LAS, 7.

108. Oliver Reagan to Lavanoux, February 23, 1929. LAS, 12.

109. Lavanoux to Cardinal O'Connell, June 30, 1930. LAS, 7.

110. J. Burke to Lavanoux, July 21, 1930. LAS, 7.

111. Lavanoux to Ides van der Gracht, et al, September 6, 1930. LAS, 7.

112. November 6, 1930.

113. See Appendix A, "Constitution and bylaws, Liturgical Arts Society."

114. Lavanoux to Ides van der Gracht, March 23, 1930. LAS, 7.

115. Lavanoux to J. Burke, August 23, 1930. LAS, 7. Lavanoux's letter concludes with the suggestion that the Cardinal might choose for the Society a person who could fill this role.

116. September 6, 1930.

117. Lavanoux to Ides van der Gracht, October 1, 1930. LAS, 7.

118. John LaFarge, *The Manner is Ordinary* (New York: Harcourt, Brace, 1954), 290-291.

119. See *LA* 32:1 (November, 1963), inside front cover.

CHAPTER TWO

1. In fact, in the very year that *Liturgical Arts* began publication, its staunch supporters at *The Commonweal* were having grave financial difficulties. *The Commonweal* itself was threatened with extinction on several occasions during that year but was rescued by private donors. See Robert Brooke Clements, *The Commonweal, 1924-1938: The Williams-Shuster years*, 178f 178ff.

2. Charles Maginnis to Everitt Harman, October 17, 1928. LAS, 188.

3. *Ibid*.

4. Lavanoux to Thomas Coakley, October 15, 1930; Lavanoux to Everitt Harman, October 28, 1930. LAS, 188.

5. Ides van der Gracht to Lavanoux, December 5, 1930, and "Minutes of Directors' Meeting, December 28, 1930. " LAS, 188.

6. Charles Maginnis to L. Bancel LaFarge, December 19, 1930. LAS, 10.

7. Ides van der Gracht to Lavanoux, December 5, 1930. LAS, 16.

8. Members of the Finance Committee were Charles Maginnis, Ides van der Gracht, J. Sanford Shanley, and Eugene Savage.

9. Liturgical Arts Society, "Minutes of the Finance Committee Meeting, December 28, 1930." LAS, 188.

10. Lavanoux to Ides van der Gracht, April 2, 1930, and February 3, 1931. LAS, 7.

11. Ides van der Gracht to Lavanoux, February 3, 1931. LAS, 188. Lavanoux explained to van der Gracht why he was reluctant to take the job: "I still have hopes of being an independent architect, and such a job as you have in mind for me is not sufficient for a bright boy like me. Not unless I should be offered something like ten thousand a year." Lavanoux to Ides van der Gracht, February 3, 1931. LAS, 188.

12. Ides van der Gracht to Charles Maginnis, February 21, 1931. LAS, 16.

13. Ides van der Gracht to Lavanoux, February 22, 1931. LAS, 7.

14. Liturgical Arts Society, "Minutes of the Meeting of the Board of Directors, April 15, 1931." LAS, 188.

15. Ides van der Gracht to Lavanoux, March 2, 1931. LAS, 16. For this work, Binsse was to be paid $6000 per year.

16. Ides van der Gracht to Charles Maginnis, April 6, 1931. LAS, 16.

17. This meeting had been scheduled for April 29 but was adjourned because of failure to achieve a quorum.

18. Bylaws Liturgical Arts Society Article VII, sec. 3b. See Appendix A.

19. Ides van der Gracht to Lavanoux, November 17, 1930. LAS, 16.

20. *Ibid*.

21. These included R. T. Townsend of *Country Life*, a "Mr. Shelton," business manager of the *Bookman*, W. N. Commons, budget director at Time, Inc., and E. J. Bill of Federated Business Publications. Binsse to Lavanoux, March 15, 1931. LAS, 7.

22. *Ibid*.

23. *Ibid*.

24. The Editorial Committee consisted of Bancel LaFarge, Ides van der Gracht, Joseph Shanley, and Donald Wood. Ides van der Gracht to Charles Maginnis, April 6, 1931. LAS, 16.

25. Ides van der Gracht, "Liturgical Arts Society, History, Program, and Object," unpublished paper, April, 1931. LAS, 8.

26. Binsse, "Report to Corporate Members," May 7, 1931. LAS, 8.

27. Lavanoux to Binsse, July 4, 1931. LAS, 7.

28. *Ibid.* and Lavanoux to Binsse, July 5, 1931. LAS, 7.

29. *Ibid.* Lefebvre himself seems not to have put his thoughts about the proposed American journal in writing, and we have only Lavanoux's second-hand report of the meeting. In later years, Lavanoux often recorded taking some delight in telling Lefebvre that the Society and the journal were still going strong. See, for example, *LA* 18:3 (May, 1950), 57.

30. Binsse to Lavanoux, July 6, 1931. LAS, 8.

31. Binsse to A. St. Luke, February 10, 1932. LAS, 8.

32. Charles Maginnis to Binsse, April 4, 1931. LAS, 10.

33. Chester Aldrich to Lavanoux, May 5, 1931. LAS, 1.

34. *LA* 1:1 was essentially the model issue which had been produced the month before.

35. Dan C. Anderson, Press Release for the Liturgical Arts Society, November 20, 1931. LAS, 188.

36. *Ibid.*

37. Liturgical Arts Society, Information Brochure, 1931. LAS, 8.

38. Lavanoux to Binsse, July 18, 1931, and Lavanoux to J. Sweeney, December 19, 1931. LAS, 7. When he sought out the names of the professors of liturgy teaching in Roman Catholic seminaries, Binsse was alarmed to find the number limited. "I carefully combed all the seminaries listed in the Catholic Directory, I only found 14 names definitely listed as professors of the liturgy. . . . . Surely there must be more than 14 such professors in this fair land!" Binsse to Lavanoux, July 20, 1931.

39. Dan C. Anderson, Press Release for the Liturgical Arts Society, November 20, 1931. LAS, 188.

40. Liturgical Arts Society to Editors, November, 1931. LAS, 188.

41. *Baltimore Evening Sun*, December 2, 1931.

42. *America* (December 12, 1931), 22.

43. See Lavanoux's own account of his early life "Never a Dull Moment," unpublished autobiography, 1972. ML, 3.

44. During this time, he worked for the architectural firms of Rocker & Vatet, and Gustave Steinbach, New York City, and Kirkhoff & Schaff, Santa Barbara, California.

45. See page 21.

46. See pages 27-8.

47. See Clements, *The Commonweal, 1924-1938: The Williams-Schuster Years*, 39 ff, and Rodger van Allen, *The Commonweal and American Catholicism*, 77ff.

48. Louis Boislinere, the Society's legal counsel, and H. Wright Goodhue, one of the incorporators of the Society in 1928, are two of those from whom nothing more is heard.

49. See page 4ff.

50. See *Who's Who in America*, 1961-1962.

51. See pages 9 and 55.

52. Clements, *The Commonweal 1924-1938: The Williams-Schuster Years*, 175.

53. *Ibid.*, 176.

54. *Ibid.*, 179-185.

55. *Ibid.*, 186.

56. Rodger van Allen, *The Commonweal and American Catholicism*, pp. 76-78.

57. Williams remained "special editor" with a weekly column until his death in 1950. Managing editor George N. Schuster, another early *Liturgical Arts* supporter, also left

The Commonweal in 1937, having received a grant from the Columbia University Social Science Research Council and the Carnegie Corporation to write the history of the Center Party in the Weimar Republic. See Clements, 176.

58. See page 1ff.

59. See pages 3-4.

60. Everitt Harman to Binsse, August 11, 1931. LAS, 188.

61. Binsse to Everitt Harman, September 14, 1931. LAS, 188.

62. Bernice Mooney to Susan J. White, May 28, 1986.

63. *AIA Membership Directory* (Washington: AIA, 1964), 198.

64. Among these were J. Sanford Shanley, John Walter Wood, L. Bancel LaFarge, and Leopold Arnaud.

65. Binsse remained in charge of the typography and layout of *LA* until 1950, when the job was assumed by Joseph Asherl of Doubleday.

66. Binsse's life ended in relative obscurity on May 21, 1971, at the age of 66. He had hoped to spend his time writing and translating books, but the revenue from this work was not sufficient to support his large family. (In addition to his own children, Binsse had adopted the children of friends who had died in an accident.) Having failed to secure steady employment, he opened a restaurant, which was unsuccessful, and his health deteriorated along with his fortunes. See "Harry Lorin Binsse — 1905-1971," *Liturgical Arts* 39:3 (May, 1971), back cover, and van Allen, *The Commonweal and American Catholicism*, 104-5.

67. "Lavanoux, Church Art Expert, Is Dead," *The New York Times*, October 22, 1974, 48:2-5.

1. J. André Fouilhoux, "Editorial,"   *LA* 6:4 (August, 1938), 170.

2. Binsse to Charles Maginnis, September 27, 1932. LAS, 10.

3. Binsse to Charles Maginnis, September 18, 1932, and November 27, 1934. LAS, 10.

4. Bishop J. McNicholas to Lavanoux, May 20, 1936. LAS, 11.

5. A. Graham Carey to Binsse, February 3, 1936. LAS, 2.

6. Binsse to A. Graham Carey, March 30, 1936. LAS, 2.

7. Bankers' Trust to Liturgical Arts Society, March 12, 1936. LAS, 188.

8. *LA* 5:3 (Third Quarter, 1936).

9. *LA* 6:1 (First Quarter, 1937), 1.

10. *Ibid.*

11. Lavanoux to Gerald Ellard, October 30, 1936. LAS, 4.

12. *Ibid.*

13. Lavanoux to John Moody, April 13, 1939. LAS, 17.

14. John Moody to Bishop James Cassidy, June 12, 1939. LAS, 17.

15. John Moody to Lavanoux, June 28, 1939. LAS, 17.

16. Lavanoux to John Moody, June 7, 1939. LAS, 17.

17. "Editorial," *LA* 4:1 (First Quarter, 1935), 1.

18. *Acta Apostolicae Sedis 36 (1903), 329-339.*

19. John LaFarge, *The Manner is Ordinary*, New York: Harcourt Brace, 1954, 289-290.

20. *Ibid.*

21. On a Monday evening in February of 1933, a small number of Society members met at the Centre Club, New York City, for the first rehearsal of what was formally called the Liturgical Arts Schola. This initial gathering seems to have been taken up with practical details, punctuated by the members' periodic lament, "But I can't *possibly* sing this stuff!"
The members seem also to have wanted a less formal name for themselves, and Fr. LaFarge suggested several possibilities. "Schola Gregoriana" was rejected because "it described the group's technical rather than religious character," but "Schola Mariae" or "Schola Marialis" merited slightly longer discussion "because the plan was to honor Our Lady by singing a Mass on her day [and] why not put it under her special patronage?" When those proposals were rejected on the grounds that the group's repertoire was not to be limited to Masses of the Blessed Virgin, LaFarge suggested the "Quilisma Club" as the unofficial name, and this proposal was quickly and unanimously adopted.
"A few minutes later," Becket Gibbs reported, "one of the number [wanted] to find a reason for the name." Here, John LaFarge's dry sense of humor is demonstrated at its most engaging. He explained that "the neum (or sign) which indicated the rugged-looking note called the *quilisma* looks very much like a crook, a shepherd's crook . . ., so that Father LaFarge was perpetrating a joke at the expense of the singers. Not that he was calling them a 'bunch of crooks,' but the implication was certainly there!"
Ibid. LaFarge appealed for his choice to the fact that the terms "gothic" and "Methodist" had originated as deprecatory terms, and so there was good precedent for such a move. Becket Gibbs, "The Quilisma Club," unpublished paper, ca. 1936 (LAS, 4). See also John LaFarge to Binsse, February 27, 1934. LAS, 7.

22. John Wood to Binsse, May 2, 1934. LAS, 16.

23. Becket Gibbs, "The Quilisma Club," unpublished paper, ca. 1936. LAS, 4.

24. John LaFarge, *The Manner is Ordinary*, p. 290.

Notes for pages 39 to 55

25. *LA* 29:2 (November, 1960), 35.

26. John C. Selener, *LA* 25:1 (November, 1956), 7.

27. John LaFarge to Becket Gibbs, March 15, 1945. LAS, 4.

28. "Editorial," *LA* 2:1 (First Quarter, 1932), 3.

29. Leo Linahen to Liturgical Arts Society, July 10, 1935. LAS, 9.

30. Binsse to M. Foy, April 24, 1933. LAS, 9. In one case, a chalice purchased by Bishop Jules Benjamin Jeanmard of Lafayette, Louisiana separated at the joint between the cup and base during preparations for Mass. It was determined that "this was due to faulty saulding [sic]", and the chalice was returned. V. Vigliero to Liturgical Arts Society, December 7, 1933. LAS, 9.

31. *LA* 3:1 (First Quarter, 1934), 1.

32. Binsse to Victor Pax, July 15, 1935. LAS, 9. Other explanations included "lack of working capital" (Binsse to Leon Dworschak, December 5, 1935) and that it "entailed far more attention than our limited facilities permitted us." Binsse to Frederick F. Schaffer, November 10, 1935. LAS, 9.

33. Binsse to Joseph Piana, July 31, 1935. LAS, 9.

34. Binsse to John J. Casey, October 17, 1935; M. Schexnader to Liturgical Arts Society, October 4, 1932. LAS, 9.

35. Binsse to T. Phillips, October 4, 1932. LAS, 9.

36. Charles Maginnis to Binsse, December 8, 1932, and December 9, 1932. LAS, 9.

37. P. Rondeau to Liturgical Arts Society, January 17, 1933. LAS, 9.

38. Donald S. Johnson to Liturgical Arts Society, April 20, 1933. LAS, 9.

39. Sisters of the Good Shepherd to Liturgical Arts Society, March 21, 1933. LAS, 9.

40. Marcella Booth to Liturgical Arts Society, March 23, 1933. LAS, 9.

41. P. Rondeau to Liturgical Arts Society, January 17, 1933. LAS, 9.

42. Luigi Ligutti to Liturgical Arts Society, September 19, 1933. LAS, 9.

43. "Editorial," *LA* 3:1 (First Quarter, 1934), 2.

44. John LaFarge, *Catalogue of a Small Church Exhibition*, 1933. LAS, 8.

45. The exhibition jury consisted of Otto Eggers, Daniel F. Higgins, Chester Aldrich, André Fouilhoux, and Lavanoux.

46. Liturgical Arts Society to members of the press, May 6, 1933. LAS, 8.

47. *Brooklyn Tablet* XXV:10 (May 20, 1933), 11; *America* XLIX:7 (May 9, 1933), 149; and *The Commonweal* XVIII:7 (June 16, 1933), 181-182.

48. John LaFarge, *Catalogue of a Small Church Exhibition*, 1933. LAS, 8.

49. Lavanoux to Gerald Carroll, June 17, 1933. LAS, 8.

50. Adam Dambrowski to Lavanoux, June 21, 1933. LAS, 3.

51. *LA* 3:3-4 (Third-Fourth Quarter, 1934), 109-110.

52. *LA* 4:2 (Second Quarter, 1935), 85.

53. *LA* 5:4 (Fourth Quarter, 1936-1937), 124.

54. *LA* 3:1 (First Quarter, 1934), 39.

55. Binsse to Matthew Britt, March 27, 1934. LAS, 9.

56. *LA* 3:1 (First Quarter, 1934), 39.

57. *Ibid.*

58. Binsse to Charles Maginnis, November 3, 1933. LAS, 9.

59. William J. Leonard, S.J., to Susan J. White, January 24, 1986.

60. *LA* 3:1 (First Quarter, 1934), 39.

61. *Ibid.* Two of the men who had been at Portsmouth Priory for the founding meetings of the Liturgical Arts Society, A. Graham Carey and John H. Benson, Newport,

Rhode Island, silversmiths, were given responsibility for the design and striking of the gold medal. It was Benson's and Carey's belief that medals of this kind should be "rescued from industrialism and Victorianism" and that the Liturgical Arts Society should lead the way. Their final product, a disk of just over one ounce of fine gold, bore the image of what Carey described as "an intellectual representation of the Church" on the obverse and the words "DILEXI DECOREM DOMUS TUAE" on the reverse. The medal, struck with apparently some difficulty, was presented to Father Clifford at a testimonial dinner on January 23, 1934, and was pictured in the April, 1934, issue of *Liturgical Arts* with a description by the makers. A. Graham Carey to Binsse, October 31, 1933 (LAS, 2), John Howard Benson to Binsse, January 10, 1934 (LAS, 1), and *LA* 3:1 (First Quarter, 1934), 45.

62. Lavanoux to Bishop Mooney, April 9, 1938. LAS, 11.

63. Bishop Mooney to Lavanoux, April 11, 1938. LAS, 11.

64. Lavanoux to Bishop Mooney, April 19, 1938. LAS, 11.

65. Binsse to Becket Gibbs, August 31, 1934, and September 15, 1934. LAS, 4.

66. Lavanoux to William Busch, May 22, 1935. LAS, 1.

67. Lavanoux to Floyd L. Begin, June 1, 1935. LAS, 1.

68. Lavanoux to Bancel LaFarge, July 16, 1936. LAS, 7.

69. See pages 22-23.

70. Lavanoux to William Busch, November 2, 1934. LAS, 1.

71. *Ibid.*

72. Lavanoux to William Busch, November 15, 1935. LAS, 1.

73. James E. Cassidy to Charles Maginnis, October 9, 1932. LAS, 2.

74. Hugh Boyle to Liturgical Arts Society, March 3, 1939. LAS, 17.

75. Bishop Donahue of New York City declined because he was the Suffragan and not the Ordinary of the diocese, and Robert E. Lucey of Amarillo because he did not "want to appear to be patronizing." Lucey went on to say that "Bishop Boyle's letter stands by itself and could not possibly be strengthened by a comparatively unknown bishop from West Texas." Robert Lucey to Lavanoux, March 29, 1939, and James Casey to Lavanoux, March 27, 1939. LAS, 17.

76. Lavanoux to Charles Maginnis, December 18, 1933. LAS, 7.

77. Eugenio Tisserant to Lavanoux, December 1, 1933. LAS, 15.

78. E. Tisserant to Lavanoux, May 7, 1935. LAS, 15.

79. E. Tisserant to Lavanoux, September 19, 1935. LAS, 15.

80. E. Tisserant to Lavanoux, May 7, 1935, and September 19, 1935. LAS, 15.

81. Lavanoux to E. Tisserant, May 19, 1936. LAS, 15.

82. Binsse to William Busch, June 5, 1934. LAS, 1. See also *LA* 3:1 (First Quarter, 1934), 41-42, 46-47.

83. *LA* 3:1 (First Quarter, 1934), 40.

84. William Busch to Lavanoux, May 17, 1934. LAS, 1.

85. William Busch to Lavanoux, May 30, 1934. LAS, 1.

86. Lavanoux to Board of Directors, June 3, 1937; Lavanoux to Charles Maginnis, December 22, 1937. LAS, 8.

87. *Ibid.*

88. The only exception is an advertisement during a subscription campaign which read "Uncle Sam wouldn't mind if you subscribed to *Liturgical Arts.*"

89. Bancel LaFarge, 1935-1937, and J. André Fouilhoux, 1937-1939.

90. Lavanoux to John Moody, October 7, 1939. LAS, 17.

1. The term "second spring" is taken from John Henry Newman's 169The Second Spring" sermon, preached on July 13, 1852, which referred to the general renaissance of Roman Catholic intellectual life in the English-speaking world. See *LA* 38:3 (May 1970), 93.

2. See pages 40-43.

3. Lavanoux to John Agar, November 25, 1940. LAS, 18.

4. This included debts of $11,884.17, assets of $1,720.88, reflecting a reduction in the deficit by $12,159.99, *Ibid.*

5. Lavanoux to Justine Ward, March 31, 1941. LAS, 19.

6. Lavanoux to Justine Ward, December 4, 1941, and December 17, 1941. LAS, 19.

7. J. Sanford Shanley to Liturgical Arts Society, April, 1944, and Lavanoux to contributors, June 9, 1944. LAS, 21.

8. Lavanoux to Charles Maginnis, November 20, 1944. LAS, 20.

9. *Ibid.*

10. Charles Maginnis to Lavanoux, November 24, 1944. LAS, 21.

11. Gerald Carroll to Lavanoux, December 6, 1946, December 15, 1947, and January 3, 1949. LAS, 192.

12. Lavanoux to Clement Lamber, September 11, 1944 (LAS, 21), and Maurice Lavanoux, "Religious Art for Servicemen," *The Marianist*, XXXVI:2 (February, 1945), 10-12. Not all of the Society's attempts to make a contribution to the war effort were as fruitful as this, however. In February, 1941, notice came out in the press that ten chapels were to be erected at Fort Dix (New Jersey). Lavanoux immediately offered the Society's services in the process, in order to prevent the possibility that "Barclay Street will invade this camp and others in the country." But this was to no avail. The manager of the Works Progress Administration informed the Society that it had been determined that "altars and ecclesiastical material will be purchased through commercial channels." Lavanoux to John LaFarge, February 27, 1941, and Audrey McMahon to Lavanoux, February 24, 1941. LAS, 21.

13. Lavanoux to John LaFarge, February 27, 1944.

14. Lavanoux to Charlton Fortune, February 11, 1942. LAS, 19.

15. Among these were the Most Rev. Edward D. Howard, Bishop of Portland, Oregon, and John J. Cantwell, Archbishop of Los Angeles. Edwin D. Howard to Liturgical Arts Society, April 19, 1940. LAS, 18.

16. Charlton Fortune to Lavanoux, May 7, 1942. LAS, 19.

17. Later Pope Paul VI.

18. Giovanni Montini to Otto Spaeth, December 10, 1946, and September 23, 1947; *LA* 16:1 (November, 1947), 1. LAS, 124

19. George Lober to Francis Cardinal Spellman, September 29, 1947. LAS, 24. Cardinal Spellman forwarded this correspondence to Lavanoux along with his own response to it, which acknowledged that the praise for the Society was "well merited." Cardinal Spellman to Lavanoux, October 2, 1947. LAS, 24.

20. In 1946, there were 176 foreign subscribers to *LA*, including members of the hierarchy.

21. Reynold Hillenbrand to Lavanoux, June 27, 1941. LAS, 19.

22. Thomas Metcalf to Lavanoux, August 14, 1943. LAS, 21. Lavanoux also gave a lecture at the opening of the exhibit.

23. "Editorial," *LA* 17:1 (November, 1948), 1.

24. "Editorial," *LA* 17:4 (August, 1949), 53.

25. Among those making such requests were Bishops Cody, then auxiliary bishop of St. Louis, and McNicholas. Lavanoux to John LaFarge, September 2, 1947. LAS, 24.

26. J. Griffin to Lavanoux, September 24, 1948. LAS, 27.

27. E. McCarthy to Lavanoux, March 22, 1944. LAS, 22.

28. "Program, Convocation of St. Vincent's College." Others honored with degrees on this occasion included Abbot Alcuin Deutsch, St. John's Abbey, Collegeville, Minnesota, and Bishop Hugh Boyle, Pittsburgh, Pennsylvania. LAS, 22.

29. See pages 48-50.

30. NCWC News Service, August, 1940.

31. When the NCWC received copies of Coakley's letter, along with the issue of *LA* in which it had been excerpted, Michael Ready, the Council's general secretary, wrote to Lavanoux, stating that he was deeply disturbed "that a publication pretending to be thoughtful, discerning, and dedicated to ideals of truth as well as of beauty should consider the discussion and spread of such fantasies that are a reflection on the good sense as well as the ideals of the Bishops in the country, who are responsible for the building."
Lavanoux responded that both his own interest and the interest of the Society in the matter of a statue of Christ the Light of the World was a "purely professional one," since certain artists had been inquiring about the statue and the terms under which it was being commissioned. He added an apology (on behalf of the Society) to the NCWC for the affront. Thomas Coakley, unpublished paper, "Some Reflections on the Proposed Statue of Christ in Washington," sent privately to Bishop John F. Noll, editor of *Our Sunday Visitor* and subsequently printed in the *Catholic Observer* and *Brooklyn Tablet*, August 22, 1940. (In the November, 1940, issue of *LA*, excerpts from Coakley's letter and Noll's response were printed.) Michael Ready to Lavanoux, October 5, 1940, and Lavanoux to Michael Ready, October 9, 1940. LAS, 18.

32. Thomas Coakley to Lavanoux, August 26, 1940. LAS, 18.

33. This committee was composed of Archbishop Mooney of Detroit, Archbishop Stritch of Chicago, and Bishop Noll of Fort Wayne (editor of *Our Sunday Visitor*, sponsor of the original fund raising campaign for the building).

34. Lavanoux attempted to explain this stunning turn of events by saying that "the choice of the Liturgical Arts Society for the competition is one of those unpredictable results of [my] lecture trips: Archbishop Mooney has always been one of my best boosters, Archbishop Stritch was the sponsor of the Chicago week, and I met Bishop Noll some years ago." Lavanoux to J. Sanford Shanley, May 8, 1941. LAS, 19.

35. Lavanoux to Charlton Fortune, May 8, 1941. LAS, 19.

36. Lavanoux to Mrs. R. L. Gilman, February 24, 1942. LAS, 19.

37. Lavanoux to Charlton Fortune, September 6, 1941. LAS, 19.

38. The jury consisted of Lee Lawrie (chair), Frederic V. Murphy (architect of the project), C. Paul Verwein, Gaetano Cecere, and Barry Byrne. Before the jury could begin its work, a serious question was raised about the way it was selected. "What I greatly fear we did," wrote long-time Society member Monsignor Philip Furlong, "is to be guilty of selecting a packed jury. One of the judges is an architect whose work is bankrupt; another is an architect who delights in being so modern that he cannot be frank; the third is a sculptor whose chief work is, in my mind, an abomination. It is my considered opinion that whoever is responsible for selecting these three of the judges erred very badly.

"I have a deep and sincere interest that any priest ought to have in the progress of the Liturgical Arts Society. When, through a blunder of this sort, we set up in the public mind the belief that we are artistically unsound, given to admiring and sponsoring extremes, then we set back the whole liturgical movement." Philip Furlong to Lavanoux, August 6, 1942. LAS, 19.

39. *LA* 10:4 (August, 1942) and 11:1 (November, 1942).

40. July 14 and 15, 1942.

41. Lavanoux to Otto Spaeth, July 16, 1942. LAS, 20.

42. *Ibid*.

43. Lavanoux to Robert I. Gannon, August 13, 1942. LAS, 20.

44. The jury met for the second time on October 1, 1942.

45. Michael Ready, the general secretary, and Howard J. Carroll, the assistant general secretary.

46. *LA* 11:1 (November, 1942), 5.

47. Upon being informed of the outcome of the competition, the winner, George Kratina, wrote to the general secretary of the NCWC, saying that he could "appreciate the feelings of the bishops" and was prepared to abide by their suggestions. "I am ready," he said, "to . . . submit other models in which I would attempt to embody other conceptions." *LA* 11:1 (November, 1942), 4.

48. Lavanoux to Mrs. R. L. Gilman, February 24, 1942. LAS, 19.

49. Not all of the Society's voyages into the world of art competition were as difficult as this one. In 1940, the National Shrine of the Immaculate Conception (Washington, D.C.) asked the Liturgical Arts Society to conduct a competition for religious Christmas cards, expenses to be paid by the Eastern Offset Company which printed cards for the Shrine. An exhibition held in connection with the seventh National Liturgical Week was another of the Society's distinct successes. Planned and executed by the Society, the exhibit drew more than 900 people to its opening on August 17, 1947, at the Portland (Oregon) Art Museum and was given most favorable reviews from the religious, trade, and secular press alike. Lavanoux to John Moody, February 20, 1948. The jury for this competition consisted of John O'Connor, Eugene Savage, John LaFarge, James W. Lane, and Leopold Arnaud. Lavanoux to Thomas Tobin, October 3, 1947. LAS, 25.

50. Lavanoux to Charlton Fortune, October 1, 1942. LAS, 19.

51. *LA* 17:2 (February, 1949), 51. The total outlay for the Statue Project was well over $25,000. The "member" who had offered to defray costs of such an undertaking was industrialist Otto Spaeth, then president of the Society.

52. Richmond Burke, Jean deMarco, Charles Cutler, Alfeo Faggi, Robert Laurent, Ivan Mestrovic, Janet deCoux, Henry Rox, Henry Kries, Helene Saideau, Oronzio Maldarelli, Charles Umlauf, Erwin W. Frei, George Kratina, and Suzanne Nicholas.

53. The five not selected were Laurent, Faggi, deMarco, Cutler, and Burke.

54. *LA* 17:2 (February, 1949), 34-50.

55. *Ibid*.

56. Siegfried Weng to Lavanoux, December 29, 1949. LAS, 25.

57. "Editorial," *LA* 18:1 (November, 1949), 1.

58. See "Editorial," *LA* 7:3 (May, 1939), 45.

CHAPTER FIVE

1. "Editorial," *LA* 30:1 (November, 1961), 13.
2. "Editorial," *LA* 18:2 (February, 1950), 28.
3. Leopold Arnaud, a very early member of the Society, was dean of the Columbia University School of Architecture; Oliver Reagan and J. Sanford Shanley, both of whom had been present at the Portsmouth Priory meetings, were presidents of their respective architectural firms; John W. Wood, another Portsmouth Priory retreatant, was serving as chair of the Architecture Department at the University of Illinois, Champaign.
4. The Michael P. Grace II Fund and the Charlpeg Foundation, both established out of profits from the Grace Steamship Company and others of the family's business enterprises.
5. Although there was no need for a major fund-raising campaign during this period, over the long term, these increases in revenue did not keep pace with increases in costs, and by 1960, the Society had once again begun to accrue a deficit.
6. It was unreasonable to expect that anyone else could be found to serve as editor, subscription and advertising manager, propagandist, and chief fund-raiser, all for about $37 per week (less than $2000 per year) in 1950.
7. J. Sanford Shanley, one of the Portsmouth Priory group.
8. Gerald Carroll served for a total of 17 years, from 1954 to 1972. The only years he did not serve were 1956-1957 and 1957-1958, during which Fordham philosophers Daniel J. Sullivan and William Dunphy, respectively, served as presidents.
9. Lavanoux to George Flahiff, June 21, 1950, and *LA* 18:4 (August, 1950), 83.
10. *LA* 18:4 (August, 1950), 83.
11. Lavanoux to George Flahiff, June 21, 1950. LAS, 26.
12. Lavanoux to Charlton Fortune, June 21, 1950. LAS, 26.
13. Richard Douaire to Lavanoux, April 15, 1950. LAS, 26.
14. This group described itself as comprising those "who feel the need of working together for the renewal of Christian Principles of Humanity and peaceful social Community, in the spirit of liberty without which the divine gift of Art cannot reap its fruits of beauty and civilization." Brochure, ICCA, ca. 1950. LAS, 26.
15. In addition to Lavanoux, the members of the United States delegation were Barry Byrne (architect), the Rev. Richard J. Douaire (director of the Liturgical Arts Society), Jean Charlot (painter), Jacques Maritain (philosopher), John J. Becker (composer), Ivan Mestrovic (sculptor), Otto Spaeth (industrialist and patron of the arts), James Johnson Sweeney (author and art critic), Leopold Arnaud (dean, Columbia University School of Architecture), and Henry Clifford (museum curator). Press release, June 9, 1950. LAS, 26.
16. The suggestion was made by Gerald Carroll, attorney for the Grace Shipping Lines. Lavanoux to Gerald Carroll, December 17, 1951. LAS, 27.
17. Lavanoux to John Douaire, April 26, 1950. LAS, 26.
18. John Douaire to Lavanoux, April 27, 1950, and Lavanoux to George Flahiff, July 19, 1950. LAS, 26.
19. Lavanoux to Richard Curtin, December 27, 1950. LAS, 27.
20. Lavanoux to Charlton Fortune, October, 17, 1950. LAS, 27.
21. Lavanoux to L. H. Tibesar, December 14, 1951. LAS, 27.
22. Lavanoux to Gerald Carroll, December 17, 1951. LAS, 28.
23. Lavanoux to Janet deCoux, April 7, 1952. LAS, 28.

24. Lavanoux to Iris Conlay, April 14, 1952. LAS, 28.

25. Lavanoux to Iris Conlay, February 2, 1961. LAS, 37.

26. Dublin, Ireland, January 4-8, 1961.

27. Held at the Katholische Akademie, in Munich, July 26-29, 1960.

28. E.g. Stained Glass Exhibition, American Federation of Arts, June, 1953. Lavanoux to Nesta Anderson, April 15, 1953. LAS, 29.

29. Consultant in Church Architecture, Columbia University School of Architecture; Lavanoux to Leopold Arnaud, December 16, 1954. LAS, 29. Consultant to the Master of Fine Arts Program, Siena Heights College (Adrian, Michigan); Lavanoux to Sister Helene, October 7, 1954. LAS, 30.

30. Contributor to the monumental *Forms and Functions of 20th-Century Architecture* (ed. Talbot Hamlin); "Problems of Religious Art" in *The Commonweal* LVIII:37 (September 18, 1953), 575; "That Elusive Commodity: Art!" in *Worship* XXVII:5 (April, 1953), 230-234; "Art Trends in Asia" in *World Mission* XI:2 (Spring, 1953), 31.

31. June 19, 1955, and November 22, 1956.

32. P. Dorsey to Lavanoux, November 10, 1953. LAS, 31.

33. Throughout this period, subscriptions hovered around 2,000. Rumford Press to Liturgical Arts Society, January 18, 1957, et al. LAS, 34, et al.

34. Lavanoux to Cecelia Hubbard, December 7, 1959. LAS, 35.

35. D. Cardinal Tardini to Gerald Carroll, October 20, 1959. During the same trip, Lavanoux also met with then Cardinal Montini in Milan and Cardinal Lercaro in Bologna, both of whom would be important to the Society's future. Lavanoux to Michael Mathis, November 27, 1959. LAS, 36.

36. In that same year, the Society awarded a citation to Ellard "in commemoration of his Golden Jubilee in the religious life, 1912-1962."

37. Three years earlier, in 1960, the Society had given LaFarge a testimonial dinner on the occasion of his 80th birthday. At the dinner, LaFarge was presented with a silver crucifix crafted by Dunstan Pruden, a disciple of Eric Gill. Lavanoux to Charles Grace, November 22, 1960 (LAS, 37), and *LA* 29:2 (February, 1960), 34-36.

38. Lavanoux to Clement J. McNaspy, December 13, 1963. LAS, 41.

39. "Editorial," *LA* 32:3 (May, 1961), 58.

40. Edward J. Bunn to Lavanoux, February 13, 1964. Of this episode, Lavanoux said: "A number of friends started the ball rolling, and it was only when I received a letter from the president of the university that I had an inkling of the affair." Lavanoux to Leopold Arnaud, October 12, 1964. LAS, 42. These friends were Clement McNaspy, Joseph Asherl, and Edmund Delaney. Lavanoux to Barry Byrne, November 2, 1964. LAS, 42.

41. Lavanoux to Brother Cajetan Baumann, October 3, 1968. The medal was awarded at a ceremony on October 6, 1968. LAS, 47.

42. Telegram, Robert Durham to Lavanoux, December 12, 1967 (LAS, 46), and *LA* 37:1 (November, 1969), 9. Awarded at the Institute's Portland, Oregon, Convention, June 26, 1968. Lavanoux was unable to attend the Portland Convention, having been hospitalized the week before, suffering from exhaustion.

43. Lavanoux to Charles P. Grace, September 23, 1961. LAS, 38.

44. Joachim Nabuco to Lavanoux, January 5, 1960. LAS, 37.

45. Lavanoux to Charles P. Grace, September 23, 1961. LAS, 38. Lavanoux, who did not read Latin, called upon the Society's chaplain for a translation of the document.

46. See Appendix C. These documents were presented to the subcommittee on April 7, 1961.

47. Joachim Nabuco to Lavanoux, January 14, 1962. LAS, 41. Lavanoux requested that he be allowed to have his name published in this regard, but he was told by Vatican officials that because he and others "were chosen directly, the general secretary thinks it wiser *not* to have names (yours and others) published, at least at the present moment." A. Bugnini to Lavanoux, November 21, 1961. LAS, 41. Nabuco further reports that the general secretary "thinks there might be trouble — but that you can show your appointment to Fr. LaFarge telling him not to pass it on."

48. Lavanoux to Charles Grace, September 23, 1963. LAS, 42. This practice of sending copies of *LA* to members of the Vatican staff continued into the papacy of Paul VI. "At the Holy Father's request, we have been mailing to him — via the Secretary of State at the Vatican — 10 copies of each issue of *LA*, airmail. It seems the Holy Father likes to pass them on to some of his visitors." Lavanoux to Patrick Quinn, February 14, 1966. LAS, 45.

49. The interaction between Lavanoux, representing the Liturgical Arts Society, and the Vatican came to a climax on July 6, 1966, when Lavanoux had a ten-minute private audience with Pope Paul VI. During the interview, Lavanoux presented the Pope with a specially bound volume of *Liturgical Arts* and a white chasuble made by Robert Bonnette of Northfield, Vermont. This final trip abroad was paid for by another private donation. Lavanoux to Ann Light, August 3, 1966. LAS, 45.

50. Lavanoux to Robert Cerny, January 6, 1964. LAS, 43.

51. Lavanoux to Joachim Nabuco, March 9, 1964. LAS, 43.

52. *Ibid.*

53. Gerald Carroll to Subscribers and Friends, April 25, 1968. LAS, 192. Lavanoux to Robert Garrity, May 13, 1968; Lavanoux to Joseph Foley, April 23, 1968. LAS, 47.

54. Lavanoux to Alice Walsh, July 13, 1967. LAS, 48.

55. Lavanoux to Joseph Calderone, October 11, 1967. LAS, 46.

56. Lavanoux to L. J. Eliner, February 6, 1968. LAS, 48.

57. Lavanoux to Fr. Gabriel Mary, O.F.M., October 10, 1967. ML, 3. Retirement for Lavanoux was out of the question. As he figured it, his total retirement income would be approximately $50 per month. He had no savings, had not been able to pay into his pension or Social Security accounts consistently, and was supporting his brother and sister, as he had done for many years. Lavanoux to Leo Tibesar, May 5, 1969. LAS, 49.

58. Lavanoux to Vital Vodusch, April 30, 1971. LAS, 53.

59. Lavanoux to Clement McNaspy, September 22, 1969. "The Quilisma Club is in a state of crisis. . . The problem is one which revolves around . . . the fact that Fr. Foley does not want to *lead*, as did Dr. Gibbs. Many meetings have been spent in endless talk, talk. . ." LAS, 50.

60. Lavanoux to Hugo Schnell, October 21, 1971. LAS, 56.

61. John P. Hanley to Lavanoux, March 2, 1970. LAS, 50.

62. Joseph Asherl to Lavanoux, no date. LAS, 51.

63. Lavanoux to C. Hanley, August 27, 1970. LAS, 51.

64. Lavanoux to Fr. Gabriel Mary, O.F.M., October 31, 1967. ML, 3.

65. "Editorial," *LA* 40:1 (November, 1971), 3.

66. John Dooley to Lavanoux, April 4, 1972. ML, 3.

67. *Ibid.*

68. Lavanoux to Peter Sidler, O.S.B., March 8, 1971. ML, 3.

69. Lavanoux to Joseph Asherl, July 7, 1972. ML, 3.

70. Lavanoux was awarded the degree of Doctor of Humane Letters, *honoris causa* , at commencement exercises, May 27, 1971. Michael F. Kennelly to Lavanoux, May 14, 1971. ML, 3.

71. "Interface," an exhibition sponsored by the Society for the Arts and Religion and held at the Interchurch Center, 475 Riverside Drive, New York City, beginning August 3, 1972. ML, 3.

72. The "Maurice Lavanoux Award in the Cultic Arts" was established in 1971 by the New England Liturgical Committee to be given annually to "the person who makes the most significant contribution to the fine arts as they apply to liturgy and liturgical usage." Press Release, Weston, Massachusetts, February 19, 1971, and William Leonard to Lavanoux, March 6, 1971. ML, 3.

73. Lavanoux to Agnes Shanley, September 11, 1972; and Lavanoux to May Ascher, September 6, 1972. ML, 3.

74. Carroll to Subscribers and Friends, September 22, 1972. ML, 3.

75. Lavanoux to Thomas Blantz, October 2, 1972. ML, 3.

76. Lavanoux to Robert Hovda, October 10, 1972. ML, 3.

77. The Society was unwilling to declare bankruptcy, believing that it was morally obligated to repay the full amount of its debt to creditors.

78. Lavanoux, diary entry, October 31, 1972. ML, 3.

79. Eugene Clark to Gerald Carroll, December 1, 1972. SRCA, 6.

80. *Ibid.* There was one final difficulty between the New York archdiocese and Lavanoux, which Lavanoux saw as further proof of the archdiocese's indifference to the work of the Liturgical Arts Society. In September, it had been discovered that Lavanoux, who had been contributing to the archdiocesan pension fund, owed a "Past Service Liability" of $896.70, since he had not always been able to afford payments into the fund. He was told that until this sum was paid he could not collect retirement benefits. The Cardinal was asked by Liturgical Arts Society representatives if he would contribute $500 to the fund in honor of Lavanoux's years of service. Cooke refused the request, but the members of the Quilisma Club donated the necessary amount to pay into the fund. John Ruvo to Lavanoux, September 27, 1972; Gerald Carroll to Terrence Cooke, October 3, 1972; Lavanoux to John Delaney, November 7, 1972; Eugene Clark to Gerald Carroll, December 1, 1972. ML, 3.

81. E.g., *The Brooklyn Tablet* LXXV:8 (June 6, 1973), 8; John Deedy, "A Man, A Movement, A Magazine," *The Commonweal* XCVII (December 6, 1972), 148-149.

82. The total of more than 114,000 items arrived a week later at the University of Notre Dame. Thomas Blantz to Lavanoux, December 18, 1972. ML, 3.

83. Lavanoux to Peter Anson, December 12, 1972. ML, 3.

84. Lavanoux had been editor of *Stained Glass* in 1928-1929 but had "run afoul of those who wanted to keep the publication a 'trade journal,' whereas I wanted to make the magazine a general publication on the *art* of stained glass. Now it seems the trend is toward my point of view." Lavanoux to Robert Hovda, March 6, 1973. SRCA, 15.

85. His column ran from 1972 to 1974.

86. Clarence Walton to Lavanoux, March 7, 1973. SRCA, 15. Again, Lavanoux accepted the honor with humility. "This is only my fourth doctorate," he is reported to have said. "Bob Hope already has twelve!" *America* CXXVII:22 (June 9, 1973), 544.

87. The archives of the Society for the Renewal of Christian Art were donated to the University of Notre Dame in 1978.
88. Lavanoux to M. Ferlin, April 2, 1974. SRCA, 16.
89. Lavanoux to Vincent Solomita, October 31, 1972. SRCA, 15.
90. Reported by John Deedy in *The Commonweal* XCVII:45 (November 22, 1974), 178.
91. Lavanoux to Gerald Carroll, September 14, 1974. SRCA, 15.
92. Among them have been *Motive, Christian Art, and Anno Domini.*

1. For analysis of the history and theology of the American Liturgical Movement, see Ernest B. Koenker, *The Liturgical Renaissance in the Roman Catholic Church* (Chicago: University of Chicago Press, 1954); Paul B. Marx, *Virgil Michel and the Liturgical Movement* (Collegeville, Minnesota: Liturgical Press, 1957); Jeremy Hall, *The Full Stature of Christ* (Collegeville: Liturgical Press, 1976); Sonya Quitslund, *Beauduin: A Prophet Vindicated* (New York: Newman, 1973); and John L. Klein, *The Role of Gerald Ellard in the Development of the Contemporary American Catholic Liturgical Movement* (Ph.D. dissertation: Fordham University, 1971).

2. Lavanoux, diary entry, December 9, 1969. SRCA, 15.

3. *Ibid*.

4. Lavanoux to Coleman Barry, October 27, 1960. LAS, 39.

5. Lavanoux to Romano Guardini, May 8, 1951. LAS, 27. "Much of my interest in this work," Lavanoux wrote to Guardini, "really began to take definite form when I read the French edition of your book *The Spirit of the Liturgy* in 1927 or thereabouts. . . . Your work has been a keystone of much of my own work since the very beginning of the foundation of our Society."

6. See pages 1-2.

7. See Everitt Harman, "Constitution and Bylaws for a Benedictine Oblate Guild . . . ." LAS, 188.

8. See page 4.

9. *Ibid*.

10. See Chapter 7.

11. William Busch, associate and friend of Virgil Michel, acknowledged that Lavanoux clearly had "deeply at heart" the principles set forth by Abbot Herwegen and the European liturgical movement. William Busch to Lavanoux, May 9, 1931. LAS, 7.

12. Lavanoux, "An Architect's Dilemma," *Orate Fratres* 3:9 (July 14, 1929), 277-281.

13. Lavanoux to Oliver Reagan, March 26, 1929. LAS, 188.

14. *LA*, Virgil Michel Retrospective, 1956.

15. Virgil Michel to Bancel LaFarge, February 14, 1930. LAS, 7. Gerald Ellard to John LaFarge, November 30, 1930; William Busch to Lavanoux, May 9, 1931. LAS, 7.

16. See John LaFarge, *The Manner is Ordinary* (New York: Harcourt Brace, 1954), 288ff. As deliberations over the future of the Liturgical Arts Society continued, Lavanoux became increasingly concerned about the degree to which his fellow founders shared a commitment to the goals and principles of liturgical renewal. "How many of the officers, directors, or charter members [of the Society] receive any of the existing publications such as *Orate Fratres*," Lavanoux wrote to Henry Lorin Binsse just after Binsse had been appointed managing editor of *Liturgical Arts*, "and how many own books on the liturgy?" Lavanoux to Binsse, July 4, 1931. LAS, 7. See also Lavanoux to Oliver Reagan, February 26, 1929. LAS, 7.

17. It is clear that the pioneers of the liturgical apostolate saw the Society as one of its own and, over the years, Society secretary Lavanoux lectured at important gatherings of the American liturgical establishment. He was an invited speaker at the first National Liturgical Week in 1940 (and of every Liturgical Week thereafter), at centers of liturgical scholarship such as St. John's, Collegeville, and at many of the early "liturgical summer schools" around the country. At one point, liturgist Gerald Ellard remarked of Lavanoux: "If all of the movers of the Liturgical Movement moved as swiftly as [Lavanoux], some movement would be perceptible!" Gerald Ellard to Lav-

anoux, March 2, 1950. LAS, 27. See also Michael Ducey to Lavanoux, June 28, 1944. LAS, 23. *Proceedings of the 1940 National Liturgical Week* (Washington: Benedictine Liturgical Conference, 1940), 96. Virgil Michel to Lavanoux, December 6-7, 1936, and P. Morris to Lavanoux, July 3, 1943. ML, 3.

18. See pages 3-7.

19. Lavanoux (like Henry Lorin Binsse before him) was rather heavy-handed in his editorial style during his 35-year tenure, generally making explicit requests for articles and then designating quite specifically their content. Very often, he would send his authors a full outline of the article as he wished it written. See, for example, Lavanoux to Bishop McNicholas, October 2, 1935. LAS, 8.

20. The Editor's Diary became a regular feature of *Liturgical Arts* in its 19:2 (February, 1951) issue and appeared in virtually every issue thereafter. It was often the single largest item in a given issue, particularly during the final years of the magazine's publication.

21. Ides van der Gracht, "Some Notes on a Movement to Make Catholic Spirit, Culture, and Liturgy More Effective and Fertile in Our Modern Intellectual and Artistic Life," May 13, 1928. LAS, 188. The idea of the liturgy as an artform, expressive of beauty and truth, was widespread among the early pioneers of the Liturgical Movement in both Europe and the United States. In *The Spirit of the Liturgy*, Romano Guardini devoted the whole of Chapter 6 to this theme, opening with the words, "The liturgy is art, translated into the terms of life."

22. Van der Gracht, *ibid.*, 8.

23. *Ibid.*, 5.

24. *Ibid.*

25. Liturgical Arts Society, brochure, 1931-1938. LAS, 188.

26. *Ibid.*, 2.

27. Represented by Everitt Harman. See page 1ff.

28. Constitution and Bylaws, "Benedictine Oblate Guild of Architects, Artists, and Craftsmen," Article II, Purpose. LAS, 188.

29. *Ibid.*

30. *LA* 3:3-4 (Third-Fourth Quarter, 1933-4), 142 and passim.

31. *LA* 2:3 (Third Quarter, 1932).

32. *Ibid.*, 111-117.

33. *LA* 6:1 (February, 1937).

34. Max Jordan to Ides van der Gracht, June 13, 1928. LAS, 188.

35. *Orate Fratres* 3:9 (July 14, 1929), 227-281.

36. *Ibid.*, 227.

37. *Ibid.*, 278.

38. *Ibid.*, 281.

39. See Appendix A, Bylaws.

40. Prospectus, "Liturgical Arts Society," 1931-1938, p. 2. LAS, 188.

41. E.g., "The Font and the Baptistry," "The Exposition of Throne and Monstrance," "The Law of Liturgical Music," and "The Textile Appurtenances of the Altar."

42. "A Chancery Letter: Reflections on the Forty-Hours Devotion," *LA* 8:2 (January, 1940), 33.

43. E.g., Eric MacKenzie, S.T.L., J.C.L., "Liturgical Requirements for Sacred Vessels," *LA* 4:4 (Fourth Quarter, 1935), 101.

44. Lavanoux, "Never a Dull Moment," 227. ML, 3.

45. *LA* 3:3-4 (Third-Fourth Quarter, 1934).

46. *Ibid.*, 157.

47. *Ibid.*, 158. See also Walter Ong, "The Renaissance Myth and the American Catholic Mind," *Frontiers of American Catholicism*, (New York: Macmillan, 1957), 52-85.

48. See pages 86ff.

49. *LA* 3:1 (First Quarter, 1934), 40.

50. *Acta Apostolicae Sedis* 35 (1943), 193-248.

51. Gerald Ellard, *ibid.*, 160.

52. *Ibid.*, 165.

53. Galatians 2:20.

54. E.g., "Editorial," *LA* 7:2 (February, 1939), 36.

55. Gerald Ellard, "Liturgy: An Old Word with a New Meaning," *LA* 7:3 (May, 1939), 47ff, and Michael Ducey, *LA* 8:2 (January, 1940).

56. *LA* 6:2 (Second Quarter, 1937), 169.

57. "Editorial," *LA* 9:1 (October, 1940), 1.

58. "Editorial," *LA* 14:4 (August, 1946), 128.

59. *LA* 6:1 (First Quarter, 1937), 3.

60. "The Spirit of Continuity in the Liturgy," *LA* 11:2 (February, 1943), 48ff.

61. Albert Hammestaede, O.S.B., "The Liturgy as Art," *LA* 5:2 (Second Quarter, 1936), 45.

62. Lavanoux to the Very Rev. Alexander Sigur, April 20, 1957. ML, 3.

63. E.g., Fernand Cabrol, "The Liturgical Year," *LA* 9:4 (August, 1941), 73ff.

64. Leopold Arnaud, "The Living Tradition in Christian Art," *LA* 9:3 (May, 1941), 47.

65. *Acta Apostolicae Sedis* 39 (1947), 521-595.

66. E.g., Lambert Beauduin, "L'Encyclique 'Mediator Dei' et le mouvement liturgique," *La Maison Dieu* 13 (1948), 7-25, and William Busch, "About the Encyclical 'Mediator Dei,'" *"Orate Fratres* 22 (1947-1948), 53-56.

67. Donald Carroll to Lavanoux, December 12, 1947. LAS, 27.

68. Gerald Ellard to Lavanoux, December 15, 1947. LAS 26. Lavanoux responded: "As you know, I have never feared that *Liturgical Arts* would get into trouble with the authorities since we are very careful not to stray from the *doctrine* of the *Church*, though we do at times run afoul of prejudices and opinions of individuals, and that is quite another matter." Lavanoux to Gerald Ellard, December 17, 1947. LAS, 26.

69. John LaFarge, "Editorial," *LA* 16:2 (February, 1948), 39.

70. *Ibid.*

71. *Ibid.*

72. *Ibid.*

73. Interestingly, *LA*'s retrospective on the work of Virgil Michel of 1956 never once mentions the Mystical-Body motif with which he was so closely identified.

74. *LA* 25:1 (November, 1956), 6ff.

75. *Ibid.*, 7.

76. *Ibid.*, 6.

77. "Notes for the subcommission on Sacred Art Lavanoux . . .," April 7, 1961. See Appendix D.

78. "Editorial," *LA* 25:3 (May, 1957), 65.

79. *LA* 34:2 (February, 1966), 38.

80. *LA* 38:2 (February, 1970), 39.

81. *Ibid.*

Notes for pages 78 to 105

82. *Ibid.*

83. *LA* 33:3 (May, 1964), 61.

84. *LA* 34:2 (February, 1966), 38.

85. *Ibid.*

86. *LA* 33:3 (May, 1965), 61.

87. *LA* 36:2 (February, 1968), 50.

88. *LA* 39:4 (November, 1971), 97.

89. See, e.g., *LA* 40:3 (May, 1972), 94.

90. *LA* 36:1 (November, 1968), 24. See also *Experiments in Community: Proceedings of the Twenty-eighth North American Liturgical Week, Kansas City, Missouri, 1967* (Washington, D.C., 1967), 42-58, for details of some of the liturgical experiments undertaken at the conference. The closing mass and "creative rites" held in hotel sleeping rooms during the Liturgical Week, although not included in the proceedings, were also the focus of considerable negative attention, both by Church officials and by the Roman Catholic press.

91. *Ibid.* Quotation from the Rev. Raymond Potvin.

92. *Ibid.* Two years later, *Liturgical Arts* would take a more humorous look at the vicissitudes of liturgical experimentation after the Council in "How to Pass for a New Breed" (37:2), offering a series of guidelines to help in answering such questions as "What color stole is correctly worn with a 'Peanuts' sweatshirt?"

93. *LA* 36:4 (August, 1968), 97.

94. *LA* 40:3 (May, 1971), 94.

95. *LA* 40:2 (February, 1970), 65.

96. *LA* 35:1 (November, 1966), 2.

97. *LA* 38:2 (February, 1970), 64.

98. See HA. Reinhold, *HAR: The Autobiography of Hans Ansgar Reinhold* (New York: Herder and Herder, 1968).

99. *LA* 10:3 (May, 1942), 53.

100. *LA* 9:4 (August, 1941), 73.

101. Peter Anson, "Mass Facing the People," *LA* 24:1 (November, 1955), 2ff.

102. Lois Malloy and Charlene Gaffney, "Liturgy and the Rural Life Movement," *LA* 9:4 (May, 1941), 52.

103. Brochure, "Liturgical Arts Society" (1932), 1. LAS, 188.

104. For example, *LA* draws readers' attention to a recent ruling by the bishop of Belleville, Illinois, directing parishes to limit their choirs strictly to men vested in cassocks. Women organists are to be replaced by men, and religious sisters are no longer to serve as organists for male choirs. *LA* 7:1 (October, 1938), 1.

105. "Editorial," *LA* 8:1 (November, 1940), 1.

106. *LA* 8:1 (November, 1940), 4.

107. *Ibid.*, 5.

108. Gerald Ellard, "Liturgy and Tradition," *LA* 10:4 (August, 1942), 56.

109. *Ibid.*

110. Lavanoux to Becket Gibbs, October 5, 1934. LAS, 4.

111. See *Orate Fratres* 15 (1941), 250.

112. *LA* 3:2 (Second Quarter, 1934), 59. In addition to those who feared that the liturgical movement was advocating a move toward "Protestantism," it was very common to find others who believed that lay participation was to be achieved *at the expense of* the ordained priesthood. This aggressive interest in the active participation

of the laity in Christian corporate worship is not surprising when one considers that the Society was founded entirely by lay persons. See pages 1ff.

113. *LA* 13:1 (November, 1944), 2.

114. "Editorial," *LA* 14:2 (February, 1946), 28.

115. See pages 44ff.

116. Becket Gibbs, "The Quilisma Club," unpublished paper, ca. 1937. LAS, 4.

117. *LA* 2:3 (Third Quarter, 1932), 111ff.

118. *Ibid.*, 116.

119. The Ward Method, developed by Justine Ward and popularized by the Pius X School of Sacred Music, Manhattanville, New York, was often the subject of *Liturgical Arts*' attention. E.g., see *LA* 7:2 and 7:3 (February and May, 1939).

120. *LA* 9:4 (August, 1941), 67. The Liturgical Arts Society saw its establishment of a Gregorian *schola cantorum* (affectionately known as the "Quilisma Club") in 1934 as its own active part in the restoration of plainchant as the normative music of the Roman Catholic Church. It was hoped that this group would serve as a model for those who wished to establish chant choirs in parishes or schools. See pages 44ff.

121. "Editorial," *LA* 10:2 (February, 1942), 31.

122. "A Layman Looks at the Liturgy," *LA* 7:2 (February, 1939), 19.

123. John LaFarge, "The Social Mission of the Liturgy," *LA* 6:1 (First Quarter, 1937), 33ff.

124. *Ibid.*, 35.

125. *Ibid.*, 34.

126. *Ibid.*, 35.

127. *Mediator Dei*, Chapter V, paragraph 63-64, as printed in R. Kevin Seasoltz, *The New Liturgy* (New York:) Herder and Herder, 1966 107ff. "Admittedly, the adoption of the vernacular in quite a number of functions may prove of great benefit to the faithful." See also *LA* 19:2 (February, 1950), 45.

128. *LA* 19:2 (February, 1950), 44.

129. *Ibid.*

130. With the publication of the *Rituale Parvum Gallicae Linguae*, November 28, 1947.

131. With the proposal of the *Rituale Germaniae* from the German bishops, in which approval was granted for the use of the vernacular by the priest in certain parts of the sacraments and occasional services.

132. *LA* 19:2 (February, 1940), 45.

133. E.g., Clement J. McNaspy, S.J., "A Plea for Intelligibility," *LA* 23:1 (November, 1954), 2.

134. Edward Sutfin, "Use of the Vernacular," *LA* 28:2 (February, 1960), 35.

135. *Ibid.*

136. "Editor's Diary," *LA* 38:2 (February, 1970), 58.

137. Lavanoux to John Spencer, March 12, 1968. LAS, 49.

138. George S. Burchill, "Some Thoughts Concerning the Language of the Mass," *LA* 34:3 (May, 1966), 84ff.

139. *Ibid.*.

140. *Ibid.*

141. Lavanoux, 133. ML, 3.

142. "Editor's Diary," *LA* 26:4 (August, 1958), 132.

143. See, e.g., *LA* 26:3 (May, 1958).

144. *LA* 21:3 (May, 1953) and 29:4 (August, 1961).

145. *LA* 36:1 (November, 1967).

146. *LA* 26:4 (August, 1958), 133.

147. *Ibid.*

148. *"Constitution on the Sacred Liturgy,"* I:2, paragraph 14. (R. Kevin Seasoltz, *The New Liturgy*, 476ff.).

149. "Editorial," *LA* 38:1 (November, 1971), 1.

150. *LA* 34:2 (February, 1966), 38.

151. *LA* 39:4 (August, 1971), 97.

152. *LA* 38:3 (May, 1970), 44.

153. *LA* 33:3 (May, 1965), 81ff.

154. Constance Parvey, "Moon People's Liturgy," *LA* 36:1 (November, 1967), 11.

155. *LA* 33:3 (May, 1965), 84.

156. "Editorial," *LA* 38:2 (February, 1970), 39.

157. "Editor's Diary," *LA* 39:1 (November, 1970), 12.

158. "Editor's Diary," *LA* 38:2 (February, 1970), 59.

CHAPTER SEVEN

1. See page 1.
2. E.g., Everitt Harman's "Proposed Constitution and Bylaws for a Benedictine Oblates Guild of Architects, Artists, and Craftsmen," unpublished paper, January, 1928. LAS, 188.
3. See page 82.
4. Ides van der Gracht, "Some Notes on a Movement to Make Catholic Spirit, Culture, and Liturgy More Effective and Fertile in Our Modern Intellectual and Artistic Life," May 13, 1928, 5. LAS, 188.
5. *Ibid.*, 6.
6. *Ibid.*, 3.
7. See pages 82-3.
8. *Art and Scholasticism with other Essays*, trans. by J. F. Scanlan (New York: Scribners, 1930). When Maritain settled in the United States in 1936, he became an important supporter of the Liturgical Arts Society and a close friend of Lavanoux. See *LA* 17:4 (August, 1949). Maritain also served as liaison between the Liturgical Arts Society and the Vatican while he was French Ambassador to the Holy See.
9. Among these was Bancel LaFarge. See, e.g., Bancel LaFarge to Lavanoux, March 4, 1936. LAS, 7.
10. See A. Graham Carey, *Pattern* (Newport: John Stevens, 1938) and *Thoughts and Things* (Newport: John Stevens, 1937). The motto at the Ditchling Common (Sussex) home of Eric Gill's own craft guild was "Men rich in virtue studying beautifulness, living in peace in their houses."
11. Lavanoux to John Douaire, April 12, 1949. LAS, 26.
12. A. Graham Carey to Binsse, February 2, 1936. LAS, 7.
13. Binsse to A. Graham Carey, March 10, 1936. LAS, 7.
14. *Ibid.* Although Lavanoux and Binsse had clearly staked out a domain for the Liturgical Arts Society and *LA* in which the formal consideration of the philosophy of art played only a minor role, there were certain factors that made them unwilling to sever utterly the relationship with Benson and Carey. One of these factors was undoubtedly money, with which Carey was rather well endowed. In 1933, during one of the Society's innumerable fund-raising campaigns, Carey had bought a $100 bond on which the Society had never paid any of the interest it had promised, and he had made outright donations of several hundred dollars more on other occasions. Clearly, there were bad feelings on Carey's part and embarrassment on the part of the Society over this issue, and although Carey wished to write off the loan as a bad investment, the Society was not inclined to discontinue its relationship until the outstanding debt had been settled. (In 1942, the Society asked Carey to cancel its indebtedness, and Carey graciously complied.) On a deeper level, Lavanoux and others certainly sensed that Benson and Carey's position had some value, even though it ran counter to prevailing opinion within the Society. There was little doubt that without occasional attention to underlying philosophical principles, superficial debates over artistic taste might indeed overwhelm the Society's program. In 1939, Lavanoux suggested that Carey renew his membership in the Liturgical Arts Society, since he felt "quite sure that [they could]work in an amicable fashion for a cause which [they] all believe is very much needed." But Carey had moved on to other pursuits and rejected what he referred to as Lavanoux's "continually extended fraternal hand." In so doing, he admitted that al-

though he and Lavanoux shared "ends [which] were the same, the means we have chosen to achieve those ends are very different." A. Graham Carey to Binsse, February 3, 1936 (LAS, 15); Lavanoux to Bancel LaFarge, March 10, 1937 (LAS, 7); Lavanoux to A. Graham Carey, October 20, 1939 (LAS, 17); A. Graham Carey to Lavanoux, October 19, 1939 (LAS, 17); see also Maureen Murphy, *Right Reason in an Unreasonable World* (unpublished Ph.D. dissertation, University of Notre Dame, 1975) for an analysis of the Catholic Art Association, to which Carey and Benson devoted substantial energy in the years that followed.

15. *LA* 2:1 (First Quarter, 1933), 28.

16. *Ibid.*, 39.

17. *LA* 7:1 (October, 1938), 2.

18. *LA* 17:1 (November, 1948), 2.

19. Binsse to A. Graham Carey, March 30, 1936. LAS, 2.

20. See especially Joseph Lonergan, "Art in the Living Parish," *LA* 10:2 (February, 1941), 36.

21. "The Nature of Religious Art," *LA* 1:1 (First Quarter, 1931), 2ff.

22. "The Living Tradition in Christian Art," *LA* 9:2 (February, 1941), 47.

23. John LaFarge, "Foreword," *LA* 30:1 (November, 1961), 14.

24. "Art and Catechesis," *LA* 25:3 (May, 1957), 34.

25. The Portland Diocese Commission on Sacred Art, "Letter," *LA* 28:2 (February, 1960), 52.

26. "Proceedings of the Twenty-first Annual Meeting, April 2, 1951," *LA* 19:3 (May, 1951), 57.

27. See, for example, A. Graham Carey, "The Craftsmanship of Sacred Vessels," *LA* 2:1 (First quarter, 1933), 28ff.

28. "Editorial," *LA* 29:3 (May, 1961), 61.

29. "Architecture and the Liturgy," *LA* 5:1 (First Quarter, 1936), 13.

30. *LA* 32:1 (November, 1963), 10.

31. In this connection, another person who influenced members of the founding group, and especially Lavanoux, was Gaspar Lefebvre, who in 1927 had himself established a fortnightly periodical, *L'artisan liturgique*. See page 31-32.

32. "Liturgical Art," *Orate Fratres* 1:6 (1927), 182.

33. *Ibid.*, 183.

34. It is written together with Gill's disciple David Jones.

35. Perhaps the closest of Gill's American friends were A. Graham Carey and John Howard Benson. See Robert Speight, *The Life of Eric Gill* (London: Methuen, 1966), 250, 291; and Walter Shewring, ed., *Letters of Eric Gill* (New York: Devin-Adair, 1948), letters 154, 160, 172, et al.

36. This brief (four short paragraphs) discussion makes the point that liturgical art is of a more public nature than other types of art and should not "flaunt the personal or private point of view."

37. E.g. Harman, "Proposed Constitution . . ., see footnote 2 above.

38. Everitt Harman to Ides van der Gracht, September 26, 1928. LAS, 188.

39. Constitution of the Liturgical Arts Society, Article II: Object. See Appendix A.

40. Bylaws of the Liturgical Arts Society, Article I: Object and standards. See Appendix A.

41. Liturgical Arts Society, brochure, 1932-1938, 3. LAS, 188.

42. Liturgical Arts Society, brochure, 1933, 2. LAS, 188.

Notes from pages 106 to 118

43. "Editorial," *LA* 2:4 (1933) 165.

44. Liturgical Arts Society, brochure, 1933, 2. LAS, 188.

45. *Ibid*.

46. "The Nature of Religious Art," *LA* 1:1 (First Quarter, 1931), 3.

47. *LA* 14:2, 43. One of the most unusual refinements of this idea is found in the 1933 prospectus of the Liturgical Arts Society, which states that we adorn the house of God "to make up for the historic neglect" suffered by the infant Jesus in the "poverty and meanness of the stable."

48. Ildefons Herwegen, "The Nature of Religious Art," *LA* 1:1 (First Quarter, 1931), 4.

49. Everitt Harman to Ides van der Gracht, November 26, 1927. LAS, 188.

50. Liturgical Arts Society, prospectus, 1933. LAS, 188.

51. *Ibid*. and "Editorial," *LA* 1:1 (First Quarter, 1931), 2.

52. See pages 49-50.

53. Liturgical Arts Society, brochure, 1932. LAS, 188.

54. See pages 119-120.

55. Liturgical Arts Society, lecture series brochure, 1935. LAS, 188.

56. *LA* 27:4 (August, 1959), 95.

57. *Ibid*.

58. John LaFarge, "A Quarter-Century Retrospect L.A.S.," *LA* 25:1 (November, 1956), 3.

59. *LA* 16:4 (August, 1948), 110.

60. *LA* 32:1 (November, 1963), 1, and 35:1 (November, 1966), 30.

61. *LA* 19:3 (May, 1951), 57.

62. "Letter to an Indian Christian Artist," *LA* 32:1 (November, 1962), 10.

63. *LA* 25:1 and John Walter Wood, "Report on the Activities of the Liturgical Arts Society," April, 1956. LAS, 72.

64. John LaFarge, *LA* 25:1 (November, 1956), 2ff.

65. *Ibid*.

66. "Architecture and the Liturgy," *LA* 5:1 (First Quarter, 1936), 13.

67. *Ibid*.

68. *Ibid*.

69. "The Liturgy as Art," *LA* 5:2 (Second Quarter, 1936), 41.

70. "The Dynamism of the Liturgy," *LA* 25:1 (November, 1956), 6-7.

1. According to Ides van der Gracht's analysis, the roots of the problem could be traced to the previous century, when the American Church was forced to abandon its traditional concern for "aesthetic expression" to devote its energies to the "rush of practical considerations" occasioned by massive Roman Catholic immigration to the United States. Ides van der Gracht., "Some Notes on a Movement to Make Catholic Spirit, Culture, and Liturgy More Effective and Fertile in Our Modern Intellectual and Artistic Life," 2. LAS, 188.

2. *Ibid.*, 3.

3. *Ibid.*

4. *Ibid.*, 2.

5. *Ibid.*, 3.

6. *Ibid.*

7. E.g., *LA* 1:1 (October, 1931); 19:3 (May, 1951), 56.

8. See pages 113ff.

9. Eric Gill, *Art* (London: The Bodley Head, 1934), 116.

10. *Ibid.*, 97

11. *Ibid.*, 119-120. See also John LaFarge, *Catalogue for a Small Church Exhibition,* Liturgical Arts Society, 1933, and Caryll Houselander, "The Liturgical Artist and the Workman," *LA* 14:3 (May, 1946), 53ff.

12. See pages 108-111.

13. Lavanoux, "What Can Be Done About It?" *LA* 11:2 (February, 1943), 43ff.; Frederic Whitaker, "We Get What We Ask For, Unfortunately," *ibid.*, 44ff; "Editor's Diary," *LA* 24:1 (November, 1955), 16.

14. Only one of the offices within the Society's leadership was designated for a member of the clergy, and that was the office of Chaplain to the Society. No member of the clergy ever served as President, Vicepresident, Secretary, or Treasurer during the Society's history. Very early, the Board of Directors which had often consisted of members of the clergy, had been stripped of its original influence in decision-making for the Society.

15. Everitt Harman, "ProposedConstitution and Bylaws for a Benedictine Oblates Guild of Architects, Artists, and Craftsmen," Article III: Membership, 1928. LAS, 188.

16. Constitution and Bylaws of the Liturgical Arts Society, October, 1928. See Appendix A. LAS, 188; ML, 3.

17. Liturgical Arts Society, prospectus, 1933.

18. *Ibid.*, 1. (In this case, the word "layman" seems to refer to non-artists.)

19. *Ibid.*, 2.

20. *Ibid.*, 3. *LA* 1:1 (Fall, 1931), 3.

21. Ides van der Gracht to Lavanoux, November 4, 1930. LAS, 7.

22. *Ibid.*

23. Liturgical Arts Society, prospectus, 5. LAS, 7.

24. Liturgical Arts Society, lecture series brochure, 1935. LAS, 7.

25. "Editorial," *LA* 8:1 (January, 1940), 21.

26. *Ibid.*

27. John Moody to Archbishop Spellman, February 7, 1940, and John Moody to Lavanoux, March 5, 1940.

28. Lavanoux to Iris Conlay, February 15, 1954. LAS, 30.

29. Particularly influential was Yves Congar's *Jalons pour une Theologie du Laicat,*

from which Lavanoux often quoted in his editorials. E.g., in *LA* 24:2: "It is certainly in accord with the mind of the Church and with current practice that the laity should not simply take a leading part but should effectively direct certain undertakings, with due safeguard for the hierarchical principle."

30. July 30, 1965.

31. "Editorial," *LA* 34:2 (February, 1966), 52.

32. *Ibid.*

33. Ides van der Gracht, "Some Notes on a Movement . . .," 3 and 6. LAS, 188. Although this seems a rather bald expression of class-conscious elitism, it is well within the perimeters of the lay intellectual revival of the 1920s, represented by such persons as Jacques Maritain and magazines such as *The Commonweal*.

34. *Ibid.*, 3.

35. *Ibid.*, 7.

36. *Ibid.*, 8.

37. Liturgical Arts Society Sec. prospectus, 1. LAS, 7.

38. Bylaws of the Liturgical Arts Society Article II Membership, sec. 1 and 2.

39. *Ibid.*, Article II: Membership, sec. 3.

40. *Ibid.*, Article IV Government:, sec. 1 and 5. It is clear also that this principle was put into practice. When founding member Wright Goodhue (nephew of architect Bertram Grosvenor Goodhue) left the Roman Catholic Church in 1930, his resignation was seen to be entirely appropriate and necessary by other founding members. Everitt Harman to Lavanoux, March 3, 1930 (LAS, 7), and Lavanoux to Thomas Coakley, October 22, 1930. LAS, 3.

41. See Chapter 6.

42. See Chapter 7.

43. The fullest expression of this is to be found in *LA* 3:2 (Second Quarter, 1934), which was dedicated to the work of Augustus Welby Northmore Pugin.

44. See "Religious Art and the Priest of Today," *LA* 14:1 (November, 1945), 2, and "An Altar Society of Wider Scope," *LA* 3:2 (Second Quarter, 1934).

45. "Editorial," *LA* 24:1 (November, 1955), 1.

46. "Editorial," *LA* 26:1 (November, 1957), 1.

47. "Editorial," *LA* 16:3 (May, 1948), 65.

48. Patrick Quinn, "Real Determinants in Roman Catholic Church Building," *LA* 31:1 (November, 1962), 2ff.

49. "Editorial," *LA* 26:1 (November, 1957), 1.

50. Roman Verotsko, "Experience in Community — The New Art," *LA* 40:2 (February, 1972), 52.

51. "The Isolated Artist," *LA* 16:1 (November, 1947), 17.

52. Lavanoux, "Never a Dull Moment," 172.

53. Gerald Phelan, *LA* 5:4 (July, 1936), 125.

54. *Ibid.*

55. Nearly twenty years later (*LA* 24:1 [November, 1955], 5ff.), Hector Velarde's "Art and Liberty" shows that little progress has been made in convincing artists that the laws of the Church can enable, rather than restrict, creativity. It describes the misapprehensions under which Roman Catholic artists continue to labor: that they are allowed to paint "only angels, virgins, and saints," that naturalism is the Church's only acceptable form of artistic expression, and that canons and rubrics unnecessarily restrict the use of the artistic product.

56. "Editorial," *LA* 16:1 (November, 1947), 2.

57. See Anthony Lauck, C.S.C., "What the Council Had to Say about Art," *LA* 32:4 (August, 1964), 111.

58. "The Homeland of Expression in Art is Still Faith, Prayer, and Religion: An Address by Pope Paul VI, in the Sistine Chapel on Ascension Sunday, May 7, 1964, at the Mass of the Artists to the Membership of the Italian Union of Artists," *LA* 33:1 (November, 1964), 2.

59. If there was one person who exemplified the qualities the Liturgical Arts Society sought in the liturgical artist, it was Georges Rouault. Although it was *LA*'s general policy not to feature articles on the work of individual artists and architects, at least three major articles on Rouault appeared, in 11:4 (August, 1943), 88; 16:3 (May, 1948), 91ff; 26:2 (February, 1958), and 47; 31:4 (November, 1963), 119ff. He also exemplified the misunderstanding that talented Roman Catholic artists suffered at the hands of the Church, having never been offered a commission to decorate a church. "Editor's Diary," 26:2 (February, 1958), 47.

60. See pages 2-3.

61. Ides van der Gracht, "Some Notes on a Movement . . .," 8. LAS, 188.

62. Everitt Harman, "Proposed Constitution and Bylaws for a Benedictine Oblates Guild of Architects, Artists, and Craftsmen," Article II: Approbation LAS, 188.

63. Bylaws of the Liturgical Arts Society, Article I tr.Object and Standards, Sec. 2.

64. Constitution of the Liturgical Arts Society, Article VI: Standards of Practice.

65. Bylaws of the Liturgical Arts Society, Article I Object and Standards: Sec. 2.

66. "Editorial," *LA* 7:4 (July, 1939), 53.

67. Kevin Seasoltz, "Elasticity in Liturgy and Law," *LA* 33:4 (August, 1965), 125.

68. Hector Velarde, "Art and Liberty," *LA* 24:1 (November, 1955), 5.

69. "Editorial," *LA* 28:1 (November, 1959), 1.

70. Paul VI, "Address to Union of Italian Artists . . .," *LA* 35:1 (November, 1966), 30.

71. "Letter to an Indian Christian Artist," *LA* 32:1 (November, 1962), 10.

72. "Editorial," *LA* 16:2 (February, 1948), 39. See also John LaFarge, "Private Opinion and Church Authority," *LA* 16:4 (August, 1948), 124ff.

73. *LA* 9:3 (May, 1941), 46.

74. "Editorial," *LA* 16:2 (February, 1948), 39.

75. John LaFarge, "Private Opinion and Church Authority," *LA* 16:4 (August, 1948), 124ff.

76. "Religious Art and the Priest of Today," *LA* 14:1 (November, 1945), 2.

77. "Editorial," *LA* 26:2 (February, 1958), 41.

78. "Editorial," *LA* 33:1 (November, 1964), 1.

79. Hector Velarde, "Notes on Architecture and Religion," *LA* 18:1 (November, 1949), 4.

80. "Elasticity in Liturgy and Law," *LA* 33:4 (August, 1965), 126. See also Lavanoux, "Never a Dull Moment," 149ff.

81. Lavanoux, "Catholics and Religious Art," in *Catholicism in America* (New York: Harcourt Brace, 1953), 201-208.

82. "Editorial," *LA* 8:2 (January, 1940), 22.

83. See pages 22-23.

84. See pages 54-56.

85. John LaFarge, "A Quarter-Century Retrospect, L.A.S.," *LA* 25:1 (November, 1956), 4.

86. *Ibid.*

87. John LaFarge, "Private Opinion and Church Authority," *LA* 16:4 (August, 1948), 124f.

88. "Editorial," *LA* 21:1 (November, 1952), 2, and Lavanoux to Gerald Ellard, October 4, 1954.

89. "Editorial," *LA* 37:2 (February, 1969), 57.

90. "Editor's Diary," *LA* 30:3 (May, 1962), 92.

91. "Editorial," *LA* 15:1 (November, 1946), 2.

92. John LaFarge, "Foreword," *LA* 30:1 (November, 1961), 14.

93. "Editorial," *LA* 22:3 (May, 1954), 74. See also "Editor's Diary," *LA* 23:1 (November, 1954), 8. "There is no question of disrespect, and the majority of artists I know, who are fully aware of the Catholic attitude in these matters will not question the *authority* of a bishop, but they are often puzzled by the vagaries of *private* opinion among prelates. It is in this area of divergence of honest opinion that artists can concentrate their objections."

94. "Editorial," *LA* 25:1 (November, 1956), 5.

95. "Editor's Diary," *LA* 38:1 (November, 1969).

96. John LaFarge, "Foreword," *LA* 30:1 (November, 1961), 15.

97. "What the Council Had to Say about Art," *LA* 32:4 (August, 1964), 111.

98. "Editorial," *LA* 33:1 (November, 1964), 1.

99. See, e.g., Thomas Geary, "A Sculptor Talks Shop with a Pastor," *LA* 9:2 (February, 1941), 125ff.

100. Ides van der Gracht to Lavanoux, November 7, 1930. LAS, 7.

101. "Editorial," *LA* 13:4 (August, 1945), 72.

102. "Editorial," *LA* 7:1 (October, 1938), 1.

103. "Editorial," *LA* 28:2 (February, 1960), 39.

104. "Editorial," *LA* 25:2 (February, 1957), 32, and Lavanoux, "Observations," *LA* 5:1 (First Quarter, 1936), 19ff.

105. Jean Charlot, "Catholic Art: Its Quandaries," *LA* 9:1 (October, 1940), 8.

106. Clement McNaspy, S.J., "The Priest as Patron," *LA* 29:3 (May, 1961), 65.

107. "Editorial," *LA* 23:1 (November, 1954), 1. Lavanoux had once told a friend: "I feel so strongly about these matters that if, perchance, I found myself the Prime Minister of a country, I would forbid the clergy to have anything to do with the building and decorating of churches." Lavanoux, who admitted that he had been, in the past, "inclined to lay the blame for all the evils of artistic aberration on the clergy," finally agreed that "perhaps the blame can be shared by all." Lavanoux to Iris Conlay, April 1, 1957. LAS, 34.

108. Among these were Fr. Edward Sutfin and Fr. John Douaire, each a scholar of both the liturgy and art, who often wrote for *Liturgical Arts*.

109. Occasionally, *LA* reported examples of what it referred to as "vandalism," such as that which took place after Fr. Edward Sutfin left his Montgomery Center, Vermont, parish.

110. Erwin Frey, "A Man Builds as He Believes" (with comments by Philip R. Adams), *LA* 13:2 (February, 1945), 25ff.

111. See *LA* 3:2 (Second Quarter, 1934), 59, and H. A. Reinhold, "Anglican," *LA* 9:1 (October, 1940), 5.

112. See pages 14ff.

113. Binsse to Lavanoux, July 6, 1931, and response, July 10, 1931. LAS, 7. Binsse ar-

gued in this case that the "Princeton set are not 'Protestants' in the accepted sense of that word" and that C. R. Morey should be encouraged to contribute to *LA*. "But," Lavanoux replied, "that is precisely the danger. You know where an out and out Protestant stands, but it is difficult to place those who profess a sympathy for all 'sects.' At any rate, I honestly believe that we should strive to do our work from the 'inside.'
"

114. The review appeared in *LA* 7:3 (May, 1939). Lavanoux to E. H. Hawks, January 23, 1940. LAS, 18.

115. Wilfrid Anthony to Lavanoux, June 8, 1934. LAS, 1.

116. See pages 51f.

117. Lavanoux to the Most Rev. Edward Mooney, April 9, 1938, and response, April 19, 1938. LAS, 16. "Whatever his merits in the field of liturgical music," wrote Mooney upon hearing that Gibbs was under consideration for the medal, "it seems to me that his present position as director of the choir of the Episcopal 'high' Church of St. Ignatius of Antioch, New York City, practically excludes him for consideration for the award. I cannot see how the award would fail to be misunderstood by many whose good will the Society actually stands in need of."

118. Lavanoux to Walter Nathan, May 27, 1947. LAS, 25.

119. Our Savior Lutheran Church, Grand Rapids, Michigan, *LA* 37:1 (November, 1968), 12, and Unitarian Fellowship, Athens, Ohio, *LA* 39:3 (May, 1971), cover.

120. Ecumenical Center, Melbourne, Australia. *LA* 36:3 (May, 1968), 70-71.

121. Lavanoux to Edward Sutfin, August 21, 1962. LAS, 42.

122. *LA* 34:2 (February, 1966), 70ff, and 34:3 (May, 1966), 122ff.

123. *LA* 34:2 (February, 1966), 70.

124. John Dwight to Lavanoux, March 26, 1953. LAS, 30.

125. Lavanoux to John Dwight, March 31, 1952. LAS, 30.

126. *Ibid.*

127. John LaFarge to Lavanoux, November 8, 1944. LAS, 22.

128. Lavanoux to John Cronin, February 23, 1945. LAS, 23.

129. "Editorial," *LA* 28:4 (August, 1960), 89.

130. *LA* 14:3 (May, 1946), 64ff.

131. Kramer cites not only Fra Angelico's admonition, "To paint the things of Christ one must live with Christ," but also the Byzantine ikon painters and the 20th-century European Benedictines such as Abbot Ildefons Herwegen in support of his thesis.

132. One of the artists Kramer offers as an example is Jewish artist Aaron Bohrod. In a letter to Kramer, Lavanoux wrote that "there is certainly no reason why a Jew cannot contribute to religious art for the Roman Catholic Church." Lavanoux to Herbert Kramer, June 16, 1946. LAS, 23.

133. "Editorial," *LA* 20:2 (February, 1952), 45.

134. *LA* 19:2 (February, 1951), 30.

135. See M.-A. Couturier, *Art et Catholicisme* (Montreal: Editions de l'Arbre, 1941); *Chroniques* (Montreal: Editions de 1'Arbre, 1947); Thomas F. O'Meara, "Modern Art and the Sacred: The Prophetic Ministry of Marie-Alain Couturier, O.P.," *Spirituality Today* 38 (1986), 31ff.; *La verité blessé* (Paris: Plon, 1984); *Art Sacre* (Houston: Menil Foundation/Herscher, 1983).

136. For a detailed history of the church at Assy and of the controversy surrounding its decoration, see William Rubin, *Modern Sacred Art and the Church of Assy* (New York: Columbia University Press, 1961).

137. *LA* 19:2 (February, 1951), 30. Lavanoux added a postscript to this commentary, answering the criticism that the church at Assy was built and decorated in violation of ecclesiastical law.

138. Richard J. Douaire, "Pilgrimage to Assy — An Appraisal," *LA* 19:2 (February, 1951), 28ff.

139. Richard J. Douaire, "A Proposal," *LA* 18:4 (August, 1950), 104ff.

140. For example, J. P. Kenny, "Towards an Aesthetic of Sacred Art: Four Canons," *LA* 35:4 (August, 1967), 146f.

141. John LaFarge, "Letter to a Critic," *LA* 18:3 (May, 1950), 67ff.

142. *Ibid.*

143. Few other serious discussions of this issue took place before the First Plenary Council of India, 1951, and the 1959 meeting of the Great International Congress in Nijmegen-Uden on the theme "Mission and Liturgy."

144. Binsse to G. Bodenwein, December 24, 1934. See also Lavanoux to Binsse, July 10, 1931. LAS, 7.

145. See page 165.

146. Lavanoux, "Never a Dull Moment," 127 and 134-5. ML, 3.

147. Lavanoux to Binsse, March 23, 1931. LAS, 7.

148. Generally, the art and architecture of England and France.

149. See page 68.

150. "Prolegomena," *LA* 26:3 (May, 1958), 69.

151. See page 68.

152. *LA* 36:1 (November, 1967).

153. Lavanoux always preferred the term 'assimilation' to 'adaptation,' on the grounds that adaptation "seems to imply a superficial veneer, a compromise, whereas assimilation means more nearly a co-penetration, a merger in which both sides, the indigenous and the European, contribute a like share." See also page 178 and "Editor's Diary," *LA* 26:4 (August, 1958), 133.

154. Lavanoux, "Preliminary Report: First International Congress of Catholic Artists," *LA* 19:1 (November, 1950), 4.

155. *LA* 24:3 (May, 1956), 63.

156. "Editor's Diary," *LA* 28:3 (February, 1953), 59. See also 24:3 (May, 1956), 63, and 21:2 (February, 1953), 39.

157. "Editor's Diary," *LA* 26:4 (1958), 133.

158. *LA* 27:3 (May, 1959), 54.

159. Joseph Periera, "Is It Possible to Integrate Indian Art Tradition into an Indian Christian Art?" *LA* 22:1 (November, 1953), 9.

160. Charles Freuler, "Is Adaptation of Church Architecture a Misunderstood Ideal?" *LA* 27:3 (May, 1959), 54ff. See also Lavanoux, "Church Building in Mission Lands," *LA* 23:4 (August, 1955), 165ff.

161. Joseph Periera, *op. cit.*, 10.

162. S. Nohonra, "The All-India Study Week," *LA* 25:4 (August, 1957), 97.

163. "Editor's Diary," *LA* 30:3 (May, 1962), 96.

1. James J. Walsh, *The Thirteenth: Greatest of Centuries*, 5th ed. (New York: Catholic Summer School Press, 1913).

2. *Ibid.*, 104.

3. Kenneth Clark, *The Gothic Revival: A Study in the History of Taste*, 2nd ed. (London: Constable, 1950), 87.

4. See James F. White, *The Cambridge Movement: The Ecclesiologists and the Gothic Revival* (Cambridge: Cambridge University Press, 1962).

5. See Phoebe Stanton, *The Gothic Revival in American Church Architecture: An Episode in Taste* (Baltimore: Johns Hopkins Press, 1968), 56ff.

6. See pages 14ff.

7. Phoebe Stanton, op. cit.

8. These included buildings for the University of Notre Dame (Indiana), the College of Holy Cross, (Worcester, Massachusetts), and Boston College (Massachusetts).

9. See *Charles D. Maginnis: A Selection of His Essays*, (New Haven: Yale, 1956).

10. The commission for the Cathedral was awarded to the firm of (C. Grant) LaFarge and (George) Heins, but on the death of Heins it was transferred to the firm headed by Ralph Adams Cram. See John LaFarge, *The Manner is Ordinary*, (New York: Harcourt Brace, 1954), pp. 389-391.

11. The fact that the editorial committee was headed by Charles Maginnis undoubtedly colored the decisions made regarding the inclusion of examples of neo-Gothic churches.

12. *LA* 1:1 (Fall, 1931).

13. *LA* 1:3 (Spring, 1932).

14. *LA* 2:3 (Third Quarter, 1933).

15. *LA* 3:1 (First Quarter, 1934), 34ff.

16. E.g., C. R. Morey, "Gothic Art," *LA* 1:4 (Fourth Quarter, 1932), 175ff.

17. *LA* 2:1 (First Quarter, 1933).

18. *LA* 1:4 (Fourth Quarter, 1932).

19. It was admitted that none of these examples of revivalist architecture were pure forms, since all were filled with stylistic anachronisms. See, e.g., L. Bancel LaFarge, "A Contrast in Romanesque," *LA* 1:4 (Fourth Quarter, 1932), 138ff.

20. Michael Trappes-Lomax, *LA* 2:3 (Third Quarter, 1933), 100f.

21. Leopold Arnaud, "The Church of the Most Precious Blood," *LA* 1:3 (Spring, 1932), 146.

22. See pages 14ff.

23. Much of the reaction against Cram, as we have seen, was the result of professional jealousy on the part of those whose architectural firms were in direct competition with the Cram firm.

24. Lavanoux to Peter Anson, August 16, 1955. LAS, 31.

25. See page 36.

26. Lavanoux, "Never a Dull Moment," 102. ML, 3.

27. Lavanoux, "Introduction," in Leroy Appleton, *Symbolism in Liturgical Art* (New York: Scribners, 1959), v.

28. Lavanoux to Lawrence J. Madden, May 26, 1969. LAS, 49.

29. *Ibid.*

30. John Walter Wood to Binsse, December 1, 1931. SRCA, 15.

31. *Ibid.* Binsse's radio lectures were delivered on the evenings of November 23 and 30, and December 7, 1931.

32. Henry Clifford, op. cit.

33. *Ibid.*

34. Henry Lorin Binsse, "Looking-Backwards Architecture," *LA* 7:4 (July, 1939), 58.

35. Henry Clifford, "Contemporary Art for the Living Church," *LA* 10:4 (August, 1942), 90.

36. *Ibid.*

37. Binsse, *op. cit.*

38. *Ibid.*

39. Andrew J. Kelly, "The Priest and Modern Art," *LA* 16:3 (May, 1948), 45. "The essence of art is creative and productive, not imitative and reproductive."

40. The Liturgical Arts Society suffered considerable embarrassment when, in 1955, the designs for the Shrine of the Immaculate Conception were published. The Shrine was designed in what might be called "eclectic revivalist" style by the Society's first president, Charles Maginnis. One longtime friend of the Society expressed his shock: "Mr. Maginnis evidently did some fine work in his time, but I am heartily sorry to see, once again, that the channels of the present can continue to inflict such pretentious monstrosities on the Catholics of tomorrow. Small wonder Catholic taste is confused. I realize that you had to pay some tribute to the Society's first president, but Maginnis' cross-section of architecture will set Catholic architecture back to 1920 at least." William Justema to Lavanoux, October 22, 1955. LAS, See pages 149-150, 166-167.

41. Lavanoux to Robert Smith, January 20, 1955. LAS, 32.

42. Leopold Arnaud, "The Living Tradition in Christian Art," *LA* 9:3 (May, 1941), 47, and "Editorial," *LA* 8:4 (July, 1940), 62. "Is it not a fact that those who belittle the art of today would have us do what no artist of the past would do if he were living today? . . . Would it be absurd to suggest that the archaeological traditionalist is rather like one who is content to let the chain of tradition accumulate rust while he indulges in sentimentality?"

43. Leopold Arnaud, op. cit.

44. Lavanoux to John Douaire, April 20, 1950 (LAS, 27), and Lavanoux, "Religious Art in the United States," *LA* 19:1 (November, 1950), 8; also, "Editorial," *LA* 8:4 (July, 1940), and 25:3 (May, 1940), 65.

45. Gregory Borgstead, "Liturgy and Tradition," *LA* 10:4 (August, 1942), 87.

46. Barry Byrne, "A Philosophy of Design for Concrete," *LA* 2:2 (Second Quarter, 1933), 54.

47. "Editorial," *LA* 24:3 (May, 1956), 49. The Society occasionally expressed disillusionment with its chosen vocation, saying that it was sometimes like "trying to breathe life into a moribund corpse of a shadowy past." "Editorial," *LA* 35:1 (November, 1966), 1.

48. See Thomas F. O'Meara, "Modern Art and the Sacred: The Prophetic Ministry of Marie-Alain Couturier, O.P.," Spirituality Today 38 (1968), 40, note 10. This organic way of thinking about architecture is criticized by Geoffrey Scott in *The Architecture of Humanism* (New York: Doubleday, 1924), cf. Chapter 6, "The Biological Fallacy."

49. Constitution and Bylaws of the Liturgical Arts Society, October, 1928.

50. Barry Byrne, "The Modern Movement in Catholic Church Architecture," lecture for the Liturgical Arts Society, May 31, 1933.

51. H. A. Reinhold, "The Modern Movement in Catholic Church Architecture," *LA* 6:3 (Third Quarter, 1938), 123ff. Leopold Arnaud, "The Living Tradition in Christian Art," *LA* 9:3 (May, 1941), 47ff. Lavanoux, "Liturgy, Art, and Common Sense," *LA* 13:3 (May, 1945), 52ff. John Henning, "Liturgy and Modern Art," *LA* 13:1 (November, 1944), 2ff. Henry Clifford, "Contemporary Art for the Living Church," *LA* 10:4 (August, 1942), 90ff.

52. Henry Clifford, po. cit., 91.

53. *Ibid.*, and John Henning, po. cit., 2.

54. John Henning, po. cit., 3.

55. Henry Clifford, op. cit., 90, and H.A. Reinhold, op. cit., 124.

56. Lavanoux, *op. cit.*, 53.

57. John Henning, *op. cit.*, 4.

58. "Editorial," *LA* 6:1 (First Quarter, 1937), 2.

59. Barry Byrne, "A Philosophy of Design for Concrete," *LA* 2:2 (Second Quarter, 1933), 54ff.

60. Lavanoux to Bishop Hugh Boyle, September 18, 1939. There were additional difficulties with the use of the term "modern" to describe the form of church architecture that the Liturgical Arts Society was seeking. In a 1950 symposium, which addressed the specific question of terminology, Leopold Arnaud summed up the problem: "Every age has labeled its current expression 'modern'; we are no exception to the rule. Our word *contemporary* is preferred by many because *modern* has come to denote a specific stylistic expression in architecture based on the 'International School' of the 1920's. "Architecture Today: A Symposium," *LA* 19:1 (November, 1950), 24.

61. See pages 149-150. *LA* 19:2 (February, 1951) was devoted to the church at Assy, featuring five pages of photographs of the decoration.

62. John Douaire, "Pilgrimage to Assy — An Appraisal ('Note by Father Couturier')," *LA* 19:2 (February, 1951), 30.

63. "Editor's Diary," *LA* 23:2 (February, 1955), 48.

64. *LA* 33:1 (November, 1964), 14, and 38:4 (November, 1970), 111.

65. See F. E. Walsh to Lavanoux, April 20, 1931. LAS, 7.

66. Lavanoux to Thomas E. Burke, January 21, 1955 (LAS, 31) and Charles Maginnis, "A Survey and a Hope," *LA* 10:1 (February, 1941), 4. "The word 'modernism' on a Catholic page looks rather formidable for a comparatively innocent idea."

67. Lavanoux, "The Fantasia of Obstructionism," unpublished article, 1973. ML, 3.

68. Lavanoux referred to this as "a sort of perpetual fear of the present." Lavanoux to Charles Maginnis, June 19, 1944. For a fuller treatment of the debate over modern art in the Church, particularly that at Assy, see William Rubin, "The Debate on Sacred Art," *Modern Sacred Art and the Church at Assy* (New York: Columbia University Press, 1961).

69. "Editorial," *LA* 9:3 (May, 1941), 45.

70. See Joseph Salerno to Lavanoux, July 19, 1947. LAS, 24. "How is it then that these artists insist on giving us sublimated representations, strictly devoid of harmony and dignity of form?"

71. Elbert Conover to the Editor, *LA* 15:2 (February, 1947), 58.

72. See Jean Charlot to the Editor, *LA* 12:2 (February, 1944), 48. "You write that many readers disliked my frontispiece, and to please tell them why I did it 'ugly.' "

73. See, for example, Harold Rambusch's extended argument against artistic "naturalism." *LA* 15:2 (November, 1947), 57.

74. *Acta Apostolicae Sedis* 24 (1932), 335; Pius XI, Address, (October 27, 1932); *Periodica*, 22-31. Also, T. Lincoln Bouscaren, S.J., *The Canon Law Digest* 3:1 (1934), 559-560, and *Homiletic and Pastoral Review* 33, (1933), 417-418.

75. Canon 1164, paragraph 1: "Ordinaries shall insure taking counsel of experts if necessary, that in the construction and remodeling of churches, forms of architecture from the received Christian tradition and laws of sacred art are used." Canon 1279, paragraph 2: "No one may place, or cause to be placed in churches, any unusual image unless it has been approved by the Ordinary." Canon 1296, paragraph 3: "Concerning the form and material of sacred furnishings, these must follow liturgical prescription and ecclesiastical tradition and be made in the best way possible according to the laws of sacred art."

76. *Acta Apostolicae Sedis* 24 (1932), 356.

77. See pages 162-163.

78. On occasion, critical letters to the Society would refer to "the Pope's dictum on modernistic architecture." (E.g., Charles Maginnis to Binsse, October 11, 1932.) As early as 1933, the Liturgical Arts Society's stance on modern art had come under direct scrutiny by the Vatican. Upon sending the first volume of *Liturgical Arts* to Pope Pius XI, the Society received the report that, "The Pope examined the book and was pleased to see the good appearance of many illustrations, but expressed some surprise seeing one of the most modern images toward the end." (Eugenio Tisserant to Lavanoux, December 1, 1933.) The Society, still searching for direction in the matter of modern art, was quite disturbed by the Pope's criticism. "We are quite concerned," Lavanoux responded, "about the remarks of the Pope on what he termed the most modern images toward the end of the book. I assume that the Holy Father referred to the mosaics of the stations of the Cross on pages 34-37. These pictures were really a bit extreme, and it is not likely that similar work will again be shown in this publication." Lavanoux to Eugenio Tisserant, December 19, 1933. LAS, 7.

79. See pages 90-91 *Acta Apsotolicae Sedis* 39 (1947), 521-595. (The material on sacred art is contained in paragraphs 195-197.)

80. "Editorial," *LA* 32:4 (August, 1964), 109.

81. H. A. Reinhold, "Liturgy and Art," *LA* 21:2 (February, 1956), 33ff.

82. Paragraph 95.

83. H. A. Reinhold, *op. cit.*, 33. The Society found further support from the Vatican for the use of modern art in the Church in Pius XII's address to the First International Congress of Catholic Artists (September 6, 1950). In his own address to that conference, Maurice Lavanoux had suggested that modern art is the "natural expression" of the 20th-century Church, and had specifically appealed to *Mediator Dei* in defense of his position. See page 68, LA 19:1 (November, 1950), 3ff, and *LA* 22:4 (August, 1954), 121.

84. *De arte sacra*, June 30, 1952, in *Acta Apostolicae Sedis* 44. (1952), 542-546.

85. From *Tra le sollecitudini*, Acta Pius X, 1 (1903), 75.

86. Canons 1164, paragraph 1; 1178, paragraph 2; and 1279, paragraph 3. See pages 170-171.

87. "We cannot but deplore and reprove those images and forms recently introduced by some, which seem to be deformations and debasements of sane art, and which at times are even in open contradiction to Christian grace, modesty, and piety and miserably offend true religious sentiment; these are to be totally excluded and expelled from our churches." *Mediator Dei*, paragraph 195.

88. *Ibid.*

89. "Editor's Diary," *LA* 32:4 (August, 1964), 109.

90. "Editorial," *LA* 27:3 (August, 1959), 73.

91. *Ibid.*

92. *Ibid.*

93. In 1956, Lavanoux edited the American edition of Anton Henze and Theodor Filthaut, *Kirchliche Kunst der Gegenwart* (Recklinghausen: Paulus Verlag, 1954), which contained photographs of modern European church buildings and furnishings. (*Contemporary Church Art* [New York: Sheed & Ward, 1956]).

94. *Constitutio de sacra Liturgia, in Acta Apostolicae Sedis* 56 (1964), 97-138.

95. "Accogliere una cosi," delivered October 28, 1961. Reported In *L'Osservatore Romano,* October 30-31, 1961.

96. *Constitution on the Sacred Liturgy,* Chapter 7, paragraph 124.

97. "Le nobili espressioni," delivered May 7, 1964. Reported in *L'Osservatore Romano,* May 8-9, 1964.

98. *Ibid.*

99. See "Fears Wild Art Gaining a Foothold," *Catholic Star Herald,* August 30, 1963, and the address at Marquette University delivered by Archbishop Vagnozzi (Apostolic Delegate to the United States), June 6, 1964. "Contemporary art as a whole has not produced works in the ecclesiastical field which have been accepted by our people as truly inspirational and conducive to a feeling of union with God." Marquette University News Service, May 14, 1964.

100. The issue devoted to an initial discussion of the question (*LA* 22:3, May, 1954), had the words "Abstract Art and Christianity" in bold letters on the front cover, along with the subtitle "Don't Be Alarmed. Read the Article and Study the Illustrations."

101. Theodore Brenson, "Abstract Art and Christianity," *LA* 22:3 (May, 1954), 76ff.

102. *Ibid.,* 77.

103. "Editorial," *LA* 28:3 (May, 1960), 53.

104. *LA* 27:1 (November 1958).

105. "Editorial," *LA* 28:3 (May, 1960), 53.

106. *Ibid.*

107. "Editorial," *LA* 28:3 (May, 1960), 65.

108. As the Society moved into its final years, its opinion of the suitability of abstract art softened somewhat. The chapel at the University of St. Thomas, Houston, Texas, decorated with large abstract paintings by Mark Rothko earned the Society's praise. Lavanoux to Howard Barnstone, August 29, 1968. LAS, 45.

109. "Editorial," *LA* 36:3 (May, 1968), 63.

110. "Editorial," *LA* 34:2 (February, 1966), 37.

111. *Ibid.*

112. Lavanoux to William Schickel, December 12, 1965. LAS, 45.

113. "Editorial," *LA* 36:3 (May, 1968), 63.

114. *Ibid.*

115. Bishop Leo Dworschak (Fargo, North Dakota) to Lavanoux, May 30, 1953. "It has become increasingly evident in recent years that the Liturgical Arts Society is encouraging a form of ecclesiastical art which departs from the traditional forms encouraged by Holy Mother Church." LAS, 28.

116. Justus George to Lavanoux, March 16, 1951. LAS, 25.

117. J. M. O'Connor to Lavanoux, June 27, 1959. "That's the trouble! You have been sold down the river, or sold *Liturgical Arts* to the modern boys!" LAS, 36.

118. Martin Hellriegel to Lavanoux, May 5, 1953. "May I suggest that you change the title from *Liturgical Arts* to 'So-Called Modern Art Society?' I can't take it any longer." LAS, 29.

119. It is difficult to underestimate the intensity of feeling surrounding this issue. "The latest copy of *Liturgical Arts* just arrived," one reader wrote. "I just happened to open it up at the 'art-rocities' on pages 11 and 12. This is not liturgical art. Maybe we should open up an insane asylum and lock up the perpetrators in padded cells with their own creations, but we should not drive good Christians crazy with such distorted kindergarten products. Christ and his mother would not be pleased to see themselves in such caricatures. I do not think it is the mind of the Church to allow such distortions to be displayed for public veneration." Aloysius Horn to Lavanoux, December 11, 1947. Over the years, a few individuals criticized *Liturgical Arts* for not going far enough in advancing the cause of modern religious art. See Thomas Coakley to Editor, November 30, 1931, and Joseph Salerno to *LA*, July 19, 1947. LAS, 7 and 24.

120. "Editor's Diary," *LA* 27:3 (May, 1959), 73.

CONCLUSION

1. For an analysis of this period in Roman Catholic history, see William Halsey, *The Survival of American Innocence* (Notre Dame: University Press, 1980) and Walter Ong, *Frontiers in American Catholicism* (New York, Macmillan, 1957).

2. One can certainly view the encyclicals *Testem Benevolentiae* (1899) and *Pascendi* (1907) and the decree *Lamentabili* (1907) in this light.

3. This flowering of Roman Catholic intellectual life in the United States and the striving for a positive Roman Catholic self-identity in the midst of Anglo-Saxon Protestant America had various manifestations in the period between the two World Wars. Several academic organizations were founded — e.g., The American Catholic Philosophical Association (1926), The Catholic Anthropological Association (1928), and The American Catholic Historical Association (1919) — and periodicals such as *The Commonweal*, and *America* served as a forum for Roman Catholic political, social, and theological opinion. A number of important Roman Catholic political and literary figures also began to come into prominence, and the European liturgical movement was transplanted to the United States. Several significant social welfare programs (such as the Catholic Worker, the Catholic Interracial Council, the National Catholic Rural Life Conference, and the Catholic Committee on International Peace) were also established. And finally, in their search for continuity with the past, and for a genuine and coherent Catholic heritage that they could call their own, many American Roman Catholics found neo-Thomism to be a vastly appealing mode of theological expression. The works of philosophers Etienne Gilson and Jacques Maritain, for example, were fast becoming required reading for American Roman Catholics seeking intellectual respectability.

4. One of the most important of those exceptions was Maurice Lavanoux.

5. For example, Ides van der Gracht, John Howard Benson, A. Graham Carey, Everitt Harman.

6. J. Sanford Shanley, John and Donald Wood, and later, John LaFarge, Barry Byrne, and Henry Lorin Binsse.

7. "Editorial (on the death of Fr. John LaFarge)," *LA* 32:1 (November, 1963), 1. See also Sister M. Aquina (for Martin Hellriegel) to Lavanoux, March 5, 1931. "The fact that the new plans [for the Society] are more promising than the original is very gratifying. What Reverend Father [Hellriegel] is looking for is a spread of the 'Liturgical Movement' and whatever serves as an impetus in that direction, be it in any phase of liturgical work, is a source of joy and encouragement."

8. Lavanoux to the Editor of *The New York Times*, September 2, 1972. SRCA, 13.

9. "Editor's Diary," *LA* 31:4 (August, 1963), 121.

10. Letter to the Editor, Louis B. LaPrés, *LA* 33:2 (February, 1965), 60. LaPrés writes to Lavanoux, "I feel you had as much to do with our final decision to build in this design as any one individual."

11. "Editorial," *LA* 24:2 (February, 1956), 24.

12. "Editor's Diary," *LA* 33:4 (August, 1965), 129.

13. Edward Sutfin to Lavanoux, July 10, 1959. LAS 36. A recent visit to Montgomery Center indicates that this vandalism has certainly not been reversed. The baptismal area has been totally dismantled, and sentimental and naturalistic plaster statues abound.

14. Lavanoux to John Ekkberg, April 21, 1960. LAS 38.

15 *Ibid*. See also, for example, Lavanoux to Alden Jewell, January 14, 1946. LAS, 23.

16. "Editorial," *LA* 16:1 (November, 1947), 1.

17. "Maurice Lavanoux 1894-1974," *Stained Glass*, 69:3 (Fall, 1974), 30.

18. A. Bugnini to Lavanoux, November 21, 1960. LAS 39. "It is my pleasure to notify you that the President of the Pontifical Commission for the Sacred Liturgy would be greatly pleased to receive your specialized cooperation in the field of Christian art, specifically in its relation to the Sacred liturgy." See pages 74-75.

19. See Appendix D. The Members of the subcommission were Valerio Vigorelli, Joachim Nabuco, Johannes Wagner, and Enrico Cattaneo.

20. Joachim Nabuco to Lavanoux, May 1, 1961. LAS, 40. See Appendix D.

21. "Instruction on the Sacred Liturgy," Chapter 5 (September 26, 1964). R. Kevin Seasoltz, *The New Liturgy*, 532.

22. "Editorial," LA 34:1 (November, 1965), 2.

23. For a graphic example of the extent and shape of the changes in Roman Catholic liturgical art and architecture, see *Enviroment and Art in Catholic Worship* (Washington: United States Catholic Conference), 1978.

Appendix A

CONSTITUTION AND BYLAWS OF THE LITURGICAL
ARTS SOCIETY

Constitution

ARTICLE I, *Name*
The name of the organization shall be the "Liturgical Arts Society,
Inc."

ARTICLE II, *Object*
The object of the Society is to increase the interest of its members in
the spiritual value of the liturgical arts, and to coordinate the efforts
of those concerned with its development.

ARTICLE III, *Membership*
Sec. 1. There shall be two classes of membership: Corporate Members and Sustaining Members.
Sec. 2. The condition of membership in either of these two classes
shall be honorable service in its respective field as defined in the Bylaws.
Sec. 3. There shall also be a body of Patrons, as provided for in the
Bylaws.

ARTICLE IV, *Officers*
Sec. 1. The officers of the Society shall consist of a President, a Vice-President, a Secretary, and a Treasurer.
Sec. 2. The above officers shall be elected from among the
Corporate Members at the Annual Meeting for the term of one year,
or until their successors are elected.
Sec. 3. The Board of Directors may at its discretion appoint such
other officers as may be necessary.

ARTICLE V, *Government*
Sec. 1. There shall be a Board of Directors, consisting of the President and eight Corporate Members.
Sec. 2. Three members of the Board shall be elected each year at

the Annual Meeting for a term of three years.

Sec. 3. There shall be an Executive Committee composed of the President, Vice-President, Secretary, Treasurer, Executive Secretary, and the Chairmen of the Standing Committees.

Sec. 4. The government of the Society shall be vested in its Board of Directors and the Executive Committee as provided for in the By-laws.

ARTICLE VI, *Standards of Practice*

The Society shall from time to time adopt a Code, or Codes, of standards of professional practice required of its members. This standard shall conform to sound liturgical tradition and the decrees of the Sacred Congregation of Rites.

ARTICLE VII, *Meetings*

There shall be an Annual Meeting of the Society at which all business affecting its general policy shall be transacted; and such other meetings as are provided for in the Bylaws.

ARTICLE VIII, *Amendments*

This Constitution may be amended at the Annual or any Special Meeting of the Society by a two-thirds vote of the Corporate Members present, provided that a notice of the proposed amendment shall have been sent not less than 10 or not more than 40 days previously to each of the above members.

ARTICLE IX, *Approbation*

The Society shall seek ecclesiastical approbation and the cooperation of distinguished professional men to ensure the soundness of its policies and activities.

Bylaws

ARTICLE I, *Object and Standards*

Sec. 1. Object. The Society devotes itself to Liturgical Art as distinct from secular Christian Art. It aims to promote the study and practice of the arts and crafts relating directly to the worhip of the Catholic Church.

Sec. 2. Standards. Strict conformity to the Liturgical Laws of the Catholic Church is expected of the Society's members. As to the artistic standards to be upheld, the Society, while advocating the study of traditional forms, aims also at encouraging the evolution study of traditional forms, aims also at encouraging the evolution of ecclesiastical art along new lines, provided that such work seems expressive of a truly Catholic spirit.

Sec. 3. Discipline.

Any member who persistently contravenes the standards of the Society as interpreted by the Committee on Standards, renders himself liable to disciplinary action by the Board of Directors.

ARTICLE II, *Membership*

Sec. 1. Sustaining Membership.

a) All those engaged in the study or practice of the arts connected with the worship of the Catholic Church are eligible for Sustaining Membership provided their accomplishments measure up to the standards of the Society. Others, actively interested in furthering the objects of the Society, are also eligible for such membership.

b) Candidates for admission shall be required by the Committee on Membership to submit evidence of their effective interest or accomplishments in the field of the Liturgical Arts.

c) A three-fourths vote of the entire Membership Committee shall elect a candidate. Such election shall take effect immediately upon acceptance thereof by the candidate and upon payment of the first year's dues as hereinafter provided.

Sec. 2. Corporate Membership.

a) Such Catholics as have notably furthered the objects of the Society may be invited to become Corporate Members as hereinafter provided.

b) Candidates for Corporate Membership must be proposed by three Corporate Members and be approved by three-fourths of the entire Membership Committee.

c) The Membership Committee may place the names of candidates before any Annual or Special Meeting of the Corporate Members and their election shall be voted at such meeting. Such election shall take effect immediately. Three negative votes shall reject any candidate.

Sec. 3. Privileges of Corporate Members.

Only Corporate Members may vote, hold the office of President, Vice-President, Secretary, and Treasurer, or serve as Chairmen of Standing Committees.

Sec. 4. Patrons.

Such persons may be invited by the Board of Directors to become Patrons as shall have signally upheld the aims of the Society. They shall not hold office and shall be exempt from paying dues.

Sec. 5. Chapters.

If in the future development of the Society the formation of local Chapters appears to be desirable, the Board of Directors shall have the power to provide for the formation of such Chapters.

ARTICLE III, *Officers*

Sec. 1. Officers.

The officers of the Society shall consist of a President, Vice-President, a Chaplain, a Secretary, and a Treasurer as provided for in the Constitution. The Board of Directors may, at its discretion, appoint such other officers as may be necessary.

Sec. 2. The President.

The President shall exercise general supervision over all the affairs of the Society. He shall preside over all the meetings of the Society, of the Board of Directors, and of the Executive Committee. He shall appoint all Special Committees and shall be ex-officio member thereof.

Sec. 3. The Vice-President.

In the case of the absence or temporary incapacity of the President, his duties, including membership on the Board of Directors, shall devolve upon the Vice-President.

Sec. 4. The Chaplain.

a) A Chaplain shall be invited by the Board of Directors of the Society to serve for a term of three years. He shall be ex-officio member of the Executive Committee.

b) He shall celebrate annually a Mass for the welfare of the Society at a time and place to be specified by the Executive Committee.

Sec. 5. The Secretary.

a) The Secretary shall compile a complete record of all proceedings of the Society; he shall keep the minutes of all meetings of the Society; and he shall conduct its general correspondence.

b) He shall issue all notices of meetings, nominations, elections, etc.

c) He shall keep a complete roll of the members of the Society and furnish the Treasurer with the same.

d) He shall prepare on behalf of the Executive Committee an annual report that shall be submitted to the Board of Directors for consideration and approval at its meeting preceding the Annual Meeting of the Society.

e) He shall be custodian of, and responsible for, all records, books, files, and archives of the Society.

Sec. 6. The Treasurer.

a) The Treasurer shall be responsible for conducting the financial affairs of the Society. He shall receive, and, under the direction of the Executive Committee, disburse the funds of the Society.

b) The Treasurer shall present a written report at the Annual Meeting.

Sec. 7. Nominations of Office.

Nominations for Officers and Directors may be made by any Corporate Member at the meeting at which such officers or directors are to be elected.

Sec. 8. Election to Office.

At the request of any Corporate Member, the election of officers and director shall be by secret ballot. A plurality of votes of the Corporate Members present shall elect.

Sec. 9. Vacancies in Office.

It shall be the duty of the President to appoint a Corporate Member to fill any office that shall have become vacant, except that of Director. Officers so appointed shall serve until the next Annual Meeting or until their successor shall have been elected.

ARTICLE IV, *Government*

Sec. 1. Board of Directors.

The Board of Directors of the Society shall consist of the President and eight Corporate Members.

Sec. 2. Election of Directors.

a) Three Directors shall be elected each year at the Annual Meeting and shall be filled by vote of the Board. Those so chosen shall serve until the next Annual Meeting, at which time the Corporate Members shall elect Directors to fill any unexpired term or terms in the same manner as provided herein for the regular election of Directors.

Sec. 3. Duties of the Board of Directors.
The Board of Directors shall be charged with the direction of the general policies of the Society. Between Annual Meetings of the Society, the board shall decide questions of interpretation of the Constitution and By laws. It shall establish qualifications for admission to Corporate Membership. It shall from time to time formulate and publish for the information of the Society such codes of professional practice as it may deem expedient.

Sec. 4. Meetings of the Board of Directors.
a) The Board of Directors shall hold at least two meetings a year: one within thirty days before and the other thirty days after the Annual Meeting, on a day designated by the President. Additional meetings may be called by the President or by any two directors. Notice of all meetings of the Board shall be mailed or telephoned to each member thereof at least two days before the meeting. A majority shall constitute a quorum of the Board.
b) Any regular or Special Meeting of the Board of Directors may be adjourned from time to time by the members present, whether or not a quorum shall be required of any adjournment at the meeting or adjournment thereof.

Sec. 5. The Executive Committee.
The Executive Committee shall consist of the Officers of the Society and the Chairmen of the Standing Committees.

Sec. 6. Duties of the Executive Committee.
It shall be the duty of the Executive Committee to carry out the policies formulated by the Board of Directors and to direct and correlate the work of the Society and its various Committees.

Sec. 7. Meetings of the Executive Committee.
The Executive Committee shall meet five times a year, in September, November, January, March, and April, and specially at the call of the President or any three of its members. A majority shall constitute a quorum.

ARTICLE V *Meetings*
Sec. 1. The Annual Meeting of the Society.

a) There shall be an Annual Meeting of the Society at which the President shall deliver an address reviewing the work of the Society during the previous year; this may be followed by other appropriate exercises at the discretion of the Executive Committee.

b) There shall be an Annual Meeting of Corporate Members of the Society for the election of Directors and Officers; the receiving of reports; and such other business as may properly come before the meeting.

c) These meetings shall be held during the last week of April on a day or days and at a place or places to be designated by the Executive Committee. Due notice shall be sent to all members entitled to attend not less than ten nor more than forty days before each meeting.

Sec. 2. Special Meetings.

Special Meetings of the Corporate Members may be called at any time by three Directors, or by the Executive Committee, or on written application by at least ten Corporate Members to the President; and not less than ten nor more than forty days notice thereof shall be sent to all Corporate Members. One third of the Corporate Members shall constitute a quorum at any Annual or Special Meeting.

Sec. 3. Order of Business.

The following shall be the order of business of all meetings of the Corporate Members, unless by majority vote the regular order be dispensed with: 1) Reading of Minutes, 2) Report of the Secretary, 3) Report of the Treasurer, 4) Reports of the Standing Committees, 5) Reports of the Special Committees, 6) Nominations, 7) Elections, 8) Amendments, 9) Unfinished Business, 10) New Business

Sec. 4. Adjournments.

Whenever at any meeting of the members, Annual or Special, notice of which shall have been duly given or waived, members sufficient to constitute a quorum shall not be present, or if for any other reason it should be deemed desirable, a majority of the members present may adjourn the meeting from time to time to any future day without notice other than by announcement at the meeting or adjournment thereof. At any such adjourned meeting at which a quorum shall be present, any business may be transacted which might have been transacted at the meeting on the date originally fixed.

ARTICLE VI, *Dues*
Sec. 1. Annual Dues.
a) The Annual Dues for Corporate Members shall be $12.00; and for Sustaining Members $7.00, payable the first of January.
b) Members in arrears shall be notified on June 1st by the Treasurer. If their dues remain unpaid on the first of the following January, they shall automatically be suspended from membership in the Society. Members whose dues remain unpaid for three years may be dropped from membership in the Society by the Executive Committee.
c) The Executive Committee may at its discretion reinstate members who have been suspended for nonpayment of dues, when such members shall have paid their arrears.
d) Religious in the vows of poverty shall be exempt from initiation fees and dues.
e) The Executive Committee may in exceptional cases remit the dues of a member in whole or in part.

Sec. 2. Disposition of Income.
The income from dues, after deducting therefrom the subscription to the Journal of the Society, and from other sources shall be applied to the running expenses of the Society as directed by the Board of Directors. The balance shall be paid into a reserve fund whose principal shall be disbursible only upon a three-fourths vote of the Corporate Members assembled at the Annual Meeting or any Special Meeting.

ARTICLE VII, *Committees*
Sec. 1. Standing Committees.
There shall be three Standing Committees, whose Chairmen, elected by their respective Committees, together with the Officers of the Society, shall form the Executive Committee, as follows:
1) Membership Committee
2) Editorial Committee
3) Finance Committee

Sec. 2. Membership Committee.
a) The Membership Committee shall consist of three Corporate

Members appointed by the President.

b) It shall be the duty of the Membership Committe to make proper and diligent inquiry as to the eligibility and qualifications of all persons proposed for membership.

Sec. 3. Editorial Committee.

a) The Editorial Committee shall consist of three or more Corporate Members appointed by the President.

b) It shall publish a Journal of the Society, which shall be an active exponent of its aims and ideals, and which shall present authentic and practical information of all kinds relative to the liturgical arts.

Sec. 4. Finance Committee.

a) The Finance Committee shall consist of the Treasurer ex officio and of three Corporate Members appointed by the Board of Directors for a term of three years, the term of one member expiring at the end of each Annual Meeting.

b) The Finance Committee shall be charged with the responsibility for developing a continuous financial program for the Society, and to submit drafts of annual budgets for the Board of Directors and the Executive Committee at their meetings preceding the Annual Meeting.

Sec. 5. Reports of Committees.

All Committees shall prepare reports upon their respective activities and shall present these, after approval by the Executive Committee, at the Annual Meeting.

ARTICLE VIII, *Waiver of Notice*

Whenever any notice whatever is required to be given by statute or under the provisions of the Certificate of Incorporation, Constitution or these Bylaws, a waiver thereof in writing signed by any person or persons entitled to said notice, whether before or after the time stated therein, shall be equivalent thereto.

ARTICLE IX, *Amendments*

These Bylaws may be altered or amended without prior notice at any meeting of the Directors or Corporate Members by a two-thirds vote of those present, provided that any alteration or amendment by the Board of Directors shall be subject to revision or repeal by the Corporate Members, and provided further that no by law adopted by the Board of Directors or Officers shall be valid unless published for at least once in each of two successive weeks in a newspaper in the country where the election is to be held, the last publication to be at least thirty days before such election.

Appendix B
BIOGRAPHICAL GAZETTEER:
LITURGICAL ARTS SOCIETY

Asherl, Joseph Paul (1897-). Typographer, production coordinator *Liturgical Arts* after resignation of Henry Lorin Binsse, 1950-1972.

Benson, John Howard (1896-1956). Silversmith and stonecarver; partner of Arthur Graham Carey and disciple of Eric Gill; member, Portsmouth Priory group.

Binsse, Henry (Harry) Lorin (1905-1971). Executive secretary, Liturgical Arts Society; production coordinator, *Liturgical Arts* 1931-1950; cousin of John LaFarge; managing editor, *The Commonweal*, 1938-1947.

Carey, A(rthur) Graham (1892-1984). Silversmith and philosopher of art; partner of John Howard Benson and disciple of Eric Gill; member, Portsmouth Priory group.

Carroll, Gerald (?-). Attorney. President Liturgical Arts Society, 1958-1972.

Clifford, Cornelius (1863-1942). Priest and author; awarded first LAS gold medal, 1934.

Cram, Ralph Adams (1863-1942). Architect author, and chief proponent of the Gothic Revival; catalyst for the Society's discussion of the role of non-Roman Catholic Christians in the Society's work.

Evans, Unity. Layout designer for *Liturgical Arts*, 1955-1972.

Foley, Joseph R., C.S.P. Priest and musician; second director, Quilisma Club, succeeding Becket Gibbs; director, Paulist Boys Choir of the Church of St. Paul the Apostle, New York.

Gibbs, H(arold) Becket (1868-1956). Musician; director of music at Covington, Kentucky, and Cincinnati, Ohio, cathedrals; founder and first director of the Liturgical Arts Schola (Quilisma Club), 1934-1946.

Harman, Everitt Radcliffe (1895-1967). Priest and architect; founding member, Liturgical Arts Society; ordained priest, Diocese of Salt Lake City, 1949.

Hayes, Patrick Joseph Cardinal (1867-1938); Archbishop of New York; first Ecclesiastical Patron of Liturgical Arts Society.

LaFarge, L(ouis) Bancel (1900-1989). Architect; founding member, Liturgical Arts Society; nephew of John LaFarge, son of Bancel La Farge.

LaFarge, (John Louis) Bancel (1865-1938). Architect; member, first advisory board, Liturgical Arts Society; son of painter John LaFarge, brother of John LaFarge, S.J.

LaFarge, John, S.J. (1880-1963). Priest and editor; associate editor of *America*, 1924-1943 executive editor, 1944-1948; first chaplain of LAS. Son of painter John LaFarge, brother of Bancel LaFarge, uncle of L. Bancel LaFarge.

Lavanoux, Maurice (1894-1974). Editor; founding member, Liturgical Arts Society; editor, *Liturgical Arts*, 1937-1972; secretary, Liturgical Arts Society, 1930-1972.

Maginnis, Charles Donagh (1867-1945). Architect; founding member and first president, Liturgical Arts Society, 1930-1934.

Michel, Virgil (1890-1938). Liturgist and monk of St. John's Abbey, Collegeville, Minnesota; early advisor, Liturgical Arts Society.

Reagan, Oliver (1891-1958). Architect; friend of Harman and founding member, Liturgical Arts Society; architect with Voorhees, Gmelin & Walsh.

Riggs, T(homas) Lawrason (1888-1943). Priest and author; Catholic chaplain at Yale University; one of the founders of the *Commonweal*, early supporter of Liturgical Arts Society.

Shanley, J(oseph) Sanford. Architect; founding member and first treasurer, Liturgical Arts Society, 1931-1933, 1936, 155-1969 president, 1941-1943, 1952-1953; architect of Mt. Saviour.

Spaeth, Otto Lucien (1897-1966). Financier and art collector; patron of Liturgical Arts Society and projects concerning ecclesiastical art.

Spellman, Francis Joseph, Cardinal (1889-1967). Archbishop of New York 1939-1967, succeeding Hayes; patron of Liturgical Arts Society beginning January, 1940.

Stevens, Mother Georgia (1870-1946). Liturgical music educator; founder and director; Pius X School of Liturgical Music, Manhattanville, New York.

Van der Gracht, Ides(bald) Walter Paulus Joseph Maria von Waterschoot (1902-1963?). Architect, and foreign service officer; founding member, vice president, Liturgical Arts Society, 1931.

Williams, Michael (1877-1950). Editor and author; founder of *The Commonweal* (1924); editor, 1924-1938, special editor, 1938-1945; member, first advisory board, Liturgical Arts Society.

APPENDIX C

Officers of the Liturgical Arts Society (1931-1971)

PRESIDENT, VICE-PRESIDENT, SECRETARY

1931. Charles Maginnis, Ides van der Gracht, Maurice Lavanoux
1932. Charles Maginnis, Hildreth Meiere, Maurice Lavanoux
1933. Charles Maginnis, Hildreth Meiere, Maurice Lavanoux
1934. Charles Maginnis, unknown, Maurice Lavanoux
1935. Bancel LaFarge, unknown, Maurice Lavanoux
1936. Bancel LaFarge, Hildreth Meiere, Maurice Lavanoux
1937. John Andre Fouilhoux, Hildreth Meiere, Maurice Lavanoux
1938. John Andre Fouilhoux, unknown, Maurice Lavanoux
1939. J. Moody, Gerald Carroll, Maurice Lavanoux
1940. J. Moody, Gerald Carroll Maurice Lavanoux
1941. J. Sanford Shanley, Gerald Carroll, Maurice Lavanoux
1942. J. Sanford Shanley, Gerald Carroll, Maurice Lavanoux
1943. J. Sanford Shanley, Gerald Carroll, Maurice Lavanoux
1944. Hildreth Meiere, Oliver Reagan, Maurice Lavanoux
1945. Hildreth Meiere, Leopold Arnaud, Maurice Lavanoux
1946. Otto Spaeth, Lauren Ford, Maurice Lavanoux
1947. Otto Spaeth, Ann Grill, Maurice Lavanoux
1948. Bancel LaFarge, Ann Grill, Maurice Lavanoux
1949. Bancel LaFarge, Barry Byrne, Maurice Lavanoux
1950. Raphael Hume, Becket Gibbs, Maurice Lavanoux
1951. Raphael Hume, Thomas Locraft, Maurice Lavanoux
1952. J. Sanford Shanley, Thomas Locraft, Maurice Lavanoux
1953. J. Sanford Shanley, John Dooley, Maurice Lavanoux
1954. Gerald Carroll, Daniel Sullivan, Maurice Lavanoux
1955. Gerald Carroll, Daniel Sullivan, Maurice Lavanoux
1956. Daniel Sullivan, William Dunphy, Maurice Lavanoux
1957. William Dunphy, Donald Wood, Maurice Lavanoux
1958. William Dunphy, Donald Wood, Maurice Lavanoux
1959-71. Gerald Carroll, Daniel Sullivan, Maurice Lavanoux

TREASURER

1931-33. J. Sanford Shanley
1934-35. unknown
1936. J. Sanford Shanley
1937. John Dooley
1938. unknown

1939-40. John Dooley
1941. Edward L. Sherman
1942. Joseph Asherl
1943-51. Max Foley
1952-53. John Asherl
1954. J. Dooley
1955-69. J. Sanford Shanley
1970-71. Joseph Asherl
*Annual Meeting and election of officers suspended in 1965.

Appendix D

"Notes for the subcommission on sacred art - Preparatory ecumenical council II April 7, 1961 submitted by Maurice Lavanoux, New York City, an editor of the quarterly Liturgical Arts."

The evolution of religious art and architecture today constitues a phenomenon, and its finest examples are evidence of a growing vitality and creativeness. In previous decades the battle of styles of architecture was fought in the nostalgic atmosphere of past prejudices and mistaken notions of architectural development. In the field of the arts (painting, sculpture, stained glass, mosaics, etc.) we labored under the delusions of post-renaissance fallacies which reduced those arts to the level of the lowest common denominator.

It is indeed providential that the opportunity should now come to inject a measure of clarity in the matter through the work of this subcommission on sacred art. In this respect it is absolutely the glories of past centuries. Instead we can meditate on the working of God's grace today, through the medium of the liturgical renewal which has thrown so much light on a sane and healthy approach to the possibilities of religious art and architecture of our times.

When we reflect on the fact that the church is a public building, set apart for divine worship and for the collective prayer of the faithful, we can realize how that building should be, by definition, a place of beauty and that therefore nothing of inferior value should be allowed in it. In truth, the church structure is the material embodiment of the Christian association. In consequence it should be clear that this material embodiment of the building, in the architectural sense, reflects the image of the Church today. We can also say that the Church — ecclesia — is not merely the place where the faithful gather; it is also the basilica — the royal palace in which our Lord renews His redeeming sacrifice, and in which He lives in the Holy Eucharist.

In the present climate of art it is unfortunate that semantics should further complicate the matter. Words such as 'modern,' 'tradition,' lend themselves to a variety of interpretations. It would help to clear the air if we could agree that we are on earth, here and now, and that the grace of God is operative now as it has been through the ages. We could also avoid the smokescreen of inveterate prejudice by pointing out that tradition is, by definition, a dynamic element and surely not a static encumbrance. It can be compared to a golden chain to which each generation must add its own link. The strength of this golden chain then resides in the strength of each link through the acceptance of the conditions which caused its fashioning in the unfolding of God's grace in the soul of man at all periods of history. It is that dynamism which should inform our understanding of the value of tradition — a value that points the way forward and is based on the distillation of accumulated knowledge.

It is understood that religious art, and more precisely sacred art, is, by its very nature, a social art. It must grow out of a common faith, thought, experience, life, and the common worship of the Church. The art of the Church today must be Christo-centric — to uplift and infuse the soul with a new life. It is obvious that art, to fulfill its total function, must achieve communication with its audience, the faithful. But it is today equally obvious that all forms of communication require two partners — the artist and his audience. In recent decades there has been a great effort on the part of the artist to reshape and rethink his language, and this has occurred in all the arts. That this is so need not surprise us unduly if we think of the world we live in and the life we must shape according to our earthly destiny — for the fact is that we live in the here and now and we must meet the challenge on the highest possible level.

In view of the above considerations I would repectfully suggest that any pronouncement concerning the evolution of sacred art be a positive one and a generous one. Such a pronouncement might state unequivocally that the Church wishes that all work on ecclesiastical buildings be entrusted only to the most talented practitioners and that only the work of the finest artists be placed in such buildings.

Architects and artists of the highest calibre are conversant with the great work of the past and with the dynamism of true tradition; and there is no need to add qualifying phrases to such a positive statement. Any negative statement can only serve as a smokescreen for the mediocre artist and the timid client. Such a

236

generous statement would surely induce many excellent artists to devote their talents and their art to bringing beauty into the house of God. There is now a vast reservoir of talent in all countries that is lost to the Church because of past timidities and misunderstandings. Hence the present need for a positive statement.

Bibliography

PRIMARY SOURCES

Liturgical Arts Society Collection (University of Notre Dame Archives, Hesburgh Library, University of Notre Dame, Notre Dame, Indiana).

Maurice Lavanoux Papers (University of Notre Dame Archives, Hesburgh Library, University of Notre Dame, Notre Dame, Indiana).

Society for the Renewal of Christian Art, Incorporated Papers (University of Notre Dame Archives, Hesburgh Library, University of Notre Dame, Notre Dame, Indiana).

Liturgical Arts quarterly magazine, volumes 1-40 (1931-1972).

Lavanoux, Maurice. "An Architect's Dilemma," *Orate Fratres* 3 (1929), 277-281.

_____. "Art Trends in Asia," *World Mission* 26 (1953), 44-46.

_____. "The Authentic Christian Tradition in Art," *Creative Art* Sister Esther Newport, S.P., ed. (Washington: Catholic University of America Press, 1955), 40-48.

_____. "Catholics and Religious Art," *Catholicism in America* (New York: Sheed & Ward, 1962), 201-208.

_____. "Introduction," *Symbolism in Liturgical Art*, Leroy Appleton ed. (New York: Scribner, 1959).

_____. "L'Evoluzione dell'architettura religiosa negli Stati Uniti," *Fede e arte* 7 (1959), 445-450.

_____. "Never a Dull Moment" (unpublished manuscript, 1972).

_____. "Parish Worship: Its Artistic Expression," *Proceedings of the National Liturgical Week (1940).* (Newark: Benedictine Liturgical Conference, 1941), 191-212.

Lavanoux, Maurice. "The Practical Aspect of Liturgical Art," *Orate Fratres* 10 (1936), 570-574.

_____. "Problems of Religious Art," *The Commonweal* 58 (1953), 575-578.

_____. "Recent Trends in Catholic Church Design in America," *Architectural Record* 85 (1939), 76-83.

_____. "Religious Art for Servicemen," *The Marianist*, 36 (1945), 10-12.

_____. "Some Sources of Ecclesiastical Symbolism," *Orate Fratres* 5 (1931), 554-559.

_____. "That Elusive Commodity, Art!" *Orate Fratres* 27 (1953), 230-234.

_____. "Uber den neuen Kirchenbaus der letzen 40 Jahre in den USA," *Das Munster* 25 (1972), 158-159.

Lavanoux, Maurice, and Sutfin, Edward. "Contemporary Catholic Architecture, ed." Modern Church Architecture Albert Christ-Janner and Mary Mix Foley, (New York: McGraw-Hill, 1962).

_____. *The Background of Sacred Art in Egypt*. (Concord, New Hampshire, 1959).

SECONDARY SOURCES

Apostolos-Cappadona, Diane. *Art, Creativity, and the Sacred* (New York: Crossroads, 1986).

Appleton, Leroy H., and Bridges, Stephen. *Symbols in Liturgical Art*. With an introduction by Maurice Lavanoux (New York: Scribner's, 1959).

"Are Protestants Catholics?" *Brooklyn Tablet* 25 (July 8, 1933), 8.

Attwater, Donald. *A Cell of Good Living* (London: Geoffrey Chapman, 1969).

Barrett, Noel. *The Contribution of Martin Hellriegel to the American Catholic Liturgical Movement*. (Ph.D. dissertation: St. Louis University, 1976).

Bayne, Wilfrid O.S.B. "Thirty-Three Years of Portsmouth History," *American Benedictine Review* 3 (1952), 315-339.

Beauduin, Lambert. "L'Encyclique 'Mediator Dei' et le mouvement liturgique," *La Maison Dieu* 13 (1948), 7-25.

Benson, John H., and Carey, Graham. *The Art of Lettering* (Newport: Stevens, 1940).

Beuron, 1863-1963: Festschrift zum hundertjahrigen Bestehen der Erzabtei St. Martin see p. 181, note 30 (Beuron: Hohenzollern, 1963).

Busch, William. "About the Encyclical 'Mediator Dei,'" *Orate Fratres* 22 (1947-1948), 53-56.

Carey, A. Graham. *Living Stones of Architecture*. Supplement to the Catholic Art Quarterly (Buffalo: Catholic Art Association, 1959).

_____. *Purpose and Pattern*. (Newport: Stevens, 1938).

_____. *The Tails Book* (New York: Sheed & Ward, 1956).

_____. *Thoughts and Things* (Newport: Stevens, 1937).

Clark, Kenneth. *The Gothic Revival: A Study in the History of Taste* rev. ed. (London: Constable, 1950).

Clements, Robert Brooke. *The Commonweal, 1924-1938: The Williams-Schuster Years* (Ph.D. dissertation: University of Notre Dame, 1972).

Couturier, Marie-Alain. *Art et Catholicisme* (Montreal: Editions de 'Arbre, 1941).

_____. *Chroniques* (Montreal: Editions de 'Arbre, 1947).

Cram, Ralph Adams. *The Catholic Church and Art* (New York: Macmillan, 1930).

_____. *Church Building* (Boston: Marshall, 1924).

_____. *My Life in Architecture*. (Boston: Little, Brown, 1936.)

_____. *Substance of Gothic* (Boston: Marshall, 1917).

Deedy, J. "A Man, A Movement, A Magazine," *The Commonweal* 97 (1972), 148-149.

_____. "News and Views: Maurice Lavanoux," *The Commonweal* 99 (1974), 178.

Diekmann, Godfrey. "In Memorian Msgr. William Busch," *Worship* 45 (1971), 179-180.

_____. "Is There a Distinct American Contribution to the Liturgical Movement?" *Worship* 45 (1971), 578-587.

_____. "Monsignor Martin Hellriegel: Holy Cross Church, St. Louis," *Worship* 38 (1964), 497-498.

Dickason, David Howard. *The Daring Young Men*. (Bloomington: Indiana University Press, 1953).

Domenach, J.-M. and Montavon, Robert. *The Catholic Avante-Garde* (New York: Holt, Rinehart & Winston, 1967).

Dwyer, J. "Maurice Lavanoux: Giant Champion for Good Art," *Catholic Sentinel*, November 29, 1974.

Ellard, Gerald. "The American Scene, 1926-1951," *Orate Fratres* 25 (1951), 507-510.

Ellis, J. Tracy. *American Catholicism*, 2nd ed. (Chicago and London: University of Chicago Press, 1969).

_____. "American Catholicism in an Uncertain, Anxious Time," *Commonweal* 98 (1973), 177-184.

_____. "American Catholics and the Intellectual Life," *Thought* 30 (1955), 351-388.

Eversole, Finley. *Christian Faith and the Contemporary Arts* (Nashville: Abingdon, 1962).

"An Exhibition of Ecclesiastical Art," *Brooklyn Tablet* 25 (May 20, 1933), 11.

"Fears Wild Art Gaining a Foothold," *Catholic Star Herald*, August 30, 1963.

Flannery, Austin, ed. *Vatican Council II: The Conciliar and Post-Conciliar Documents* (Collegeville: Liturgical Press, 1975).

Garner, J. Patrick. *The Vision of a Liturgical Reformer: Hans Ansgar Reinhold* (Ed.D. Dissertation: Columbia University, 1972).

Gaunt, William. *The Pre-Raphaelite Dream* (New York: Schocken Books, 1966.)

Gill, Eric. *Art* (London: The Bodley Head, 1934).

_____. *Autobiography* (New York: Devin Adair, 1948).

Gleason, Philip, ed. *Catholicism in America* (New York: Harper & Row, 1970).

Godfrey, Aaron. "Maurice Lavanoux: 1894-1974," *Liturgy* 21 (1976), 31.

Hall, Jeremy. *The Full Stature of Christ* (Collegeville: Liturgical Press, 1976).

Halsey, William M. *The Survival of American Innocence* (Notre Dame: University of Notre Dame Press, 1980).

Hellriegel, Martin. "Survey of the Liturgical Movement," *Orate Fratres* 3 (1929), 333-340.

Henze, Anton and Filthaut, Theodore. *Contemporary Church Art* ed. Maurice Lavanoux (New York: Sheed & Ward, 1956).

Kervick, Francis W. *Architects in America of Catholic Tradition* (Rutland, Vermont: Charles Tuttle, 1962).

Klein, John L. *The Role of Gerald Ellard in the Development of the Contemporary American Catholic Liturgical Movement* (Ph.D. dissertation: Fordham University, 1971).

Koenker, Ernest B. *The Liturgical Renaissance in the Roman Catholic Church* (Chicago: University Press, 1954).

LaFarge, John. *The Manner is Ordinary* (New York: Harcourt, Brace & Co., 1954).

_____. "The Liturgical Arts Society," *America* 46 (1931), 221.

"Lavanoux, Church Art Expert, Is Dead," *The New York Times* (Wednesday, October 22, 1974), 48.

"Liturgical Briefs," Orate Fratres 5 (1931), 144-145.

Madden, Lawrence. *The Liturgical Conference of the United States of America: Its Origin and Development, 1940-1968* (Ph.D. dissertation: Trier, 1969).

Maritain, Jacques. *Art and Scholasticism with Other Essays* (London: Sheed & Ward, 1946)

_____. _Creative Intuition in Art and Poetry_ (New York: Pantheon, 1953).

Marx, Paul, O.S.B. _Virgil Michel and the Liturgical Movement_ (Collegeville: Liturgical Press, 1957).

McManus, Frederic R. "American Liturgical Pioneers," _Catholics in America_ Robert Trisco, ed. (Washington, D.C: National Conference of Catholic Bishops, 1976).

McNaspy, Clement J. "Remembering Maurice," _America_ 130 (1975), 326-327.

Michel, Virgil. "Apostolate," _Orate Fratres_ 2 (1928), 221.

_____. "The Liturgical Arts Society," _Orate Fratres_ 11 (1937), 182-184.

Morey, C. R. _Christian Art_ (London and New York: Longmans Green, 1935).

Murphy, Maureen T. _The Search for Right Reason in an Unreasonable World: A History of the Catholic Art Association, 1937-1970_ (Ph.D. dissertation: University of Notre Dame, 1975).

"News and Views: An Old Story," _The Commonweal_ (1974), 426.

O'Meara, Thomas F. "Modern Art and the Sacred: (cf. p. 225) The Prophetic Ministry of Marie Alain Couturier, O.P.," _Spirituality Today_ 38 (1986), 34ff.

_____. _Romantic Idealism and Roman Catholicism_ (Notre Dame: University of Notre Dame Press, 1982).

Ong, Walter S.J., _Frontiers of American Catholicism_ (New York: Macmillan, 1957).

O'Shea, William. "Liturgy in the United States: 1889-1964," _American Ecclesiastical Review_ 150 (1964), 189.

Pichard, Joseph. _L'Art Sacre Moderne_ (Paris: B. Arthaud, 1953).

Proceedings of the 1940 National Liturgical Conference (Washington: Benedictine Liturgical Conference, 1940).

Quitsland, Sonya A. _Beauduin: A Prophet Vindicated_ (New York: Newman, 1973).

Reinhold, H. A. *The American Parish and the Roman Liturgy* (New York: Macmillan, 1958).

_____. *Dynamics of the Liturgy* (New York: MacMillan, 1961).

_____. *H.A.R.: The Autobiography of Father Reinhold* (New York: Herder & Herder, 1968).

_____. "The Liturgical Movement to Date," *Proceedings of the National Liturgical Week, 1947* (Boston: Liturgical Conference, 1948 11).

_____. *Liturgy and Art: Religious Perspectives* New York: Harper & Row, 1966).

_____. *Speaking of Liturgical Architecture* (Notre Dame: Liturgical Programs, 1952).

Rengers, Christopher. "Headstarter in Liturgical Revival: Interview with Martin Hellriegel," The *Priest* 24 (1968), 866-874.

Rubin, William Stanley. *Modern Sacred Art and the Church at Assy* (New York: Columbia University Press, 1961).

Ryan, Richard. "One of the Last of the Pure Poor," *Brooklyn Tablet*, July 26, 1973.

Scott, Geoffrey. *The Architecture of Humanism* (New York: Doubleday, 1924).

Seasolz, Kevin. *The New Liturgy: A Documentation, 1903-1965* (New York: Herder & Herder, 1966).

Shewring, Walter ed. *The Letters of Eric Gill* (London: Devin-Adair, 1948).

"A Small Church Exhibition," *America* 49 (1933), 149.

Speight, Robert. *The Life of Eric Gill* (London: Methuen, 1966).

Srawley, J. H. *The Liturgical Movement: Its Origin and Growth* (London: Mowbray, 1954).

Stanton, Phoebe B. *The Gothic Revival and American Church Architecture: An Episode in Taste, 1840-1856* (Baltimore: J. Hopkins University Press, 1968).

_____. *Pugin* (New York: Viking, 1971).

Tegels, A. "Chronicle," *Worship* 46 (1972), 573.

Thompson, Raymond. *Maritain and Tillich: On Art and Religion* (Ph.D. dissertation: Boston University, 1962).

Van Allen, Rodger. *The Commonweal and American Catholicism* (Philadelphia: Fortress, 1974).

Verdon, Timothy Gregory, ed. *Monasticism and the Arts* (Syracuse: Syracuse University Press, 1984).

Walsh, James J. *The Thirteenth Greatest of Centuries* 5th ed. (New York: Catholic Summer School Press, 1913).

White, James F. *The Cambridge Movement: The Ecclesiologists and the Gothic Revival* (Cambridge University Press, 1962).

Wilson, Winefride. *Christian Art Since the Romantic Movement* (London: Burns & Oates, 1965).

Yorke, Malcolm. *Eric Gill: A Man of Flesh and Spirit* (New York: Universe Press, 1982).

Index of Persons